RSKing

CW01021343

the MAN *who*
DISCOVERED FLIGHT

the MAN *who* DISCOVERED FLIGHT

George Cayley and the First Airplane

RICHARD DEE

McCLELLAND & STEWART

Library and Archives Canada Cataloguing in Publication

Dee, Richard
The man who discovered flight : George Cayley and the first airplane / Richard Dee.

ISBN 978-0-7710-2971-4

1. Cayley, George, Sir, 1773–1857. 2. Flying-machines. 3. Aeronautics – History.
I. Title.

TL670.5.D44 2007   629.130092   C2006-906855-0

We acknowledge the financial support of the Government of Canada through the Book Publishing Industry Development Program and that of the Government of Ontario through the Ontario Media Development Corporation's Ontario Book Initiative. We further acknowledge the support of the Canada Council for the Arts and the Ontario Arts Council for our publishing program.

Typeset in Jenson by M&S, Toronto
Printed and bound in Canada

This book is printed on acid-free paper that is 100% ancient-forest friendly
(100% post-consumer recycled).

McClelland & Stewart Ltd.
75 Sherbourne Street
Toronto, Ontario
M5A 2P9
www.mcclelland.com

1   2   3   4   5   11   10   09   08   07

To my dad, Harry, the source for my love of flight. This is despite him scaring me half to death by his constant repetition of that story where the wing fell off his Vampire jet aircraft and he nearly died; or perhaps, in part, because of it.

CONTENTS

ACKNOWLEDGEMENTS

The list of those who have assisted me in writing Cayley's life story is a long one, but without the following contributions this work would not have been possible.

I'd like to thank Sir Digby and Lady Cayley, who were my first contact with the Cayley family and who provided so many of the leads for other sources of information. Also Mark and Belinda Evans for all their continuing work in preserving the Cayley legacies, for the excellent roast pheasant lunches, and for allowing me to reproduce the portraits of Cayley, his wife, and Miss Phil. Mark, Belinda, and their close family also put me on to innumerable other sources on the Cayley family story. My thanks go to Angela, Lady Frank, for her time and her permission to reproduce the early Cayley portrait, and to Sir Marcus Worsley and his assistant Kathryn Lamprey for their time in seeking additional Cayley leads. Brian Riddle, librarian, is a fount of knowledge, trusted gatekeeper to the unique records of the Royal Aeronautical Society and the man with whom I got to share the finding of the Cayley "cartoons." My deep appreciation goes to all the staff at the North Yorkshire County Records office in Northallerton; my time there was a real pleasure – what a great team. The Cayley family archive could not be in better hands. Thanks also to Brenda Weeden, archivist at the University of Westminster, who so generously allowed me to photograph the Cayley-related sources in

Westminster's excellent archive. My time with Allan Morrison of the University of Westminster was also highly productive, especially his colourful and informative *Cayleyana* anecdotes. Mark Mihkelson, head teacher of Brompton School, gave his time and allowed me unfettered access to the Brompton Hall and its grounds – my thanks for that. Ian Reed, director of the fascinating Yorkshire Air Museum at Elvington, provided several other avenues of research that I would have missed, as did the Reverend Leonard Rivett, who has spent some forty years (or more) as a spokesman for the Cayley cause. Dr. Clare Rider, archivist at London's Inner Temple, provided the background on George John and Edward Cayley's legal studies. My appreciation goes to Mrs. Green, the secretary of St. Peter's School, York, who confirmed that Cayley did not attend there in his teens (which is a pity – I would have liked to have found that piece). Thanks also go to Brian Luskey of the University of Northern Colorado, who directed me to the George John Cayley archive at the New York Historical Society, and to Andrew Nahum at the British Science Museum for the invaluable microfilm copies of the Cayley notebooks. Other leads to the story came from Dick Swann, executive secretary of the Newcomen Society, and Mr. Barry Thomas of Low Hall, Brompton. Finally, I'd like to thank Jesse Taylor Wallace for the genealogical information concerning the Robert B. Taylor episode, the most satisfying piece-finding of them all.

The process of research and writing was undertaken around and in between my day job, and I'd like to thank my boss, Laurence Harris, who has been so understanding, not to mention supportive and enthusiastic, about the whole process. Due acknowledgement has to go to Chris Bucci, my editor at McClelland & Stewart, who had the idea of writing the Cayley biography in the first place. Chris's guidance and the excellent copy-editing of Wendy Thomas made the book as good as it could be. The whole endeavour would not have come about had it not also been for the tireless work of my agent, Sally Harding. It goes without saying (but I'll say it anyway) that none of the above would have amounted to much had it not been for the loving support of my wife, France.

I'd point out that, despite the best efforts of everyone involved, if there are errors remaining, they are mine alone.

All illustrations derived from Sir George Cayley's exercise book, notebooks, publications, and correspondence are provided by the Royal Aeronautical Society Library. The image of the Cayley silver disc is reproduced with the permission of the Smithsonian Institute. The portrait images of Sir George Cayley, Lady Sarah Cayley, and Miss Philadelphia Cayley are reproduced with the kind permission of Belinda and Mark Evans. The two images of the Royal Polytechnic Institute are reproduced with the permission of the Westminster University Archive. It is the author's belief that all other images are either in the public domain or else are original images generated by the author himself who hereby releases his copyright to those images with the request that, if reproduced, their source is duly acknowledged.

PROLOGUE

On a November day in 1925 an elderly woman entered Richard Smith and Sons Watchmakers and Silversmith in the small seaside town of Scarborough, in northern England. She was reluctant to give her name but let slip in conversation that her mother had once been a member of the aristocratic Cayley family from the nearby Brompton-by-Sawdon Estate. She offered a selection of blackened silver oddments and broken jewellery that Smith, feeling a little sorry for the woman, reluctantly purchased.

Some time later, while idly cleaning one of the pieces – a silver disc about the size of a British shilling – Smith discovered an engraving dated "1799." On one face was a simple but obscure trigonometric design; on the other was the date and what appeared to be a covered boat with a curiously elaborate rudder. Underneath it were the initials GC, which Smith immediately recognized as those of Sir George Cayley, the Brompton-by-Sawdon baronet who had died in 1857.

The disc was, in fact, both the design for an airplane and the description of the forces by which a wing can fly. This small coin documented both the scientific principle for and the practical application of heavier-than-air aviation fully a hundred years before the Wright brothers' historic flights at Kitty Hawk, North Carolina.

Cayley's dated and initialled silver disc.

I

CAYLEY'S ENGLAND

Although not necessarily the best way to start a life story, this one begins with something of an unknown – George Cayley's place of birth. We do however know whereabouts: North Yorkshire, northern England. More specifically, in Scarborough, a town perched on cliffs overlooking an aptly named cold and usually grey North Sea. Exactly where in Scarborough Cayley was born is not really known, though a best guess would be a solid but comfortable townhouse owned by the Cayley family in the old town centre where his parents are thought to have wintered. This is where the local government placed its official blue plaque of commemoration, but whether they got it right no one knows – even the wording on the plaque is unusually vague, leaving Cayley's exact birthplace still something of a mystery.

These days Scarborough is a tourist centre for day trippers who come to enjoy its bracing air and seaside charms, but it retains the echoes of the fishing town and market that are its origins. You can still find the small harbour and a smaller fishing fleet; a ruined fort overlooking the harbour and town acts as a reminder of a less peaceful history with raiders from any of a dozen European neighbours depending on the century, decade, or sometimes *month* in question. In Cayley's day, the town was a bustling and relatively prosperous municipality. Like everywhere else, there was poverty and hardship, but for

3

the more affluent resident and the moneyed visitor Scarborough offered a close approximation to the much sought-after retreat by the ocean. For the wealthy – and though not extravagantly rich, the Cayley family was certainly on the better side of very comfortably off – the town was a place for business and pleasure, politics and socializing. The land-owning aristocrats and gentry of the area, including the Cayley family, were the movers and the shakers of the town, which was in turn a low-key but dominant influence in the surrounding area. However, although Scarborough and its affairs would periodically dominate Cayley's life, the source of the most enduring influences lay some nine miles to the west, toward the sheltered hinterland and the Cayley family seat in the small village of Brompton-by-Sawdon.

Inland from Scarborough the countryside rises steeply over the heathered moors of North York, which themselves overlook the green Yorkshire Wolds to the south. Between and beside these roughened hills are the richly fertile Dales of Pickering and York, and here agriculture dominates. This is a rural region and clearly distinct from the heavily populated northern English counties that were the birthplace of Britain's most significant revolution, the industrial one. Even into the early twentieth century, farm rents provided the income that sustained scores of local dynasties and made the rolling landscape home to a sizeable portion of the English aristocracy. The land and the histories of those who owned it can be traced back through dozens of generations – Cayley was born to a family that could follow its ancestors back to the first Christian millennium.

We do know the date of Cayley's birth: December 27, 1773. This was a time when the United Kingdom did not exist and Great Britain (a term then barely seventy years old) was in the process of losing its first empire. A poorly performing economy and the cost of trade-inspired wars with numerous European empires had driven Britain to the brink of bankruptcy. In order to address its insolvency, the government decided to impose a series of spectacularly unpopular taxes on the American colonies, ironically to pay for defending those same colonists from the marauding French in the previous decade. The taxes, twinned with the incompetence of amateur politicians and absentee landlords, led to the colonials finally galvanizing themselves into action after decades of infighting. Zealously taking up the sentiments that abounded at the time, the brand-new Americans righteously quoth, "No taxation without representation," and the rest is history. As it happens, there was considerable popular support for the revolution in Britain, and this led to a number of issues, not least the reluctance of British troops to fight fellow countrymen engaged in a seemingly just rebellion. In part, these sympathies stemmed from exactly the same reasons as had made the New World revolt in the first place.

At the time of Cayley's birth, the electorate in England and Wales consisted of fewer than a quarter of a million people, less than three per cent of the total population. In Scotland, fewer than one in a thousand could take part in the electoral process. In Ireland, no one could vote if they were Catholic, which the vast majority were. No women anywhere in Britain had any right of influence in the political process. Thus, over five hundred years after the groundbreaking Magna Carta was signed, the birthplace of modern democracy limited that very process to a tiny group of land- or property-owning English men who were openly bribed to vote for their members of Parliament. These M.P.s represented constituencies whose boundaries bore no resemblance to the number of people in them: a notorious case had one of these "rotten boroughs" containing twenty-six constituents who between them elected two of the nearly six hundred British M.P.s. In most cases, though, the electorate was a little larger and so, with perhaps a couple of hundred eager voters all with palms to grease, it cost a small fortune to stand as a candidate. As a result, though hardly unique to Britain, the chamber of elected representatives was populated exclusively by those with access to considerable sums of money. This meant that they were either the landed interest themselves or those who sought to foster their future well-being and patronage. As if the rights of British man were not sufficiently hard done-by, the unelected House of Lords and monarch retained the practical means to stop or delay, redefine, or dilute any legislation that Parliament chose to put before them. Though taxed just as punitively as the colonial Americans, and as equally unrepresented, the average Yorkshire man and woman, like everyone else in the nation, had to hope that whoever held sway over their lives was relatively benign. Fortunately for the tenants of late eighteenth-century Brompton-by-Sawdon, their patriarch would be something approaching a saint; fortunately for Cayley's life story, he also possessed a number of redeeming flaws.

Cayley's place in society, the niche he would occupy from birth, though eventually transcend, was determined by the point in the pecking order earned by his ancestors. More practically, it was tied to the estates the family owned in and around Brompton, as well as in more distant Lincolnshire. With regard to his title, Cayley occupied the lowest rung of the hereditary aristocracy: he was a baronet. This designation meant that the family's male heir was entitled in perpetuity to the epithet of "Sir" and his wife to that of "Lady." The title is one of privilege that stands one degree above those who were knighted (which is merely a title of honour). A baronet cannot claim the right to be called "My Lord" nor does he sit in the Lordly House. This privilege is reserved for the upper five tiers of the aristocracy, namely, in ascending order of seniority, baron, viscount, earl, marquis, duke. Up until the late twentieth century, these ranks, along with higher orders of the British Anglican clergy, filled the British Parliament's upper chamber, the House of Lords.

Originally an aristocratic title was earned for some service to the Crown. If the deed was deemed significant enough, the rewarding rank could be made heritable by being initiated at or upgraded to one of the levels from baronet or above. The Crown used the granting of aristocratic status and associated revenue-generating land and pensions to reward the faithful servant of the monarch. This practice was aimed at maintaining a stratum of society specifically created by and dedicated to the preservation of the status quo; it was the embodiment of conservatism. This form of social grading was further reinforced by the relationship between the state and the other powerhouses of preindustrial society. It was no coincidence that the three professions most closely associated with the younger and largely disinherited sons of the nobility were the church, the army, and the navy – listed here in descending order of preference as a result of their being in ascending order of the likelihood of getting oneself killed. Illustrating something of the deep sense of personal duty that runs through the history of the Cayley family, its pedigree (the rather grand name for a family tree) is littered with individuals marked as being in "H.O." (Holy Orders) and "R.N." (Royal Navy). The mutual support between the church and monarch stemmed from each institution's claim as being both Divinely Elected and the necessary source of moral guidance to a nation of potentially wayward subjects. The military formed the third pillar of the ruling triumvirate, with the army and navy representing the practical means by which the authority of the ruling classes was often enforced. Heads of aristocratic rural households were both the religious focus and the legal authority for their local domains. Thus Cayley was destined to become a prominent member of two bodies: the Anglican Church and its close cousin the English aristocracy, though he was a typical example of neither, and the era that was bracketed by Cayley's life saw both these institutions, and Britain as a whole, change almost beyond recognition. Over the course of Cayley's eighty-four-year lifespan, he was not just an observer of Britain's transition from pre-mechanized agrarianism to industrialization; he was an active, if at times idiosyncratic, agent of the process. Throughout these radical times, the one constant in his life was his family home, his family estates, and most importantly his family itself. Reinforcing these ties was the ancient traditions associated with the family name.

One rather quaint aspect of aristocratic prestige is the age of the title itself. In order to trace a family back through time requires documentary evidence of its roots. It was thus something of a self-fulfilling prophecy that the nobility alone could follow its lineage back through the ages: if you neither owned property nor were involved in politics, the likelihood of your name ever being mentioned in a largely illiterate and media-free past was essentially nil. In fact, the Cayley pedigree had more going for it than even its most illustrious peers, in particular because the Cayleys could say they came across the English Channel with William the Conqueror in 1066. A second factor associated with a title's kudos is the history of the associated land, and in this the Cayleys score again: Brompton had been around a long time too. The story of Cayley the family, the baronetcy they gained, and Brompton their home formed the ancient history that would have a profound influence on the young Cayley, his family, and their lives.

One of the earliest references to a Cayley forebear is Bernard "the Dane," whose son Rollo became the 1st Duke of Normandy in about AD 860. By coincidence the Danish nation as a whole had taken something of a fancy to Britain around this time, and the Danes had occupied what was quickly becoming Danelaw, the northern and eastern portion of England under Danish control. A corner of this region emerged later as Yorkshire and within that lay Brompton. The first wooden church in "Bruntune" ("the farm where the broom grows") was built around AD 1000. The construction was a by-product of the Danes permanently settling into British life and adopting Christianity.

At the same time, back in Normandy, although its 2nd Duke, William, didn't seem to do much of note, his son Richard at least had the postscript "the fearless" appended to his title of 3rd Duke in around AD 960. Fearless Richard was the great-grandfather of both William the Conqueror and Osbern de Cailly, the latter being born some time around 1040. The appearance of something approaching a recognizable surname is the result of the family having gained stewardship over the town of Cailli outside Rouen in the Seine-Maritime district of Normandy. It was either Osbern or his son Guillaume who crossed "La Manche" in 1066 to join the invasion of Britain. Who sailed, when they sailed, and whether they were with the original invasion force is unverifiable, but some member of the Cailly family added his ancestral mark alongside the other undersigning nobles on the highly speculative venture to attempt to take the British Isles. The fact that it paid off makes one of them being at the Battle of Hastings something of a moot point: the Caillys had been part of the original "spoils of war" sharing-deal that had put the invasion fleet together so the family had just made it big in Britain. With extensive properties in Normandy and now with land gifted to them in southern England as well, Guillaume's four sons decided among themselves where they'd like to take up residence. William and Humphrey went native in the splashy fens of English East Anglia while Osbern Jr. and Roger remained largely continental.

On defeating the incumbent and acquiring the crown, William Duke of Normandy, now William I, King of England, sent forth civil servants so that he should know exactly what it was he had just conquered. The resulting Doomsday Book of 1086 notes that the village of Bruntune had a church and priest associated with the land of a certain Berenger de Toni. A stone fortification known as Brompton Castle was built in the village at some time around 1120, presumably as a visual reminder to the locals of the recent change in management. It was constructed by Eustace Fitzjohn the Baron of Alnwick who had gained a reputation as a constant harrier of the still unconquered Scots. However, by the time of Eustace's death in 1157 the Brompton stronghold was already a near ruin whose dungeon was being occupied by a monk named John. The disintegration of Brompton Castle is not thought to have been as the result of war. It is more likely that the ungarrisoned fortress was stealthily pillaged for much-needed building supplies. It may be purely coincidental that the first stone church in Brompton appeared shortly after the castle dissolved, and mere chance that a twelfth-century remnant of a Norman chevron moulding can be found embedded in its tower wall. A note in the Cayley family archive concerning the church refers to "a large Norman column dating from circa 1150 which may have been brought from somewhere else." That "somewhere else" seems not such a hard thing to guess: those rural Yorkshiremen may not have known how to militarily engage a conquering Norman army, but they sure could lift heavy things.

Back in Norfolk, the "Cailly" family had become the more anglicized "Cayley" and some had also become the Earls of Beckenham, though the male line died out within three generations, taking the title with it. The direct line to the Brompton Cayleys emerges again in 1280 in the person of John Cayley, son of Sir William Cayley of Owby. On realizing that his elder brothers held almost exclusive control of the family purse strings, John decided to head up to Yorkshire "in search of good sheep country." Bearing in mind his French heritage, John decided on the rather aptly named Normanton in West Yorkshire (current population 250). This is where John settled in and the begetting began. He begat another John, who begat William, who begat Edmund, who moved to the tiny enclave of Thormanby (population 118) in what is now North Yorkshire. Here things continued in a similar vein with another William and then another John, who appears to have been the first to live in the area of Brompton itself. He was followed by an Edward and then yet another William. This particular William Cayley seemed to have even better business sense than his forebears – he married the heiress Joan, daughter of Richard Gouldthorpe, past Lord Mayor of the nearby metropolis of York (population in excess of 10,000 souls). William and Joan produced Edward, who continued the good work of building the Cayley family fortune by gaining the patronage of the Brompton Parish from King James I at some point in the early 1600s. Edward proceeded to buy the whole Brompton Estate lock, stock, and barrel in 1622 and was buried rather grandly in Brompton's fine stone church twenty years later. The Cayley family and Brompton had become as one.

At this point the family fortunes seemed to rather take off as both of Edward's sons did even better for themselves than their father. The younger son became Sir Arthur Cayley of Newland, Coventry, Knight-at-Arms. The elder son climbed even higher when, as the result of war and intrigue, the Cayley family once more showed its mettle and won its spurs. William Cayley was knighted by King Charles I at Theobalds, in Hertfordshire on March 2, 1641. It has been suggested that the reason for the honour was "services to the crown during the Civil War." This seems unlikely because the English Civil War didn't start until August 1642. We can only hope that Sir William wasn't being rewarded for any part in the despicable, bloody, and wholly incompetent campaigns waged by King Charles against the nearby and all too Presbyterian Scots during the previous two years. The 1640s were not a decade of stability for anyone in Britain; however, the revolutionary removal and beheading of the King must have been a particularly unpleasant blow for anyone recently knighted by him. The cause of these events was the English Civil War, with the Parliamentarian Roundheads engaging the King's Cavaliers in a power struggle that lasted for nearly four years. After a series of military defeats, King Charles emerged the overall loser and suffered the consequences when he was executed in 1649. The Royalist defeat had come in spite of the stalwart support and conspicuous bravery shown by a whole swathe of the Cayley family – particularly during the northern English battle of Marston Moor, where three Cayley sons fell for the King's cause. Despite the death of the monarch and the loss of the monarchy itself during the brief period of dour British Commonwealth under Oliver Cromwell, the political tide soon turned again.

Charles's eldest son was in exile in France, where he was declared King of England. Once Cromwell's Commonwealth collapsed, Charles returned to England, gaining the unique accolade of being crowned a second time following a largely bloodless coup. The whole country celebrated the Reformation of the Monarchy in 1660. The celebrations continued for years, and Sir William Cayley cashed in his favours while the party was still in full swing by being elevated to the rank of the near peer as the 1st Baronet of Brompton on April 26, 1661. The Cayley family, title, and home estate were now all in place.

The first Sir William, Baronet (Bt) produced another William (2nd Bt), who tragically lost six children to the outbreak of the Black Death while living in the city of York in 1665. It was a time of fear for many of the major cities, a fear compounded by the devastating Great Fire of London in 1666 whose cleansing properties (as far as the plague-spreading fleas were concerned) wasn't appreciated at the time. Britain's incidences of the plague finally died out, though the pits in which the countless bodies of its victims were buried around the York City Walls remain to this day undisturbed for fear of letting free the bubonic menace. Life for the Cayleys began to recover from their loss, and the family began to thrive and prosper once more.

This generation of Cayleys also saw the first conspicuous sign of a greater than usual intellect within the family as two of William Cayley's brothers, Cornelius and Arthur, became barristers-at-law within the famous Grey's Inn, Middlesex – later absorbed within what became Greater London. All in all, the Cayleys seemed to be doing very nicely, and the stability of local rule within their tiny enclave was ensured as the line of the baronetcy remained uninterrupted for the next two centuries. The family continued the tradition of intermarrying with nearby dynasties, so that individuals were multiply related to one another. Sir Arthur, 3rd Bt and one of the few survivors of the plague that wiped out his brothers in 1665, married Everilda of nearby Fixby, and their son was Sir George Cayley, the 4th Bt, grandfather of the George in our story.

The first Sir George was, by all accounts, a cad and bounder of the highest order. The wife of the 10th Brompton Baronet describes him as "irascible, domineering, determined and selfish." He appeared to have little compunction in using his influence for his own convenience, including an attempt to have the main road between Pickering and Scarborough moved some half a mile so as to make his carriage rides a little less trying. Sir George lived to be eighty-four, retaining the baronetcy until his grandson was well into his teens and acting as a passing, though not necessarily positive, influence on young George's early life. Fortunately grandfather George occupied the High Hall in Brompton, which was, on a village scale, conveniently distant from The Green, a drafty farmhouse that was the home for George Cayley Jr. for the earliest part of his life. It was to The Green that his mother, Isabella, and father, Thomas, returned with George's four elder sisters in February 1774 from somewhere in Scarborough.

Finding the Pieces I – Talking in Tongues

Legend has it that at some point in the 1100s a Norman ancestor of George Cayley's named William d'Albini was betrothed to a certain Madam Adelina. In those days, prominent members of society could be engaged *in utero*, and not surprisingly, such marriages were more political than romantic, more mercenary than emotional. Nevertheless, in our world of legend, William and Adelina's betrothal arose from the wellspring of love unsullied by any potential financial, political, territorial, religious, or constitutional benefits that might have accrued for either party or their parents.

During this particular period of history, Europe found itself, as was often the case, beset by wars, so William was sent off to fulfil his noblesse oblige, leaving his fiancée behind. At some point during his military service, William was standing on the parade ground with his troops when they were suddenly inspected by an unnamed Dowager Queen of France. The country of France didn't really exist back then, so she could have been one of the Capetian dynasty who occupied the Ile-de-France, but the legend is vague on the issue. In any case, the dowager made an undisguised pass at our heroic nobleman, who, being previously engaged, resolutely declined her advances. William thought that was the end of it, but as is often the way in such tales, it wasn't.

The Queen secretly arranged for William to be trapped in either a cave or a pit (depending on which version of the story you read), which was inconveniently inhabited by a lion. William, armed only with his trusty battle-axe and protected only by chain mail, helmet, chest plate, pointy steel boots, teeth-proof gauntlets, and an overdose of righteous indignation, not only smote the savage beast but returned to the wicked dowager and presented her with its recently excised and bloody tongue.

Henceforth the Cayley family coat of arms bore the image of a tongue-less lion "rampant" holding the aforementioned battle-axe. It makes a nice story.

Imagine my surprise, then, when I spotted the tomb-mounted family crest of Edward Cayley in Brompton Parish Church that seems to have a lion, rampant, with what could be a battle-axe, but also quite obviously *avec tongue*. Maybe back in 1642 (when Edward was buried) they just got it wrong and accidentally included one.

Then I ventured into Brompton Hall itself, the country pile of the Cayleys since the seventeenth century and there, above the fireplace in the main sitting room, is another Cayley family crest, with another heavily armed lion rampant, and this time he's positively thrusting out an all-too-present tongue with complete disregard for the demands of our legendary Cayley forebear. Looking through the family archive, I found dozens of illustrations of their coat of arms, and every one of them seems to have lions, axes, and clearly visible and intact tongues. Could they have got it wrong this often? It doesn't seem likely. It looks like that tongueless lion legend was made up or was someone else's story that got misattributed to the Cayleys.

Then I got to thinking . . . the Cayleys owned Brompton Hall until the 1920s. Up until that time, if anyone had idly brought up the tongue legend, it would have been pretty easy to refute it: one would need to simply walk across the room and point to the family crest as it adorned the warming hearth and ask, "What's that then?" However, the cachet of having an interesting legend associated with the family is something many see as having its advantages – you can't buy that kind of publicity. So the legend seems to have survived in spite of, rather than supported by, the evidence.

This would not be the last time when legend would seem to overtake verifiable fact when it came to the Cayleys.

Left: Close-up of the lion on the family coat of arms – they seem to have gone out of their way to *add* a tongue.

Right: A more detailed rendering of the lion in steel above the fireplace in the dining room of Brompton Hall.

2

ENLIGHTENMENT *and the* PUPIL'S RESPONSE

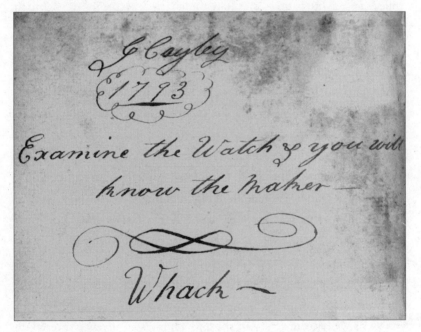

G Cayley

1793

Examine the Watch & you will

know the Maker —

Whach —

Front piece to Cayley's notebook on "Motive Power" started during the closing years of his schooling.

On the announcement of George Cayley's birth, his father, Thomas, paid each bell-ringer at Brompton Parish Church the peculiarly English monetary unit of a guinea (a pound plus a shilling) to peal out the good news. Thomas's generosity is particularly noteworthy when one realizes he was still plain Mr. Cayley at the time, with his own father, Sir George, holding on tightly to the estates and their finances. Whereas Sir George, 4th Bt, was as bombastic and self-centred as his position allowed (and his position allowed a great deal), son Thomas had a reputation as quiet, reserved, and charming when the occasion demanded it. Under the shadow of his overbearing father, Thomas's asthma had been a constant concern, though he may have used it as a convenient excuse to spend as much time abroad as he could. Thomas's mother, Philadelphia, was also known to be as strong willed as her husband – she had the chancel of Brompton Church pulled down and remodelled because it spoiled the view across to the hall at Ganton where her sister, the Lady Legard, resided.

Bearing in mind the rather incestuous aristocratic habits of the time, particularly within the Cayley family, Thomas's most daring act seems to have been marrying the far-from-typical Isabella Seton, a descendant, like most Scottish aristocracy, of Robert the Bruce. The Seton family seat was originally in Parbroath, Scotland, though the family had radiated, mainly in a southerly direction, on dispersion of the family fortunes. In general, daughters of the Seton line married rather well, perhaps as a result of the Seton family motto of "Ever Gay," which in those more innocent times took the original meaning of the word and was related to their renown for both artistic and musical endeavours. Isabella seemed to slip effortlessly into her husband's habit of spending much time abroad; she was gifted in languages as well as the arts, and she and Thomas regularly wintered on the continent, with Florence being a particular favourite. During a visit to Ferney, they met Francois Marie Arouet (pen-named Voltaire), the anglophile French philosopher, writer, and liberal of his day.

Though as a couple Thomas and Isabella seemed to share much, what is in little doubt is that it was Isabella who took charge of the young George Cayley's formative years and indulged the intellectual talents he seemed to possess from an early age. That Isabella took the lead on the subject may in part be the result of the poor role model Thomas had been presented by his own father. Thomas and his siblings were farmed out in the village to be nursed and raised "rather like foxhounds."

VIEW from the GARDEN

High Hall as illustrated in the 1920s on its conversion to a hotel, close to how it looked in the mid-nineteenth century.

Enjoying the small, but significant separation from his grandfather up at Brompton's High Hall, the young Master George was allowed some unusual freedoms by his parents. Not least of these was that of befriending local villagers, including the watchmaker, whose work captured the imagination of the technically leaning youngster. Cayley's youth appears to have been that country idyll much loved of contemporary poets, including the briefly imported Jean-Jacques Rousseau. This was an age that idealized the simple outdoor pleasures and familial indulgences. Cayley was a keen and accomplished fly fisherman, as well as a practised marksman; two skills he later turned to good use in gathering specimens for his investigations into flight.

Cayley was often accompanied in his fresh-air endeavours by his younger cousin Philadelphia Frances Cayley, who became a prominent, though enigmatic component of Cayley family life at Brompton. Philadelphia, or "Miss Phil," lived in the Low Hall, situated to the south and west of the village. "The Low" was an extensive manor house a little under a mile from High Hall; the two houses were joined by a sunken lane that passed by Brompton's church to what was effectively the back door to the main Cayley family residence. Low Hall had for generations housed the manor-born relatives of the extended Cayley clan, and during Cayley's childhood it was the home of his deceased aunt's husband, the Reverend John Cayley and his two children, John and Philadelphia. Despite being related to George through the female line, Miss Phil was also a Cayley by virtue of the fact that she sprang from another of those country-cousin marriages for which the family became renowned. Cayley and Miss Phil had been close from an early age, particularly after the untimely death of her mother while Miss Phil was still young. Bearing in mind the family tradition of keeping the gene pool to a minimum, it would not have been surprising if more than one family member regarded Miss Phil, just four years his junior and well within commuting distance of Brompton central, as an eligible mate for the young George. It was not to be, though the exact nature of the relationship between them is obscured by something of a mystery. Many letters from Cayley to Miss Phil have survived, and each, perfectly amicable, acts as a record of the almost six decades' worth of the family matters with which each was absorbed. The correspondence in the opposite direction is almost completely absent; one biographer suggested the letters had been exorcised from the family archive to conceal some indiscretion. However, there is no evidence to support the idea that the cousins were ever anything more than platonic. It is more likely they remained close but non-kissing throughout their lifelong friendship.

The absence of much surviving correspondence between family members during Cayley's youth leaves us with little first-hand information about his early years. A family anecdote tells of young Cayley being sent to an unnamed school in the county capital of York at some point during his teens. Here he developed a "low fever," which caused him to become so ill it was feared he would die. It is claimed his recuperation was the result of

Philadelphia Frances Cayley – Cayley's cousin "Miss Phil."

his escaping from his sickbed and an enforced starvation to gorge himself on a round of beef hidden in a nearby pantry. It sounds more like the propagation of country lore (and promotion of the local cattle industry) than fact but it remains one of the few stories we have about his early years. It also adds to the evidence that his parents sought a fundamentally different education for their son than was the aristocratic norm.

Cayley's formative years occurred during an age when attaining literacy was viewed as an unseemly distraction from proper pursuits (for the common man at least), and an extended academic education was something limited almost exclusively to the few existing professions of cleric, lawyer, and physician. Although there were mighty works of engineering – ship and architectural construction, canals, aqueducts, docks, and bridges – and the ingenious products of highly skilled craftsmen, such skills were acquired through decades of apprenticeship and application rather than through bookwork and abstract reflection. Unlike the higher reaches of the English aristocracy, a country squire of

George Cayley aged around nine, painted by his aunt, Lady Synnot (Jane Seton), in 1782.

Cayley's station required little in the way of schooling. A grasp of literature, an understanding of the basics of English common law, and a knowledge of the rudiments of bookkeeping are really all that were required to meet the demands of his stratum of noblesse oblige. As a result of the Enlightenment movement from the culturally influential French court, a nodding acquaintance with the principles of the Renaissance could prove something of a social asset, but the absence of such knowledge was hardly unusual, particularly among provincial males. This social standard began to change as the effects of an increasingly educated, vocal, and more economically powerful new class emerged. In Britain this group eventually changed from being the merchant class to the rather blander middle class, but whatever the label, it was from this breed that the powerhouse of liberalism and revolution materialized. "Self-made men" would have the confidence and influence to stir the political pot, and in many ways their emergence as a political force sounded the death knell for a British society that still bordered on the feudal. In the late eighteenth century, dissent, both religious and political, was in the air. The recent debacle of the American Revolution illustrated all too clearly that the existing social order could and would change. The likelihood of an impressionable young baronet-to-be finding himself exposed to the uncouth ranting of a bunch of political troublemakers was pretty small, and from the country hollow of Brompton it must have seemed that Master Cayley was nearer to the equator than the corrupting influences of liberalism. Thanks to his mother, things didn't stay that way for long.

The first major event in Cayley's education involved his leaving home for the city of Nottingham in 1790. This kind of move was not unprecedented for a son of the well-to-do, especially with Cayley being at the not very tender age of sixteen years. It was his mother's choice of teacher that raised some eyebrows. The encounter with his first tutor, George Walker, would change Cayley's life in more ways than he could have imagined.

George Walker was a professor of theology at Manchester College and a Fellow of the Royal Society (FRS), the prestigious organization that seeks to promote the sciences and philosophy, as well as the reputation and careers of its members. There is no doubt that Walker had the brains to join the club, and he was admitted without much fuss in 1771. What might have been in doubt was whether such a radical thinker, outspoken liberal, and challenger of the status quo was the kind of chap a society with "royal" in the title ought to be encouraging. Fortunately, there was a long line of boat-rockers in the auspicious hall of fame that constituted the organization's past membership. Even the initially anglophile then loudly revolutionary Benjamin Franklin was forgiven his role in the unpleasantries surrounding American independence on the back of his work in linking the terrifying phenomenon of lightning to the more amenable one of static electricity. Though rather unkindly dubbed "The Patron Saint of Self-Interest" and still unpopular back home as a result of personally helping to impose the hated Stamp Tax in Pennsylvania, Dr. Franklin maintained his popularity and correspondence with other Royal Fellows in England throughout his years in France during the Colonial War. Then as now, the scientific community was both intimate and strongly non-partisan. Another contemporaneous example of an FRS's intellectual independence was that of Sir

John Pringle, physician to Queen Sophia, wife of King George III. Pringle declined to endorse the imposition of blunted lightning conductors over pointed ones at the monarch's palaces. The change had been suggested simply because the latter was the traitorous Franklin's invention and the former that of a loyal Englishman. Pringle punctuated his refusal to carry out his instructions with the statement that "the laws of nature are not changeable at Royal pleasure." It was a fine example of the emerging attitude that some things transcended aristocratic etiquette. The resulting dent made in Pringle's career by his being fired was a similarly fine example of what happened when such a sentiment was expressed out loud. The trick to speaking up while remaining solvent was to have either independent means or a regular paycheque underwritten by one of the big players of the day. George Walker went the latter route by becoming a prominent cleric.

Even though Walker ate, lived, and breathed dissent, and revelled in the title "most heretical minister in the neighbourhood," he attained a series of high-profile positions from which the volume of his advanced liberalism would only increase. In 1772, Walker became a tutor at the famous "dissenting academy" in Warrington, Lancashire. Warrington Academy had been established by the founder of modern education in Britain, John Aikin, and was notably free of traditional teaching methods and their obsession with the ancient classics and disregard for the modern world. With its strong emphasis on mathematics and science, Warrington became a template for the serious study of the "hard philosophies" and even promoted the alien notion of not only serious academic female education, but serious female educators. This included Aikin's own daughter Anna Barbould who became a noted poet, teacher, and proto-feminist. In 1774, Walker also became minister of High Pavement Chapel in Nottingham, a post he retained for twenty-four years. From this solid organizational foundation, with its attendant financial security, Walker went on to become an outspoken spokesman for the Unitarian Church in England.

Unitarianism, along with other emerging branches of the Christian church, was challenging the autocratic methods of Anglicanism. The Unitarians in particular attracted many extreme liberals of the day as a result of their encouragement for a revisionist view of even the holiest of fundamentals. Unitarianism itself started from the bottom up with the view that Jesus was not divine and the Trinity of the Father, Son, and Holy Ghost was something of an after-the-fact invention by later Christian followers. For the liberal Unitarian, this made worship of either Jesus himself or the Holy Spirit a form of idolatry; it also made just about every other denomination within the Christian fold mad as hell. Though Unitarians were in the forefront of the new ministries of their day, their point of view was neither as radical nor as modern as it sounded, for the exact nature of the divinity of Jesus of Nazareth had always been a subject of heated discussion. The issue was debated at the Council of Nicaea in AD 325 and the resulting Nicene Creed became embodied in the holy oath sworn to by all subsequent congregations. It was to this creed, absorbed into the Anglican liturgy, that Unitarians such as Walker "dissented," and the notion of challenging religious dogma sat well with many of those who also chose to do the same in the secular domain. Though perhaps not having as high a profile as Joseph Priestley (the co-discoverer of oxygen) or the outspoken pro-American Richard Price, George Walker remained a member of the furthest fringe of religious liberalism in Britain at the time.

Walker's modernist and modernizing views were not restricted to religion; he promoted active political debate and spoke out whenever he saw the hand of institutional bigotry. In Britain, the unevenly applied Test Acts became a focus for his and others' protests. This legislation required a religious oath to the Anglican Church to be taken by anyone in public office. Effectively all non-Anglicans – Primitive

Protestants, Quakers, Presbyterians, Methodists, Catholics, Jews, and anyone else attesting to a "nonconformist" faith – were out of luck as far as potentially lucrative government jobs were concerned. These posts were particularly sought after because lining the private pocket while being salaried from the public purse was not only permitted but actively encouraged. M.P.s, ministers, and their civil servants made fortunes from influence-peddling and insider dealing. However, in a nod to the *realpolitik* of a limited number of skilled and educated professionals, non-Anglicans were allowed to attain government-sponsored positions if their abilities and popularity warranted it, though they could be removed from office and prosecuted if they subsequently fell from favour. Despite the protests of an articulate and morally unassailable lobby, the issue of officially sanctioned and legally enforceable religious discrimination remained unresolved in Britain until long after Walker's death.

A third strand of Walker's life was that of science and philosophy, and most importantly the teaching of principles grounded in natural law. Although the majority of Walker's publishing output was in the form of sermons, his *Treatise on conic sections in five books*, though not an easy read, at least proved his skill in mathematics. In addition to his publications, Walker also helped found the Manchester Literary and Philosophical Society, whose presidency he assumed in the years just prior to his death. In and among these activities he also invented a new form of clock and an improved drill press that allowed holes to be driven through a material precisely perpendicular to its surface.

George Walker's robust, hands-on approach to science, religion, and politics made for a fearsome reputation, and he was soon prevailed upon to take on a small number of private students. This venture allowed the offspring of the budding liberal movement to experience a rounding education that combined the muscular practicality of the emerging sciences with the socially advantageous grounding in the classics. Though hardly a typical example of his generation to start with, following his enlistment into Walker's tutorial ranks Cayley would never be the same.

That Cayley ended up gaining the unique and highly personalized education he did stems in part from the fact that the educational system in late eighteenth-century England doesn't really warrant the label of being a system at all. Although Scotland voted tax revenues to pursue the goal of universal education as far back as 1633, the idea of general education was regarded in England as being as potentially dangerous as it was intellectually beneficial. As late as 1807 the English M.P. Davies Giddy publicly attacked the idea of universal education, suggesting it "would teach them [the poor] to despise their lot in life, instead of making them good servants in agriculture and other laborious employments to which their rank in society has destined them; instead of teaching them the virtue of subordination, it would render them factious and refractory."

Even for the well-heeled, an education in a school environment remained something of a gamble. Many of the grammar schools of the day had been founded by wealthy benefactors with an eye to educating the children of the lower classes in order that they might gain a trade. These schools were, by their very nature, difficult businesses to manage from the point of view of profit, but many headmasters realized that they were allowed (or else not expressly forbidden) to take on paying pupils from more moneyed parents, and many of England's prestigious "public" (i.e., fee paying, *private*) schools arose from such beginnings. However, the quality of the education to be had in such schools was of a desperately inconsistent quality. The surer bet was to secure the personalized attention of a studious tutor with an established reputation, and George Walker had this and more.

Cayley's experience under Walker was a combination of rote learning, as was still the norm, and the far more rarely practised application of what had been learned. Most importantly, it was Cayley's first experience of practical experimentation, of technical designing, of the trial-and-error craft of fabricating and testing machines. The few details of what exactly Cayley built in this era are sketchy, though there is a later reference to Cayley's ideas on an embryonic caterpillar track that emerged decades later as one of his few patented designs. For the most part, Cayley's education remained academic, as he and his fellow pupils studied under the steady hand and steely glare of their tutor.

One of the teenage Cayley's earliest descriptions of Walker was that he was "irritable, but just," though Cayley eventually warmed to his company. Cayley would always regard Walker as an intellectual authority and continued to consult him over matters of science and engineering until well into the next century. Cayley's studies concentrated initially on mathematics, though there are no records of Walker's opinions as to Cayley's talents in the subject. Some clue to his abilities in the area can be inferred from the notable absence of algebraic calculations from Cayley's later notebooks and published work – despite aerodynamics being singularly suited to their application. Instead it is Cayley's raw intellect that shines through: he had a prodigious capacity for arithmetic and geometry and managed to complete even the most involved of his later calculations through the use of little more than handwritten addition, a stopwatch, and a protractor. Cayley's approach developed into a hybrid of the examples set by both his mother and tutor: Cayley would decide on his method of achieving a goal, and if it seemed likely to fall short, rather than modifying his approach he would merely redouble his efforts. It was a facet of his approach to problem solving that generated both spectacular successes and serious errors.

Cayley's general education also included navigation, mechanics, and developing his proficiency in the workshop with hand tools and lathe, another skill-set he maintained and developed throughout his adult life. Other areas of study were theology, philosophy, and what has been described as "human rights." This latter subject was undoubtedly one close to Walker's heart, but one that must have been a complex affair at a time when slavery, though uncommon in mainland Britain, was the chief means by which England's all-important Caribbean-derived wealth was generated.

The small group of students in Walker's class comprised Cayley himself, a fellow Yorkshireman named Mr. Duncombe, and an apparently gifted "Blanco" White, whose talents were cut short by an early death. The fourth member of their class was, rather unusually, Walker's own daughter, Sarah. Sarah's mother had died some years before, and she had been raised almost exclusively by her father. Sarah captured Cayley's attention almost immediately, perhaps through her good looks, but most certainly because, initially at least, she outshone him academically. This gender-crossing frisson, the first one recorded concerning Cayley, began initially with a form of intense competitiveness between the two. In this arena, Sarah appears to have had a number of advantages: she was naturally very bright and not shy about showing it, and her native intelligence had been cultivated through years of formal study, certainly longer than Cayley. Also Sarah had honed her skills in emotional stage management to an edge fine enough to be admired by even the most gifted tool-smith. She was, in short, a highly attractive, clever, but fiery-tempered siren. The talented Mr. Cayley consequently found himself besotted.

There has been some fairly uninformed speculation as to the genesis and progression of this young romance, speculation that arose in the absence of any surviving correspondence between the two from this time. Scattered references to Sarah are found in Cayley's correspondence to his mother, however:

Sarah, although not yet fully reconciled to the reversal of our respective positions, I mean in relation to what obtained [pertained?] when I first entered under Mr. Walker, no longer enters into tantrums in consequence. Indeed she seems to be making valiant efforts to control this quick temper of hers. . . .

George Cayley, aged around twenty-one.   Sarah Walker.

After this bout of adolescent jealousy, Cayley's feelings for Sarah seem to have done an about-face. Then events within the Cayley family added their own impetus to the relationship.

At some point, Sarah accompanied George to Brompton, perhaps around the time of the death of Sir George, 4th Bt, in September 1791, and during the transfer of aristocratic power to the new Sir Thomas, 5th Baronet. It seems unlikely that the first time Sarah met Cayley's parents was at the funeral itself – not even as rebellious a teenager as Cayley would think to bring a date to such an occasion – but in any event the visit was during a period of heightened tension as the baronial reins were being passed from the eighty-four-year-old Sir George

to the fifty-eight-year-old Sir Thomas. Along with the bittersweetness
of personal loss and financial independence, Thomas and Isabella were
suddenly faced with the prospect of their son and heir doing that most
uncharitable of things, marrying beneath his station. Isabella, newly
made Lady of the Manor, was acutely conscious of her son's failure to
undertake the tradition of walking the full length of the matrimonial
counter before choosing. She tried to help Cayley widen his perspective
by moving him from Nottingham and the Walkers to London, where
she engaged a second tutor to keep Cayley suitably occupied. It was
assumed that the distance and change of air would cool the ardour and
focus the mind of the intense adolescent Cayley. It spectacularly failed
in both respects. Isabella could have chosen neither a place nor a time
less likely to keep a young man's attention on his Latin primer.

London in 1791 was the eye of the storm as far as European politics was concerned, and the continental traumas racking France in
particular seemed to be getting uncomfortably close. The source of
discomfort was the recent spate of blue-blood decapitations that had
broken out there during the late 1780s. Although there was a minor-
ity in Britain who thought these events perhaps served the French
right for their despicable support of the revolting Americans a decade
before, the less myopic observer foresaw a future less than rosy for
anyone with long-term investments in real estate and the established
hierarchy. The pillars of stability on which European power had so
firmly rested were being assailed on all sides by troublemakers raising
issues ranging from the rights of man to the universality of societal law.
The whole episode smacked of an irritating preoccupation with the
responsibilities, rather than the privileges, of power. And so, against a
chorus of institutional teeth-grinding, the issues of social reform
began to be seriously discussed in Britain. It was not so drastic a
measure as "adapt or die," but more the acceptance that a refusal to
change was likely to have marginally less appealing consequences than

actually changing. Although things like this didn't usually happen in Britain (or if they did, then only under the cloak of night), there grew a vocal and increasingly influential body of opinion that espoused the radical sentiment that "new" might actually be better than "old." Heady times, indeed, though it would not be achieved without a long and bitter struggle. At the centre of this political cauldron was Cayley's new London tutor, George Cadogan Morgan.

Morgan was a man cast in the same mould as George Walker; in fact, the two were close friends. Morgan was another vociferous reformer who, like many of his fellow dissenters, had supported both the American Revolution and the early days of the French one. Morgan had been present at the storming of the Bastille in 1789 and is reputed to have been the first to bring the news of it to England. He was also a member of the group of Unitarians that had included Walker, Priestley, Aikin, and another high-profile supporter of American independence (and Morgan's uncle), Dr. Richard Price. As with his like-minded contemporaries, Morgan had been a correspondent with Benjamin Franklin on scientific matters, and Morgan's published articles included two volumes of lectures on electricity, as well as a small work entitled *Directions for the use of a Scientific Table in the collection and application of Knowledge*. He had even communicated to the august Royal Society concerning his *Observations and Experiments on the light of bodies in a state of combustion*. Morgan was in the vanguard of the liberal *cause célèbre* in also opposing the Test Acts and had helped establish a highly regarded dissenting academy in Hackney, Middlesex. He had then "retired" at the age of thirty-seven to take in private pupils at his home in Southgate, London.

Cayley joined the ranks of Morgan's students at a particularly stressful time. Morgan's friend Priestley had just had his home, library, and scientific laboratory sacked and burned by a mob incited to believe that Priestley was seeking to bring down the church and the monarchy, as was being so ruthlessly done in France. Priestley was lucky to escape with his life, and dissenters began to fear not only social ostracism, but for their safety. Priestley briefly found sanctuary as a religious minister in nearby Hackney before leaving for a new life in post-Franklin Pennsylvania.

Cayley's arrival in London from Nottingham was not quite as traumatic, but the change in environment could not have been more striking. Cayley found himself in a London flooded with French refugees brimming with the news of the emerging Terror. He was also surrounded by a radical peer group struggling to balance their support for the principles of reform and even revolution, while in general deploring its current horrific outcome.

Even as he began to settle into his new home, Cayley found his domestic circumstances performing yet another somersault. Barely six months after Cayley's father had inherited the baronetcy, Sir Thomas died suddenly, making George the 6th Baronet in March 1792; he was barely eighteen years old. Despite his ascendancy to the title, Cayley, still a minor in the eyes of the law, remained at the financial mercy of his mother, who held control over the Brompton estate until he achieved his majority at age twenty-one. After a brief visit home to attend his father's funeral, Cayley returned to London and Morgan's tutelage. His education was not the only place in which Cayley sought refuge from the sudden traumas at Brompton. As Walker and Morgan were friends, it seems likely that Walker visited the capital with his daughter during this period, further stoking the teenage couple's forbidden love.

Cayley's prospects of imminent independence, to be attained at an age forty years younger than his father, must have fuelled his sense of liberty. But the next few months were filled with examples of how limits to that very concept affected those having the most influence on his instruction. Following the execution of Louis XVI in 1793, Britain's prime minister, William Pitt, expelled the French ambassador, and Britain quickly found herself, once again, at war with France. Britain and more specifically London were in turmoil, with open talk of revolution filling the streets and taverns. In May the British Commons suspended habeas corpus – the common-law right to trial – and many leading reformers were arrested and imprisoned. That same month Cayley penned a letter to his mother that seemed to suggest a rising rebellion of his own concerning a subject close to his heart. Though his passion is there for all to see, he could perhaps have started the letter a little more diplomatically.

> My dear crazy mother ... you have entered so largely on the subject of matrimony – one that I am fond of! – that I will tell you of my ideas, and of the conduct I mean to pursue in respect of it. In the first place, it is a point agreed by all philosophers that in a good state of society men should be married at eighteen, the woman at sixteen, but that the circumstances of their country do not admit of it. . . . Now according to the second of my Articles, I hope you will admit that the sooner these gratifications take place the better. This determines me to marry early. It seems to frighten you somewhat about Town life. I assure you that I was not a little mortified to learn you thought me in danger of being in love with every little girl I meet – like a schoolboy – especially those near town, whom I would not have if there were not another woman in the world and the race of human beings likely to become extinct! But be assured that, when I choose a wife, she shall not be a woman from near that Map of Country that is contained in your letter, nor fond of coaches and diamonds, nor helpless and pallid. . . . Once and for all I swear never to play the gentry of England. I am not tied to England; I am a citizen of the world – I shall settle in that part I like best if, "Sir" shall be changed to Citizen Cayley. . . .

He signed off with the charming but equally unusual "I remain in <u>Love</u> with you, your son, G Cayley." Having informed his mother he would marry whom he wished, that it wasn't going to be the traditional Cayley cousin or even someone local, and that he was expecting to live neither necessarily in Brompton nor under the title carefully nurtured by his family through five generations via an aristocratic heritage going back seven hundred years, just adding "by the way I love you" seems a barely adequate blow softener for his espousal of the revolutionary cause. Isabella's reply was, if anything, even more surprising than the original. It exemplifies the intimate, loving, and strikingly liberal relationship that existed between mother and son.

> My most dear & affectionate George – how shall I sufficiently thank you for your friendship in so speedily relieving my anxiety about your dear self – your sensible & explanatory letter was an unexpected cordial that banished all fears & made me resume my sanguin [sic] hopes of joy & happiness for you in a moment. . . .

Isabella later added this letter to her small personal archive of correspondence, though not before appending the suffix "I put this letter by to keep it as a vindication of my self against the unjust charge of my having exirted [sic] myself to prevent my dear George marrying. . . ." This same afterthought, in Isabella's hand, revealingly refers to another letter that does not survive in which she "expressed my fears of his affections being engaged to some fond deceiver." It seems that although Isabella now accepted her son as master unto himself (and "with pleasure look up to you as our conductor & protector through life . . ."), her concern over some of young George's life choices, in particular his all-important future wife, still left her in a state of some apprehension.

As Cayley's London education continued, he was increasingly exposed to the sharp end of British politics. He attended reform meetings at the famous Crown and Anchor Tavern in the Strand, London, where the most prominent liberal figures of the day would meet. Its clientele was made up of the first team of the reform movement. There was Charles Fox, the fierce political opponent of the embattled prime minister, William Pit. There was the Reverend John Horne Tooke, a man tried on the charge of high treason for printing the phrase "equal, active citizenship was a right of man." One of the most prominent members of this band was the "Father of Reform," Major John Cartwright, a man who had refused a commission in the navy on the grounds of his opposition to the colonial war. Cayley's meeting with him foreshadowed later events, when Cartwright became the subject of Cayley's pamphleteering as a prelude to Cayley's own political career.

As Cayley approached the end of his schooling, the finishing line being defined by the point at which he would take on the legal responsibility of his inheritance, he seemed to be ensuring that his workload was as unburdensome as possible. Not long after his return to Brompton, he received a request from his erstwhile tutor for upwards of a hundred pounds in monies owing as a result of Cayley's habit of throwing lunch and dinner parties for his friends and fencing partners. His time in London had not been all academic drudgery.

Though Cayley refers in later life to the fact that his earliest thoughts on mechanical flight occurred during his time in London, there has, up until now, been little to document that fact. Recently, a school exercise book from the period has been rediscovered that documents the first of his thoughts on the theory and practice of flight. These schoolboy doodles represent some of the first of their kind in the history of aviation, and hidden within the dozens of sketches is the one that would change Cayley's life, and the future of aviation, forever.

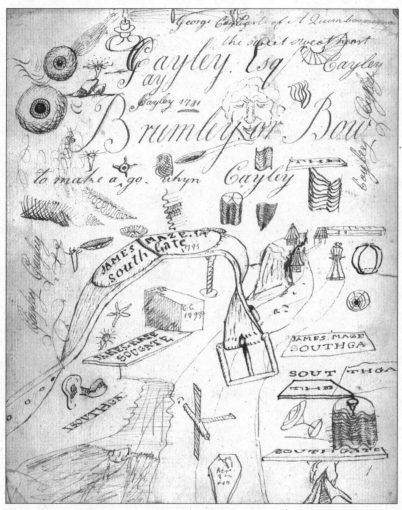

The inside front cover of Cayley's school exercise book: the record of a schoolboy's rambling thoughts over a number of years. Included are early exercises in practising his signature; fellow student James Maze Esq. seemed to have made an impression; the coffin shows the date one year after his father's death. Other details include the action of light upon the eye (top and left); on the lower left is a sketch of the auditory canal. Down the left-hand edge are the repeated representations of wind-carried seeds, a subject that was included in Cayley's treatise on flight a decade later.

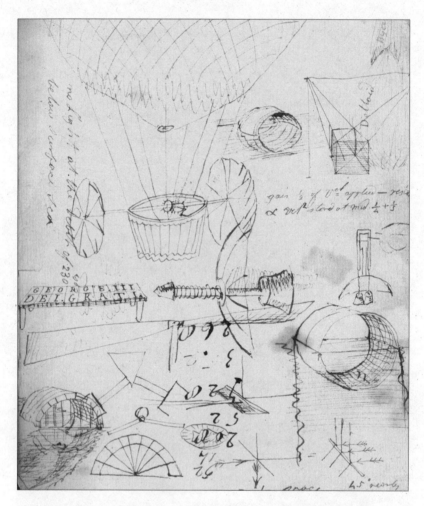

The inside back cover of the same exercise book. The hand-cranked gears driving the
propellered-balloon follow an idea for this by Frenchman Jean Pierre Blanchard in 1784.
The umbrella-like dart below it appears to be the prototype "spinning top," which Cayley
developed a few years later. Just below that is a large two-bladed propeller, which also
featured in some of his designs. The curious sketch to the propeller's right appears to be
Cayley's first attempt to draw another later design for a gunpowder-fuelled, bow-string-
return internal combustion engine. Above that, in the topmost right corner, a rough sketch
of deltoid and bicep ("bycept") muscles for arm-powered flight. The number of small bridges
is a foreshadowing of one of his earliest works: a large-scale drainage scheme for Brompton
and surrounding areas.

These doodles have lain hidden in the archive of Britain's Royal Aeronautical Society for almost forty years. At least one previous researcher has viewed them and noted the date of 1781 on the front cover. We know this because the researcher also, rather shamefully, underlined it in pencil, even though this is almost certainly not the date on which the sketches were made. In 1781 Cayley was eight years old, so it is far more likely that these are from around 1793 when the nineteen-year-old Cayley was in Southgate. In among the cartoons of the back page are a remarkable series of clues to Cayley's later work. The most extraordinary are three figures to be found, upside down and obscured by later additions. The first shows an inclined plane on

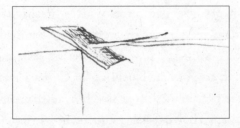

A computer-enhanced detail from the inverted back cover of Cayley's exercise book shows an inclined plane pushing against a resisting airflow.

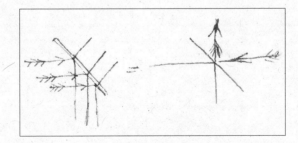

A similarly enhanced and inverted detail shows how Cayley has deduced that an inclined plane, driven up against the air, will generate an upward force – the first ever documentation of the forces of wing-borne flight.

a shaft with two perpendicular lines intersecting it. This represents a wing, with the wind resisting horizontally against it generating another vertically acting force. The other two nearby figures are a schematic of the resultant forces acting on a wing; Cayley's inspired discovery was that the force of lift that makes wing-borne flight possible results from driving an inclined plane up against the air. Cayley had extracted the fundamental of flight. Flight was not achieved through some complex interplay between a mass of feathers and the flapping of their supporting wing; the wing beat in order to generate thrust, while at the same time acting as the angled surface that pushed against the air to generate lift. Nature's stunningly elegant means of achieving flight concealed the fact that there were *two* independent factors involved. The separation of these two forces and the realization of how an artificial structure could mimic their effects is what made wing-borne flight possible. These images predate by over six years the famed silver disc of 1799, and acted as the blueprint for Cayley's later detailed calculations on the possibilities of *manned* heavier-than-air flight. While drawing a doodle as a bored teenage student, he had unravelled a puzzle that had baffled humankind for millennia.

Finding the Pieces II – What's All This About an "Inclined Plane"?

If, like me, you learned the rudiments of aerodynamics from picture books on the subject, then the news that Cayley had simply taken a horizontal board, tipped it slightly, and then pushed it up against the air seems a world away from how an airplane flies – surely it is the airfoil that keeps a plane in the sky? The explanation I grew up with talked about the wing's cross-section having the upper surface bulged and the lower one flatter. The science was that the air has to travel farther to get over the longer upper surface, so it spreads out, lowering the pressure above the wing and so the whole surface gets "sucked" up into the air.

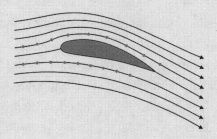

The iconic representation on how a wing generates lift. The stretched air on the upper part of the wing causes lowering of pressure, which means that the higher pressure underneath pushes the whole surface upward, generating lift.

This classic explanation is called the Bernoulli effect, and it was known even before Cayley, though not applied to aerodynamics until the twentieth century. If this was the only means by which a wing generates lift, then Cayley would have discovered a whole lot of nothing – but that's not the case. Although Bernoulli can account for some of the lift generated by an airplane's wing, it doesn't account for all of it, and sometimes not even much. If the Bernoulli effect were the only thing keeping an aircraft up in the air, no airplane could ever fly upside-down: an inverted airfoil would *add to*, rather than subtract from, gravity and the result would be a smoking hole at the end of the runway. I don't know if you've ever seen an aerobatics display, but the ones I've seen have airplanes flying upside-down without a second thought. So what's keeping them up there?

The answer is Newton's Third Law. If you push against something, it pushes back with an equal and opposite force. So if you push a piece of paper against the air, the air resists. If you place that piece of paper at an angle, most of the resisting force is acting backwards, but a proportion is acting upward – and so an inclined plane, driven against the air, generates lift just like a kite. The Wright brothers referred to their early machines as kites, and the term remains a quaint, though oddly appropriate nickname for an aircraft. Many airplanes designed for aerobatics have symmetrical wings with upper and lower surfaces equally curved specifically to *remove* the Bernoulli effect. High-speed aircraft have wings that are almost flat, and these too generate most of their lift through being angled and pushed against the airflow. It is the *angle* of the wing relative to the flow of air (Cayley's *inclined* plane) that is critical. In fact, every form of wing, either flat or curved, has an angle at which it produces no lift at all. Even the word "airplane" means a plane moving against the air.

The icon of the airfoil is a handy cartoon for explaining one element of lift, but it's much less than half the story. The inclined plane is a large part of the remainder. It is this phenomenon that made the first man-made, winged flight possible.

3

FLIGHT *before* CAYLEY

Cayley found himself growing up in the first-ever era in which man-made flight of any kind had been achieved, thanks largely to the Montgolfier brothers' successes of 1783. Though this was a relatively early stage in aviation, human attempts at flight had been around for some time, and there were no lack of claimants for having invented flying machines. However, the answer to the question "Who invented artificial flight?" is less than straightforward, owing to the fact that it depends on what "flight" means.

The Australian Aboriginals can probably lay claim to the earliest form of an aerodynamic machine: the boomerang is a remarkably sophisticated variant of a rotary flyer. Early boomerang-like artifacts have been found in North America, northern Europe, central Africa, and Asia – they even appeared in the tomb of Tutankhamen. However, many of these were essentially "throwing sticks" – a hybrid of a club and an edged weapon whose effective range was extended by it being thrown and spun through the air. There was no anticipation of such a weapon returning, it was a "fire-and-forget" device, along the lines of an arrow or javelin. These throwing sticks achieved their effect through blunt trauma, the sharpened edge merely providing improved stability to make them more accurate. They were most useful in the pursuit of small game, when an animal could be captured simply by injuring it enough to slow it down.

It was the Australian Aboriginals who invested more effort in these weapons than was strictly required for hunting when they crafted the blade profile and arm geometry to enable the stick to complete an elegant arc. At some point, an early Australian must have wondered at the attraction of throwing something whose path through the air could be both predicted and influenced. The practice became something akin to a performance art, the boomerang itself gaining an intrinsic value far beyond that of mere utility. There is no evidence to suggest that the Aboriginals understood the mechanisms of flight in any kind of modern academic sense, they simply knew the physical characteristics required of a stick to make it fly.

The science that keeps the boomerang in the air is a combination of gyroscopic precession and differential lift, neither of which was documented until perhaps five thousand years after the first boomerang glided back to hand. "Gyroscopic precession" provides stability; the same mechanism prevents a moving bicycle from falling by providing an "automatic" resisting impetus in the direction opposite to any force trying to tip the bicycle over. The same self-stabilizing effects are found in the eponymous gyroscope, which when spinning will push back against any attempt to change its angle of inclination. "Differential lift" refers to the difference between the forces generated by the "upper" and "lower" arms of the boomerang – for it must be thrown with the boomerang oriented vertically (one arm above the other) for it to return. The upper arm of the boomerang travels faster through the air than its lower twin because it is both moving and spinning forward, whereas the lower arm is spinning backwards relative to the air around it. As a result, the upper arm produces more lift than the lower one, twisting the boomerang in the air and forming the curving flight that is the boomerang's claim to fame. This little flying marvel has long been overlooked by aviation historians. It was regarded as little more than a curiosity when introduced to northern hemisphere culture – an exotic curiosity, perhaps, or an example of native charm and guile, but of little significance in the civilized world.

The boomerang joined any number of examples that acted as a major irritation for early aviation researchers, for the mystery of flight appeared hidden in plain sight. And it was Nature that mocked the human observer most. A thousand breeds of fowl and ten thousand species of insects were capable of effortlessly launching themselves into the ether. If birdbrains and lacewings could fly, how could it be beyond the grasp of the tamer of fire and the creator of the wheel? Every generation seemed to throw up individuals fascinated by (or obsessed with) emulating nature's aviators. There was no shortage of people willing to try – in fact, taking to the air was simplicity itself; it was staying there that was the problem. Although the earliest forms of aviation had little obvious connection with later attempts to fly, in fact each formed some precursor to the development of the all-important wing.

The first written records of aviation concern the venerable kite. Though, like the boomerang, it is viewed as little more than a toy, a kite demonstrates the crucial principle of an inclined plane generating lift, one of the fundamental aspects of wing-borne flight. Trivializing the kite as a model for flight stems from a poor understanding of how a wing generates lift. Before beginning to build their gliders, the Wright brothers tested their future control systems on large biplane kites, which they flew at their home in Daytona. Years later, on days when the Kitty Hawk winds were too strong, the brothers tethered their full-scale gliders and practised flying them like a kite in a natural wind tunnel.

Legends concerning the origins of kites centre in China. Depending on whose account you believe, they were invented when a farmer's hat blew off in the wind, with the owner clinging to the unravelling thread as it sailed skywards, or else through the more romantic notion of a leaf observed clinging to a hedge by a gossamer strand. The earliest written records of kites begin with the legendary accounts of Han Xin, a second-century BC general who was supposed to have used a kite as a trigonometric measuring tool. Later and more reliable reports concern the sixth-century AD Emperor Wu of Liang, who used a kite as a distress signal during the siege of Tai-cheng. Though Wu's attempted SOS amounts to little more than taking a flag from its pole and holding on to the rope, it was at least a conscious attempt to apply the technology for a specific purpose. Unfortunately, Liang's attempts at summoning help proved to be unsuccessful. The besieging army, realizing the significance of the kite, unleashed "a thousand arrows" until one finally tore the fabric and the kite fell to earth. Eventually Liang and his army were defeated, but his attempts at summoning help were at least recorded for posterity.

"Man-carrying kites" were used as a form of execution by Emperor Kao Yang in the city of Leh in the mid-sixth century. One political prisoner named Yuan Huang T'ou successfully traversed the drop from the city tower to the ground on an owl-shaped kite and was subsequently rewarded by being imprisoned and starved to death. Though the first recorded successful flight of its kind, T'ou's experience is better viewed as a parachute trial than aviation as such, the parachute being yet another piece in the flying puzzle.

The first form of powered flight, the rocket, also hails from China. In the mid-ninth century, Chinese chemists produced black powder from saltpetre, sulphur, and charcoal, a mixture that made for a slower burning form of gunpowder. The powder was later used as a horrific weapon by being packed into long bamboo canes and used as a short-range flame-throwing "fire-lance" during the tenth century. By turning the fire-lance around and allowing the expanding gases to act as a propellant, the fire-lance was eventually developed into a rocket-powered projectile. The rocket's career was largely military: from its first use in AD 1232 during the Mongol siege of K'ai-feng, through development under the Ming and Ch'ing dynasties, to its widespread use in Europe, until it was superseded by the smooth-bored cannon of the early sixteenth century. Its use in massive quantities by Tipu Sultan proved an embarrassing re-introduction to the rocket for the British army during their campaigns in India at the end of the eighteenth century. The see-saw in dominance between cannon and rocket swung briefly in favour of the firework during the Napoleonic Wars, when Britain's use of Sir William Congreve's stick-stabilized rockets was widespread – 25,000 of them setting Copenhagen alight in 1807.

The principle of a more easily recognizable form of aviation – the flying rotor (which went on to become the helicopter) – also has its first recorded incidence in China. In the third century AD a common pastime was the construction of what were known as "dragonflies." By angling a pair of leaves atop a bamboo stem and then spinning the central spindle with the fingers or between the hands, the leaves acted as a lift-generating rotor with the mass of the stem providing a weighted "pendulum" stability. This design kept the centre of gravity of the whole machine directly beneath the centre of lift generated by the spinning leaves. This critical combination of stability and lift allowed the dragonfly to gently rise an entertaining few feet into the air and then with equal grace descend to earth. The development of such little craft gave Europe its first recorded contribution toward flight, though once more it would emerge in the form of an entertainment. A draw-string helicopter is first illustrated in a Flemish psalter now in the Copenhagen Royal Library and dated around AD 1330. The illustration shows the more familiar four-bladed propeller on a shaft with a length of twine attached. By wrapping the twine around the central shaft, a much higher rotational speed could be attained than was possible with the hand-twisted dragonflies. The smoothness with which the additional force could be applied allowed it to be delivered to the spindle without upsetting the steadiness of the craft, preserving that all-important balance between stability and power. These toys became a favoured aristocratic gift in middle-age Europe; in France they were known as *moulinet à noix* (little windmill with a pulley wheel). The helicopter remained as little more than a plaything until the 1940s, but its inspirational power proved nothing short of profound, most notably on Cayley and later the Wright brothers. Only in hindsight can this toy, like the kite, be recognized as a "model" – the building block of not only aerodynamics, but mathematics and science. It was the safe, simple, and replicable technique of modelling designs for aircraft that eventually made flight possible. Before this, however, the hazardous, complicated, and idiosyncratic variations of the ornithopter (flying machines with bird-like flapping wings) dominated much of aviation history.

The ornithopter long remained a stubbornly persistent aberration in the search for manned flight. Even today, the Ornithopter Society seeks to solve the almost intractable engineering demands of making an artificial beating wing simultaneously generate sufficient lift and thrust to take off. Historical examples of this pursuit include two highlights typical of their time. Abu'l-Quasim 'Abbas Ibn Firnas (a "Moorish physician and rather bad poet") adopted the classic "feather-covered arm" followed by the "tower-leaping" approach in the ninth century AD (he broke his back). Britain's Benedictine Brother Eilmer became "the Flying Monk of Malmesbury" in the eleventh century, using wings framed with willow-wand and covered with light cloth (he broke both legs). More famous, and certainly more prudent, was Leonardo da Vinci, whose early sixteenth-century notebooks include numerous illustrations of not only bird wings, but winged and helicopter mechanisms for flight. It is not known whether any of these machines were ever contemporaneously manufactured – in fact, a hard-nosed examination of da Vinci's designs indicates that none of them could ever have flown. Da Vinci suffered from the classic under-estimation of the muscle power required to get an ornithopter off the ground, and his design for an "airscrew" (derived from the Archimedes fluid screw) was a dead end as far as flight was concerned, despite the fact that working toy helicopters had been around in Europe for over two centuries before da Vinci's birth.

Another pair of Italians, Marcello Malpighi and Giovanni Alphonso Borelli, were the first to scientifically discredit the idea of flying like a bird. Their 1680 publication "The movement of animals" was uncompromising in its conclusions that the man-powered ornithopter would never make it into the air with arm power alone. However, rather than abandoning the flapping wing, later pioneers simply attempted to amplify human muscle power through the mechanical advantage of levers. It never did work. It was not the wing or the emulation of nature's living flyers that provided the biggest breakthrough in aviation. It was the balloon.

Archimedes is the most likely candidate for the title "grandfather of the balloon" for it was his observations on displacement that are the principles of lighter-than-air flight. He recognized that an object forcibly immersed in a fluid of higher density is driven up with a force equal to the difference between its own weight and that of the fluid displaced. Of course, there is no substance lighter than a vacuum, and so it seemed obvious to Jesuit priest Francesco Lana de Terzi to suggest in 1670 using vacuum-filled balloons to hoist a ship into the air. His vow of poverty and fear of the ungodly imbalance such a machine would create prevented him actually trying it out. If he had, we would have discovered that the weight of an encasing "balloon" strong enough to withstand the external air pressure around an effective vacuum would be more than the lift it produced – but it was a neat idea.

The eventual route to practical ballooning had once more been recognized, first by the Chinese and then rediscovered by the French in the 1700s, in the form of a culinary conjuring trick. An emptied then resealed eggshell would float when gently heated on a stove; it was the prototype hot-air balloon. Another priest – the Brazilian-born, Portuguese resident Bartolomeu Lourenço de Gusmão – was the first to publicly fly a balloon-proper on August 8, 1709. On that day, a small brazier hanging beneath a wooden-framed paper balloon soared above an audience, including King John v and the future Pope Innocent iii, until a worried courtier grabbed it before it set fire to the drapes. Although de Gusmão died in 1724, poor and friendless (having destroyed all his papers and designs following the religious and political upheavals of the Inquisition), news of his achievement had already spread throughout Europe – though not apparently as far the ears of either of the two Montgolfier brothers in France.

In November 1782 Joseph Montgolfier, recuperating from the recent hospitality of debtor's prison, was warming himself in his rooms at the University of Avignon and watching the smoke rise into the chimney when inspiration struck. He built a small, square cross-section balloon from taffeta stretched over a wooden frame, held it above the fire and then watched the smoke-filled balloon rise to the ceiling. He persisted for years in believing it was the smoke, rather than heated air, that generated the necessary lift – no matter; he summoned his brother Jacques-Étienne, and they began to experiment with larger and more elaborate designs. It was the very scalability of lighter-than-air flight that made progress so fast. In fact, as far as lift alone is concerned with balloons, the bigger the better: doubling the diameter of a balloon generates eight times the lift – this is why later airships would get so huge. On December 14 a large Montgolfier balloon rose to over 1,000 feet and alighted nearly a mile away from a stunned crowd. Six months later, another spectacularly successful demonstration of their now 35-foot-diameter craft left the market square in Annonay and reached 3,000 feet up and two miles distant. It was time for the Montgolfiers to visit Paris – they arrived just too late.

The Montgolfiers themselves had alerted the French Académie Royale des Sciences as to their successes. This news provided the impetus for the considerably better funded Académie to speedily complete its own parallel and independent experiments into the construction of a balloon filled with the recently discovered hydrogen. It took days, during which iron filings boiled with the addition of sulphuric acid to generate the required volume of the lifting gas. Finally the small 12-foot-diameter craft was furtively guided through the narrow, darkened Paris streets from Place de Victoires, across the Seine, to Champ de Mars. On August 27 at five o'clock (using two rather ill-advised cannon shots to herald the event), the hydrogen-filled balloon was set free in heavy rain. An enraptured audience watched until it disappeared into the clouds, still going heavenwards in an accelerating spiral. The crowd (including an aging Benjamin Franklin and John Quincy Adams) went wild, as did the terrified group of innocent locals in Ecouen, where the balloon landed. They severely mauled the demonic gas-sack with anything sharp or heavy that came to hand. Not to be outdone, the Montgolfiers' now 70-foot-high balloon (after only one false start) rose from Versailles on September 19 carrying a sheep, a duck, and a rooster. Over 100,000 Parisians, including Louis XVI and Marie-Antoinette, rubber-necked to watch as the balloon headed toward the horizon and a landing in the Forêt du Vaucresson.

These events were followed in quick succession by numerous others in hot-air and hydrogen vehicles. Each demonstrated that getting off the ground was now a reality, but ballooning was seen as more of a

fairground novelty than a form of transport. No immediate flying revolution followed these achievements. Instead, the French Revolution
interceded to delay and diffuse the considerable interest in French aviation and to shorten rather than stretch Royal necklines.

Cayley was little more than a month short of his tenth birthday
when Jean François Pilatre de Rozier and François Laurent climbed
into a Montgolfier balloon and became the first men to fly free from
the earth on November 21, 1783.

4

TOYS *for the* BOYS

Even Cayley himself seems unsure about exactly when he began his first serious work on flight; initially he quotes the date as being in 1796, later changing this to 1792, when he was a mere eighteen years old. The discovery of his exercise book aviation doodles suggests the earlier date is nearer the truth. What is clear is that on completing his formal education with George Morgan in London, Cayley threw himself into a myriad of scientific interests, though to start with he prudently kept his thoughts on flight to himself.

Following his permanent return to Brompton in late 1793, the only record we have of Cayley's scientific activities comes from the sparse entries of his notebook "Motive Power." However he had other, more pressing, activities to occupy him throughout 1794 in preparation for taking legal responsibility for the Brompton estate in December. It was shortly afterwards, in early 1795, that Cayley began to document his thoughts once more in his notebooks. Through his entries we can see that it was his responsibilities as a country squire and his enthusiasm for his new roles of landowner and farm manager that were on his mind, though his notes are an almost haphazard and certainly irregular record. His notebooks are not necessarily a straight chronology of events, for he would revisit them, appending further ideas at later dates, making it more difficult for a reader to decide *when* Cayley had his initial thoughts on any given subject. The note-book known simply as "number one" is the easiest to place in time as the inside cover bears the useful inscription "George Cayley 1795." This was a pivotal year. Cayley had just turned twenty-one, and on reaching his majority he began to exercise his new-won independence both socially and intellectually. His notebook captures a mind in a whirl of ideas.

> . . . fact on the fecundity of sheep . . . construction of roots and veg-etables . . . the effect of age on the nutritive power in the vine . . . fact on the structure of the seed . . . on the anomalous propagation of the nut . . . on the soil in Flanders . . .

His notes then run through divorce in ancient Rome, the power of both the navy and the priesthood in tenth-century England, origins of the longbow, and a catalogue of historical British earthquakes. Some entries border on the odd: the chastity of nuns; nature's design for placing a goose's rectum just above water level while floating; "My own Thumb nail grew half an inch all but 1/20th in the space of 3 exact calendar months. . . ."

Another emerging range of interests, which with the 20/20 of hind-sight seem to orbit around a common theme, are those concerning the materials required for building strong and light machines, the engi-neering principles of engines, and the continuation of his fascination with the air and the creatures that fill it:

> I tried the following experiment with the best fir timber I could get. . . . All experimentalists agree that the law of resistances in an elastic of fluid such as Air is as inversely as the space it occupies. . . . I dissected a Jay on the 2nd of April 1795 the Esophagus is very long. . . .

As well as text, there are numerous sketches of his ideas and experiments, drawn in ink and hatched in what would become his characteristic manner. In many ways Cayley's sometimes rough but always energy-filled drawings are the most vivid expression of his psyche. There is an immediacy about them that is lost when his diagrams are professionally re-rendered for public consumption. Each sketch captures a specific moment of discovery or else the first glimpses of a considered idea, and though he was no great artist, he had a raw talent for illustration. The drawings often end abruptly at the paper's edge because, in his zeal to get them down, he'd simply failed to realize there wasn't room to fit them within the constraints of the page; Cayley was never comfortable with constraint. More importantly for his research, he never let the limitations of his artistic skills or his mastery of grammar or punctuation inhibit his thoughts. He would not, perhaps he *could* not, edit himself, and it is this quality that allows him to throw off any intellectual inhibitions that would stem the flow of ideas. In the secure privacy of his personal notebooks, each hastily drawn sketch and scribbled note represents a unique and specific moment of Cayley's mind at work.

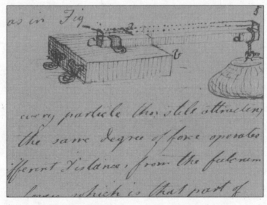

Cayley's 1795 notebook sketch of his experiments in firwood strength. Cayley has started drawing from the left-hand side and then simply run out of paper on the right to complete it.

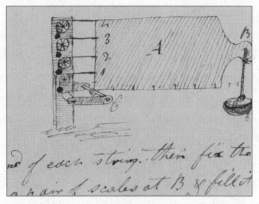

A more sophisticated experiment on the breaking point
of a wooden plane, again just squeezed in on the page.

At first his notebook reads as if it might head off in a dozen directions but get nowhere, but then things change. On page 129 (he
numbered them himself for later reference), appearing within pages
that are a clutter of other subjects, comes the undated and almost
casual beginning of a life's work. Cayley has finally been experimenting
with his inclined plane idea, and the results are startling.

> A surface of 33 3/18 sq feet carried through the air in an
> Horizontal direction and presenting an angle of the fifth part of
> Radius with the Horizon sustained a weight of 17lb – at the veloc-
> ity of 12 miles and a quarter p^r Hour. Now from the nature of the
> inclined plane and its passage through a fluid . . .

And then off he goes with barely a thought for the fact that he had
just initiated the study of aircraft aerodynamics. Like his interest in
how the plimsoll line of a goose intercepts with its rectum, Cayley
simply lets the outpourings from his head spill onto the page regard-
less of where they would lead. But he's excited, that is obvious; you can
sense his mind tumbling through the geometry and arithmetic.

Cayley's 1795 note entry showing the forces acting on a lifting plane, echoing his earliest illustrations of the same idea in his school exercise book. These are his record of the first-ever experiments on a lift-generating wing.

> ... therefore if such a surface were made and a conveyance car were suspended from it below the Centre of Bulk and the weight of the man and surface were equal to 200 lb and that this man had the power of resisting or pushing against the air with a force of 40 pounds either by Wing or another contrivance that man could convey himself through the air ...

And so winged flight was born, or more accurately, the first example of it with any hope of getting an adult human into the air and keeping him there. But Cayley's train of thought couldn't stop and it's not until five ink-blot-and-correction-ridden pages, and at least one change in pen nib, later that he finally draws an almost breathless conclusion:

> ...hence it is demonstrated that when the plain [the wing] is large enough and the angle [of its inclination] small enough 1lb [of thrust] might support a million – 2 million or any number whatever....

Cayley had just proved that a jumbo jet would fly. Actually, he hadn't quite done that because there were issues such as three kinds of drag that would demand a much more powerful engine than he at first thought, as well as issues of control and stability, of taking off, of landing, and a dozen other as yet undiscovered complications, but he'd seized hold of the basic idea: there was no theoretical limit to the weight that could be lifted into the air using an inclined plane. Anyone else might have called it a day, but Cayley didn't leave it there. Even in the exhilaration of discovery, he realized there was a catch that would cast a shadow over all his future endeavours even into the ninth decade of his life: "but this extent can only be true in theory as such a surface would be scarce capable of construction."

Cayley was a man living in the eighteenth century. The railway engine hadn't been invented yet, never mind the automobile. The steam engine was in its infancy, the internal combustion engine a pipe dream; the invention of the paper clip was a century away. In 1795 wood, iron, and stone were the working materials for construction. Leather, canvas, or even silk offered durable and flexible alternatives, but how could anyone build a plane of such strength and lightness as to allow it to safely support, on air alone, its own weight and that of man? This eureka moment came with the realization that it was in that most infuriating class of ideas: it was two or three generations ahead of its time. Within the course of six scribbled pages in his notebook, Cayley had shown that man-made flight by wing was a theoretical possibility, but practically, with engineering constraints as they were at the time, it was a non-starter. So having discovered that it *could* happen and then almost immediately proving that it couldn't happen *yet*, what next?

He got married.

Eccentric though his hobby may have seemed to his contemporaries, it was not his growing interest and experiments in aerodynamics that caused his widowed mother, Isabella, most concern. It was the news that Cayley had retained his affection for Sarah Walker over the three years of their enforced separation, and at some point they had become engaged, though when is not known. As part of Isabella's documentation of events surrounding her son's marriage, she notes cryptically, "I knew not who it was who had engaged them," suggesting that some formal agreement to marry had been entered into by George and Sarah and that the event had been overseen by some third party without either the knowledge or consent of Isabella. That the event was described in such formal terms stems from the fact that an engagement could be more than merely a statement of intent. It was a legally binding agreement, with the possibility of the male being sued for breach of promise should he subsequently renege. An engagement could also mark the point at which sex between partners became socially acceptable, though there were no hard and fast rules on the subject, and no indication one way or the other as to whether Cayley and Sarah were lovers as well as fiancés. At some point, Cayley broke the news of his engagement to his mother, though there is no record of when or how her reactions to it. As would become a pattern for many aspects of George and Sarah's later relationship, even its inception was unconventional.

George and Sarah were married at All Saints, in the Parish of Edmonton, London, on July 9, 1795. Both were aged twenty-one years. The service was conducted under special licence as neither party was being married in their home parish, the ecclesiastical division used for the practical administration of many of the local laws in eighteenth-century Britain. Even their reception was a little unusual. It was held not within the traditional home estate of the wealthy groom at Brompton, but at a London social landmark. The post-wedding feast took place at the Bell Inn, an eatery made famous through the highly popular and lengthy comic verse by William Cowper, "The Diverting History of John Gilpin; Showing How He Went Further Than He Intended, And Came Safe Home Again." The wedding's location in faraway London meant that there was no customary presentation of the new Lady Cayley around the Brompton and Sawdon district. Because of the war with France, a sojourn abroad in the tradition of Cayley's father and mother was also out of the question. Instead, immediately after their marriage they took the coach trip up the main communication artery from London to Scotland, branching off at York and then on to the joys of family life at Brompton's High Hall. Cayley was leaving his life as a single man and a student behind and taking on the responsibilities of a husband, aristocrat, and estate manager. He would not, however, be putting away all his childish things.

On his arrival at Brompton, Cayley set about three specific goals. He would take control of the Brompton estate and see to its improvement; he would begin an intense period of private experimentation into the mechanisms of flight; he and the new Lady Sarah would start producing a family. An ancillary project would be Cayley's attempts to balance his maturing love for his young wife with his deep affection for his recently bereaved mother, a task made all the more difficult because the two women were far from the closest of companions. The strong-willed and increasingly unconventional behaviour of them both became a major part of Cayley's complicated life.

Isabella had moved into High Hall on the death of her father-in-law in 1792. However, with the arrival of the newlyweds, she decided that, grand though it was, the main family residence was just a little too small to accommodate two Ladies of the Manor for tradition dictated that she was still the *Lady* Isabella despite her husband's death. So the Dowager Lady Isabella returned to The Green to enjoy the benefits of an independent old age sourced from the considerable endowment she received from Sir Thomas's will. She also further pursued her religious work in the parish. Such an action could have made for a smoothing of the Brompton waters had not her religious fervour drawn her into the arms of a recently emerged cult. Isabella had embraced the New Methodism, a creed that some considered but one step away from the accursed atheism that had swept much of the late eighteenth-century upper classes.

According to the *Methodist News*, at age fifty-two Isabella saw the light and found that "a deep seriousness possessed her spirit." This occurred around the time her father-in-law and then husband had died in quick succession, and her son had announced that he was a revolutionary republican and was marrying a non-related commoner. With these events in mind, it's not hard to believe that Isabella's soul was in need of a little moral support. From that point on, though previously no slouch when it came to her religious devotions, Isabella took to her new faith with an avid enthusiasm. For the time being, Cayley was content to accommodate, though not condone, his mother using the family name and title in the commissioning of her evangelism. Eventually, though, there was a serious clash between Lady Isabella and the new squire about the estate.

In the meanwhile, the little time Cayley could spare from lordly matters of estate and procreation, he devoted to discovering the secrets of the air's resistance. One of his first steps in his search for the

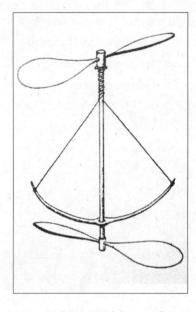

Launoy and Bienvenu's *hélicoptère* of 1784.

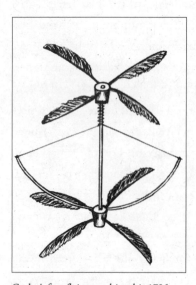

Cayley's first flying machine, his 1796 adaptation of Launoy and Bienvenu's design.

secrets of flight involved something he had brought back with him from London, a toy with a little history of its own.

In 1784, barely a year after the Montgolfiers had achieved the world's first manned flight by balloon, two Parisian gentlemen named Launoy and Bienvenu demonstrated an updated version of a toy helicopter at the Académie Royale. Their model had two twin-bladed rotors attached at opposite ends of common shaft, which was made to rotate using a small bowed wooden stave. The result was a little flyer capable of charming, though for most onlookers, superficially pointless flight. A decade later, along with the many possessions the fleeing French bluebloods had brought to London had been an example of the original Launoy and Bienvenu toy helicopter, and Cayley had just happened to be around to catch sight of one. His insight was the realization that scale was militating against his exploration of flight, and the new toy acted as a focus for his consideration of the problem. Getting a man and his enabling machine to fly meant getting two hundred pounds or more into the air and, as Cayley had already calculated, this was currently an engineering impossibility. His solution was typically practical: he downsized the problem and rebuilt the elegant little Launoy and Bienvenu toy to demonstrate something that *was* achievable. The double helicopter he created was an amusement, but it proved a point. From then on, Cayley would describe, to any guest or family member showing even the slightest interest, how eight feathers, two corks, a length of twine, and a bent twig could be used to build a flying machine. Its construction became one of the many Cayley hobbies and a source of entertainment for his guests. But such things could be little more than a distraction, for he had a serious piece of real estate to lick into shape in order to guarantee that future Cayleys would enjoy the same opportunities he had.

Cayley started with an assault on the inefficiencies of local agriculture. A disastrous series of harvests throughout Britain was bringing the country to its knees. This urgent problem, combined with an economic blockade of Britain by France and her allies, had led to a food shortage, which sparked off hunger riots in many of the major British cities. Opening Parliament in October 1795, King George III was greeted with missiles and cries of "Bread, peace and no Pitt." Taking what political advantage he could from the event, Prime Minister William Pitt immediately passed a new Sedition Bill redefining the law of treason in an attempt both to quell the popular discontent and as an aid to his own personal security. No one was quite as crass as to suggest that the hungry masses should "eat cake" but there were few options available in the short term to deal with the food shortages. The efficiency with which the French were enforcing their maritime siege was obvious; they had already seized as prize-of-war some two hundred American ships attempting to land goods in Britain. Cayley set about making his own contribution to resolve the crisis in a typical manner: through studying the available texts and then applying the knowledge gained as best he could. He sought to introduce a string of minor changes in cultivation, from the beneficial effects of adding lime and sand to arable fields to the application of large volumes of blubber secured from the nearby whaling port of Hull. However, Cayley always saw the importance of scale in his endeavours and when applied to farming he knew that the best way to think was to think big. So he embarked on his first major engineering project: drains.

One of the things with which Britain in general and Yorkshire in particular is well endowed is moisture moving in all directions: it falls from the sky like anywhere else but it also swirls around in clinging mists or rain or hail or snow and it rises from the ground in timber and health-wrecking damp. With the effects of gravity, all this water has to go somewhere, and in Yorkshire it by and large heads east to the sea. Its sometimes tortuous route is through the valleys making up the most fertile land in the region, but the rivers that formed them were prone to sudden and spectacular flooding, leaving large tracts of land unavailable for cultivation. Cayley became the young catalyst for encouraging the landowners of the area to embark on a large-scale plan not only to drain and clear the sodden land, but also to maintain the extensive series of canals, culverts, and embankments that would protect the newly reclaimed fields from future flooding. It was an undertaking requiring considerable diplomacy and politicking, as well as organization and practical application of proven agricultural method. Messrs. Walker and Morgan's recently graduated pupil seemed to have learned his lessons well, as Cayley was elected chairman of the charmingly titled Muston and Hunmanby Drainage Corporation: he served as a director until he was eighty. In order to acquire the necessary rights to land and property, an Act of Parliament was required and it was passed in 1800 under the Muston Drainage

Act. The groundwork for the act became the first of Cayley's lifetime involvement in central governmental politics. Cayley joined with neighbouring aristocrat Sir John Legard, who, being nearby and wealthy, was naturally a relative by both blood and marriage (one of Cayley's daughters later married into the Legards once more). It is suggested that Cayley himself was the chief architect of a novel form of drainage whereby the width of the artificial floodplain and the height of the embankment to contain it were tailored to the known flooding behaviours of any given stretch along the rivers to be tamed. This plan resulted in substantial savings as the length of the rivers Derwent and Hertford in need of flood control was considerable. Cayley's involvement may have been pivotal, but it seems likely that Cayley, ever the eager student, did more learning than leading, the work being managed by the highly accomplished William Chapman, an engineer with a sound reputation in the construction of piers and harbours. The result seemed like a win-win for all concerned: more than ten thousand acres brought into cultivation, the value of land increased for anyone holding it (Cayley, Legard, etc.), and a growing reputation for Cayley as a can-do kind of chap. The benefits of better drainage also induced an early example of the trickle-down effect as Cayley decreed that henceforth each cottage rented from him should have at least half an acre of land for the tenants to use for their own subsistence.

In the meantime, Lady Sarah had been making her own contribution to Cayley's local ambitions. Following their marriage, she was soon pregnant and their first daughter, Anne, was born on June 6, 1796. In another break with tradition, the birth took place neither at Brompton nor one of the nearby towns but back in Sarah's hometown of Nottingham. The birth of their first daughter was soon followed by a second, the diplomatically named Isabella ("Bell"), on November 8, 1797, once more in Nottingham. A third daughter, Emma, made her entrance on June 6 (again) in 1799, this time within the confines of the

High Hall. The production of numerous strong, healthy daughters turns out to be something of a Cayley family specialty – of course, the impressive number of female offspring in the aristocracy was partly as a result of the need to generate one or preferably a couple of sons in order for the title to survive. Fortunately, unlike his grandfather, *this* Sir George seems to have had his full complement of paternal instincts and by unanimous account he adored and was loved by each and every one of his daughters. Four decades' worth of letters act as testament to their mutual and tender affection.

In between daughters two and three, during the later stages of his work initiating the Drainage Act and his other landlordly duties, Cayley somehow found time to ponder on his ideas about how air acts on a moving body. It is unclear what substantive findings he made in his first few years, but in 1799, he was prompted to commit his thoughts not to paper, but in the form of a homemade medal. In the stone work-shop at the northeast corner of High Hall garden, Cayley struck a commemorative silver disc to illustrate his ideas. On one side is a repro-duction of his earlier thoughts on the triangulation of the forces of flight: lift, thrust, and drag. The obverse contains another classic Cayley sketch in the form of his early ideas on a powered airplane.

Though the quality of the art leaves something to be desired, the content of the image itself is nothing short of revolutionary and boasts no fewer than four world firsts. The craft shows a single lift-generating wing that appears like a canopy above the seated pilot. The wing shows a noticeable "camber"; it is concave to the airflow, an idea that seems to have sprung from his earlier notebook thoughts on "An umbrella being carried through the Air. . . ." Lift and thrust generation are separated into two distinct mechanisms: the wing for the upward force and the oar-like flappers for propulsion. Control of both left-right motion (yaw) and vertical motion (pitch) is effected by a single control surface – the elongated rudder/aileron at the rear, though how the pilot, rowing with both hands, was to guide it is a mystery.

There are a number of unsolved puzzles surrounding Cayley's silver disc, not least why he would think to mint it in the first place. It could have been intended as a present for someone or simply as an outlet for his thoughts in general, with this particular artifact being one of the few durable enough to survive to the present day. A second puzzle is the capital letter "R" placed between and below Cayley's initials "GC." Cayley had no middle name, so it was not a third initial. It might be the beginning of an unfinished word or phrase, but what it might mean is unknown. The intended recipient of the disc, if there was one, is also a mystery. The disc's significance lies in the fact that it clearly dates the design from 1799. This is a crude but principled blueprint for an air-craft with all the theoretical prerequisites for sustainable winged flight. That it should appear over a hundred years before the Wright brothers' even earliest designs makes it something of a gift to posterity – perhaps we were the intended beneficiary all along. But Cayley did not stop at simply sketching his ideas, even in precious metal. In spite of his pes-simism concerning the limits of construction, he wanted to see if he could build a machine that would fly. So, as well as the silver disc, he started working on the detailed design for an airplane.

The plans for his first flyer show how Cayley envisioned the full-scale machine operating. The sketches and attendant notes reveal how he had extrapolated from the measurements he had made on bird flight using their weight and wing area to calculate a wingspan that would support both the bulk of the machine and the intended aviator – "my own weight 160lb." Charles Gibbs-Smith, a historian with a particular interest in the invention of the airplane, examined Cayley's flying machines in detail in 1962 and was the first to tie the flyer of the silver disc to the more detailed plans in his loose papers, which are assumed to be roughly contemporaneous. Gibbs-Smith noted that the cambered wing so prominent in the disc is in fact formed by the upward stretch of the single-ply canvas that Cayley had proposed as the wing material. The wing would fill forming the concave surface much like a canvas sail, paper kite, or fabric hang-glider. The most obvious departure of these plans from what we imagine as the typical airplane is the short fat wings, or wings of a low-aspect (length-to-width) ratio. Cayley's initial concern over the structural strength of the wing, dating from his musings in 1795, never left him, and the short wings persisted in his designs throughout his life. There is no evidence that Cayley either built or flew the planned design, and there is no reference from him to suggest as much. The disc flyer of 1799 and the paper designs that were elaborations on it rank among many others from Cayley's catalogue of aircraft as a concept rather than a construction, another mental plaything of sorts. Cayley needed more time and, most importantly, more data before he could take the process to the next stage.

The preamble for the experimental work that followed the disc flyer designs can be seen during the early years of the nineteenth century as once more his notebook entries chart the ideas running through Cayley's head. As usual, general thoughts and observations are sandwiched among those most pertinent to flight:

> This year 1800 I gaged [gauged] a field of Standing corn in the following manner. . . . If birds when in that act of flying, which may well be called skimming oppose their wings to the horizontal current of the air in any given angle say for example that of the tenth part of radius and that the resistance upon the wing is sufficient to support their weight. . . . I measured the velocity of several Crows in flying during a calm day. . . . On Wednesday the 10th October 1802 at 10 o Clock at night there was a perfect circle or Halo surrounding the moon. . . .

Cayley includes within his aviation notes the leisurely observation that the amount of lift generated by an inclined plane varies as the square of the velocity multiplied by the density of the air. Cayley predicts that as the speed of his craft increases, the upward force generated by the wing would increase at an even higher rate: doubling the speed meant four times the lift, so getting his machine to travel quickly through the air became the critical requirement. He also realized that the thinner the air, the harder it would be to fly in it, a fact that pilots today are acutely aware of when flying in very hot conditions (when the air is significantly less dense) or in the thin air of higher altitudes. These observations are another pair of aviation world firsts, if they needed counting. As a counterbalance, Cayley's notes also conclude that a bird generates lift and thrust on alternate wing beats – which is also a world first, but unfortunately it is also wrong, which probably means that this one doesn't count. By way of coincidence, the date of his final quoted entry in his journal, 1802, was another turning point for the country, the Cayleys, and even, in its own small way, the village of Brompton.

The year 1802 saw matters military taking the fore on the world stage with the establishment of both America's West Point and Britain's military academies at Great Marlow (later moving to the more famous Sandhurst). The year also saw Britain and France temporarily resolving their differences with the Treaty of Amiens. The treaty followed the decisive defeat of the French fleet at Copenhagen by the British Navy, helped conspicuously by Horatio Nelson turning a "blind eye" to his superior's signal to disengage the enemy. Though the peace would be short-lived, it relieved both the British government and the people from the ravages of the continental blockade. This was also the year in which a young English writer of verse tied the knot with a local Yorkshire lass in Brompton Church, making Mary Hutchinson of Gallow Hill the very happy Mrs. William Wordsworth. June of this year also heralded the birth of Cayley's first son, also named George. Cayley's unbounded happiness is captured in the letter he sent to his mother Isabella up at The Green.

> I sit down in high glee to inform you that Lady Cayley is safe in bed with a very fine fat BOY who arrived here this morning at two o'clock. . . . I have so many letters to write that you must excuse more at the present, dear mother. P.S. I will send them a guinea for them to ring for this day and will make a feast for the village on my rent day.

Of course Cayley's glee did have *some* bounds; the new and ever fiscally aware Sir George paid the village bell-ringers considerably less than the guinea each that his own father Sir Thomas had paid on the equivalent occasion. The announcement of a "feast upon rent day" must have been cheering news for all concerned, though it may have had the added effect of reducing the number of defaulting tenants as a purely coincidental by-product. These signs of conservatism came alongside other indications that reaching the ripe old age of twenty-eight years had tempered the revolutionary zeal of his youth, as Cayley's private journal of the time records:

> The great bulk of the Nation is made up of men not competent to decide on the simplest political questions and therefore the will of such a majority would probably be wrong.

The birth of a son was a considerable relief for all concerned, and the release of tension allowed Cayley to throw himself into his work on aerodynamics. The eight years from 1803 to 1810 were, as far as his development of flight theory was concerned, nothing short of remarkable. During this time, Cayley finally built a winged flyer, but before he could do so he needed what every subsequent aircraft designer would require: aerodynamic data on the components of the craft that would keep it in the air.

Before the first recorded work on aviation aerodynamics could begin, Cayley had to come up with the machine to do it. Ever the scientific opportunist, Cayley ingeniously combined the inventions of earlier British scientists in ballistics and windmill design to build his homemade "whirling arm," which he mounted at the top of the High Hall staircase.

Cayley's apparatus comprised an arm pivoted on top of a swivel. The arm acted as a balance, and the swivel allowed this balance to rotate. At one end of the balance arm, he fixed a tensioned flat sheet of fabric that acted as one of his planes; at the other end was a weight. The arm was fixed to a spindle around which a cord had been wound, like a spinning top or the toy *moulinet à noix* helicopters of four hundred years before. However, Cayley wanted to apply a known force to spin his whirling arm, so instead of pulling, he used the most convenient force available: gravity. By attaching a weight to the end of cord around the spindle and then allowing it to drop the forty-five feet from the top of the High Hall stairwell to the floor, Cayley could rotate the spindle at a known speed. If the balancing arm is level while the apparatus is spinning, the plane is generating an upward lifting force that is equal to the downward pull of the counterweight. By varying the surface area of the plane and its angle of inclination, Cayley could calculate the lifting force of a whole series of potential wings. Cayley was quantifying the lift that a plane would impart, finding the wing's best *angle of attack* into the airflow, the ideal inclination that would give the upward push that keeps a plane in the air. It was not only simple, it worked. Cayley's calculations on the coefficient of lift (a fundamental concept in flight aerodynamics) are remarkably close to the accepted modern values derived from wind tunnel and flight experimentation. All the details of the design and testing are in his notebook, and they might have remained there, unknown to anyone, had not external events driven Cayley to consider publicly presenting his findings.

The catalyst for Cayley to think about airing his ideas was the publication of a Professor Danzel's "Bases of the Mechanisms for Directing Air Balloons." Danzel's fourteen-page article appeared in one of Cayley's favourite reads, the *Monthly Magazine*, of October 1804. In it the German professor expounded on a stylized oar that could be used for making balloons travel more toward the direction required than in the direction dictated by the wind. Fearing that he would be scooped, Cayley produced his first formal writing on the subject of wing-borne aviation: "Essay upon the Mechanical Principles of Aerial Navigation," dated October 6, 1804 – only a week after reading his rival's suggestions for balloons. The essay was never published, and in fact it was rediscovered only by chance when Laurence Pritchard, a Cayley enthusiast and biographer, found it among the Cayley family papers in 1960. Unpublished or not, the firsts in Cayley's essay just trip from his pen.

Cayley starts by christening the new mode of travel resulting from flight "Aerial Navigation" – that is, a practical mode of transport, not a curiosity or academic exercise. He foresees its rapid development, though with a *début de siècle* optimism, his premonition is exactly a hundred years early: "Aerial Navigation will form a most prominent feature in the progress of civilisation during the succeeding century." Though not an expert on balloons, Cayley reveals another of his insights through noting the need for balloon streamlining to form a "true solid of least resistance."

He also draws on his designs from his 1799 flyer by proposing controls for a new semi-rigid and steerable craft: "to the hinder

extremity of the balloon must be fixed upon a universal joint a rudder of considerable length opposing both an horizontal and vertical surface...."
Cayley includes his confirmation that arm power alone for flight was an impossibility "and always must fail when it is considered that the pectoral muscles of a bird exceed 7 or 8 times in proportional strength the whole power of a man's arm" and then the realization that winged flight required power for it to succeed "and the result is that a first mover [a powerful engine] which I shall have occasion to describe may possess the power of a horse with less weight than a man...."

Just when he seems to have hit his stride Cayley seems to be suddenly cut short: "I shall proceed to analyse the action of flying birds, and conclude with applying the principles thence deduce to the object of aerial navigation. I shall –"

The Brompton Hall stairwell – the first laboratory for aerodynamic research on a wing.

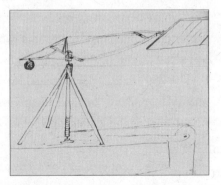

Cayley's roughly sketched whirling arm apparatus dated 1804.

And there it stops. We don't know why. Perhaps Cayley realizes that he actually *can't* deduce the principles of bird flight just yet. This seems a credible explanation because 1804 marks the start of an intense series of flight testing, both theoretical and practical. The most tangible result was the earliest winged flyer in human history – Cayley's first glider.

Cayley needed to build a glider to compare his whirling arm results with the real thing. He realized that the circular motion of his experimental device would not be the same as the straight-line motion of a genuine flying machine. What Cayley built was a simple, elegant glider looking much like a kite on a stick – which is exactly what it was. It isn't much to look at; generations of school kids have made model planes at least as complicated, though perhaps not quite on the same scale – Cayley's was over a foot wide and nearly six feet long. That such a simple idea had never been thought of before is testament to Cayley's understanding of why it flew, and fly it did. Cayley recorded his joy in seeing the craft "skim for 20 or 30 yards. . . . It was very pretty to see sail down a steep hill, and it gave the idea that a larger instrument would be a safer conveyance down the Alps than even the surefooted mule."

His pessimism from nearly a decade before had proven groundless, a plane could fly, or at least a model of one could. But just when he might have begun the work on scaling up his new discovery, there was yet another interruption to his work as world events once more impacted on the sleepy Brompton hollow.

The year that Cayley watched his glider float down Brompton Dale and William Blake penned the poem "Jerusalem" (bringing "green and pleasant land" and "dark satanic mills" into the British geo-social vocabulary), the rather less poetic Napoleon Buonaparte (later Bonaparte) was crowned Emperor of France by a worried Pope Pius VII. The Pope and just about everyone else had good reason to be concerned, for just as Napoleon had seized the crown from the pontiff's hand to anoint himself emperor, he had similar plans to grab the rest of the known world. One piece of recently acquired French real estate had gone sour, however, when a slave revolt in the Americas proved to be an unpleasant hurdle to Napoleon's plans for establishing an empire on the continent. France had secretly gained ownership of what was named Louisiana from the Spanish on a promise that the Iberian Peninsula would not come under French attack (it would be devastated less than five years later). However, Napoleon found himself seriously short on cash, and with his intention of taking over the world he needed some liquid reserves to fund his impending adventures. The recently re-elected American president Thomas Jefferson sent Vice-President James Monroe to France with an offer to buy what land he could in order to secure river passage to the Gulf of Mexico from the American north. On

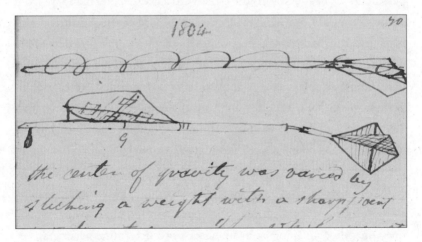

Cayley's notebook sketch of his glider from 1804. The kite-shaped wing was a typical "short-fat" aspect ratio and is set at a slight upward angle from the fuselage. An adjustable weight at the front shifts the centre of gravity (marked "G") toward the wing's centre of pressure (the point through which the lifting force of the wing acts). The adjustable tail allows both "yaw" (left-right) and "pitch" (up-down) to be adjusted.

arriving in Paris, Monroe was told that he could have the whole Louisiana Purchase for a bargain-basement $15 million – just under 4 cents an acre (though at the time no one had any idea how much land was involved). Unfortunately, the Americans didn't have $15 million or anything close so Britain helpfully offered the Americans a loan at an equitable six per cent so that the newly liberated Americans could double their nation's surface area. This meant that France now had the funds required to beat seven bells out of the rest of Europe, including Britain. In 1805, as Napoleon's invasion fleet swarmed around the port of Boulogne as a prelude to doing what William the Conqueror had done 740 years before, the British rued their rather ill-advised off-shore loan and cast around for every means they could to fight the threatened invasion.

Cayley's response to these events was immediate and typically personal – he headed off to the coast with a clandestine mandate from Henry Phipps (Lord Mulgrave, later First Lord of the Admiralty and later still the Master-General of Ordnance) in order to determine whether his recent research on aerodynamics could extend the range of the British Navy's cannon shot. As it happened, ordnance in general was going through something of a revolution at the time, with Colonel Henry Shrapnell's invention of the evil exploding shell, as well as Sir William Congreve's development of the spectacular, though wayward rockets.

Cayley used a six-pound gun, a great deal of gunpowder sourced from the governmental stores at Scarborough, and a group of artillerymen, including an aging ex-army observer to determine what shape of shot would provide the best means of dropping long-range unpleasantness on the French fleet. Cayley conducted a series of lengthy trials using increasingly sophisticated aerodynamic forms for the artillery rounds. He reported his results to the Admiralty Board but there was no public acknowledgement of this secret work until Cayley himself published his findings some forty years later in July 1846. His motivation in revealing the results, even so long after the fact, was as a response to the publication of similar findings by contemporary experimenters at London's Woolwich Arsenal. This publishing reflex, whereby Cayley would almost always require some external impetus to prompt him to publicize his findings, became part of an established pattern throughout his life. As a result of the secrecy, and perhaps because of the singular inertia involved in the British Admiralty's adoption of innovation, Cayley's cannon-shot experiments had little if any known influence on munitions development. The only reason we know about them at all was Cayley's inability to keep the information to himself once the subject had become a topic of discussion in the popular press four decades later.

During this period of genuine fear, Cayley did more than experiment with weaponry. He brought all his faculties to bear at his country's time of need with a published pamphlet explaining how to convert the entire male population into an effective militia. Cayley went a stage farther by forming his own army of locals with himself as colonel-in-chief. As the immediate threat of invasion subsided, the Cayley's Volunteer Company was eventually disbanded with their commander's praises ringing in their ears. Cayley's private opinions concerning his fellow militia-men he kept to his private correspondence: "They have never been called upon to sabre more than roast beef, or bleed other than port in drinking Loyal Toasts to the Ladies."

Thankfully Cayley's military work, though laudable, proved unnecessary as Britain's safety from immediate invasion was secured in 1805 when Lord Nelson wiped out the French fleet off the coast of Africa near the little-known Bay of Trafalgar. The absence of an armed fleet to escort the invasion squadrons into British waters meant that

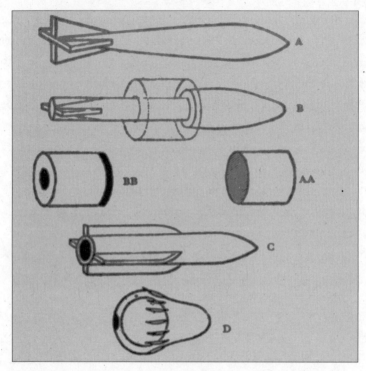

Variants of the cannon shot used by Cayley to determine the best range and accuracy for the British Navy. Though the least sophisticated, the lower "sugar-loaf" shaped shell (D) turned out to be the most effective. The wooden collars placed around the modern-looking projectile (B) would be used in the late twentieth century for the tank-fired "sabot"-shrouded finned rounds used in anti-tank munitions.

Napoleon gave up his immediate plans for southern England and redoubled the land-based campaigns that dominated continental Europe for another decade.

In the perceived breathing space provided by Nelson's victory, Cayley threw himself once again into his scientific work with a series of designs, discoveries, and inventions. There was also the further development of his family, with the birth of his fifth child, another daughter named after her mother, though the youngster's full title, Sarah-Philadelphia, hints at a potential duality in Cayley's affections.

Even as his family grew and his responsibilities as local squire mounted, his work on flight continued, and from 1805 Cayley's aviation plans focused on a series of fanciful winged inventions.

The first of these used "flappers" as the means of propulsion along the classic lines of the ornithopter. These were powered through a series of hand-driven levers placed at the flyer's fingertips, but with the whole machine now mounted on top of a wheeled undercarriage. His 1805 design remained unbuilt and untested as far as can be determined but even this doesn't stop the machine from exhibiting another first for aviation. Cayley's observations on bird flight had brought him to the conclusion that both wing tips should be raised above the central fuselage, making a V-shaped dihedral.

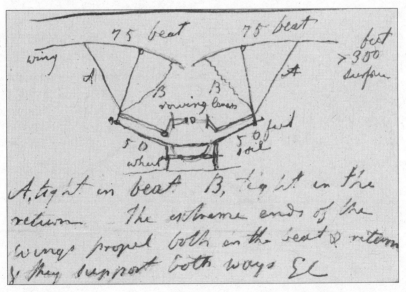

The 1805 flyer, with Cayley's instructions for the pilot on the type of wing beat required for flight: "A, tight in beat, B tight in the return – The extreme ends of the wings propel both on the beat up and return and they support both ways." The design shows two major innovations: the dihedral V shape of the wings (for stability in flight) and the presence of a fixed, wheeled undercarriage.

This configuration provides an inherent stability to the structure and is a design still incorporated in modern aircraft for that very purpose. Cayley seems to have been biding his time and consolidating his ideas. He still had some reluctance to publicize his findings; the subject was, after all, not openly considered by any prominent member of the scientific community. Cayley's first true scientific publication, though in retrospect an obvious first toe in the aviation water, was concerned not with aviation directly but with the means by which sustained flight could be made possible at all: the engine.

Finding the Pieces III – The Naming of the Parts

One of the problems in deciphering Cayley's notes and even some of his published articles results from not knowing what exactly he means by a particular word or phrase. This is understandable when you realize that Cayley was inventing the vocabulary as he went along, but even Cayley was inconsistent in his use of certain terms.

Take the word "wing," for instance. By "wings" Cayley means the mechanism for supporting a plane (like the modern meaning of wing) but he also means the flappers used to push the plane forward.

Cayley never uses "plane" to describe an airplane. He uses "plain" and "plane" (almost interchangeably) to mean either the flat geographical feature found at the bottom or top of slopes (down which he sometimes flew his machines) or the inclined surface that is generating lift through resistance to the air (i.e., a wing).

By "resistance to the air," Cayley means both the modern usage (the drag or backwards force of the air as you push forward through it) and the upward force (lift) generated by an inclined plane. All Cayley's winged machines relied on the simple principle of an inclined plane generating lift as it glided down to the plain below.

Cayley never uses the word "glide" but prefers the word "skim" to describe the flight of a bird or plane that is flying without flapping its wings. Similarly, Cayley never uses the word "glider" but instead uses "parachute," meaning anything that is passively falling through the air, even if that falling involves considerable motion forward as well as down. However, sometimes he *does* mean "parachute" in the modern sense of the word, and when he does, he means a plane that is skimming straight down, generating a resistance to the air with a car slung underneath.

A "car" is what contains a pilot or a passenger, something like a gondola. One reason for using a car is to make the whole vehicle more streamlined.

Cayley never uses the word "streamlined" but instead he uses variations of the term "solid of least resistance," meaning lowest drag in this context rather than lowest lift. The main reason for streamlining is to reduce drag but also to increase stability.

Cayley uses the term "equipoise" rather than "stability," though this refers to the intrinsic stability of the machine rather than the ability of the pilot to control its direction in the air. In order to do that you need to control the direction of motion up-down (using "elevators") or left-right (through using the "rudder").

When Cayley uses the term "rudder," he is referring to the elevator (i.e., opposite to the modern term), whereas he labelled his rudder descriptively as a "vertical sail." Cayley's use of rudder continued until the twentieth century, and even the Wrights used rudder in this way.

Cayley never uses the word "aviation." He christened it "aerial navigation." The word "aviation" was coined by Frenchman Gabriel de La Landelle in 1862 from the French for "like a bird."

5

CAYLEY INVENTS AVIATION

O ctave Chanute was an early flying pioneer who built and then flew the first American gliders. His own investigations into flight had a long pedigree, though his greater claim to fame was as a paternal influence on and then a minor irritant to the Wright brothers. Chanute was instrumental in arranging the first meeting of serious American would-be aviators at the Conference on Aerial Navigation held in Chicago at the beginning of August 1894. Chanute's opening address includes what proved to be one of the most perceptive lists in aviation history.

> It is a mistake to suppose that the problem of aviation is a single problem. In point of fact it involves many problems ... the motor ... the propelling instrument ... the form, extent, texture and construction of the sustaining surfaces ... maintenance of the equipoise ... the method of getting underway, of steering the apparatus in the air and of alighting safely. They each constitute one problem, involving one or more solutions, to be subsequently combined.

In order to fly, all the problems raised by Chanute had to be resolved. Unknown to Chanute and everybody else at the time, by the end of 1809 each and every one of these issues had been at least thought about by Cayley – and in most cases they had been considered, experimented on, and some part solution tested and applied. Though he would get some things terribly wrong, Cayley would get most of them spookily right. The oddest thing of all was that Cayley's secret notebook reveals that he had set about solving these problems in almost the exact same order as Chanute would list them eighty-five years later. Cayley even spotted a few problems that Chanute had missed. But Cayley started with the heart of the matter: power.

All early aviators realized that practical flight meant powered flight but to get off the ground at all required that whatever flew had to be light. Thus aviation made a unique pair of demands for a light yet powerful motor and no such engine existed. Although the steam engine of Cayley's day was evolving into a reliable and economical power plant, it was hardly compact. Everything about the steam engine was in the super-heavyweight class, from the iron-plated boilers, flywheels, and pistons to the coal to drive it and the water to generate the steam and yet more water to cool the steam again in the condenser. For stationary engines, the ones used for pumps in the mines or as generators driving machinery for the factories, the issue of weight was a non-issue – make it as heavy as you like just as long as it works. For the emerging use of steam as a locomotive force, this weight was more of a problem, but hard-packed roads or, better still, iron railways could be made more than strong enough to cope with these massive engines. Cayley was the first person to grasp that the harder you forced an inclined plane up into and against the air, the more likely it was to stay there. Over 130 years later, Sir Sidney Camm, the designer of the leg-endary Hawker Hurricane fighter, observed, "You can make a barn door fly if you put a big enough engine on it." But Camm had a petrol-driven internal combustion engine generating over a thousand horsepower: to generate less than one-tenth of that power in Cayley's era required a steam engine the size and weight of a small house.

Cayley's 1793 schoolbook reveals that he had been thinking about the subject of engines for some time – the cartoon of his gunpowder-fuelled engine was one of his earliest ideas on the subject. His tutors, Walker and Morgan, were more than proficient mechanics who no doubt encouraged his investigations, but what Cayley needed for his "first mover" was help from a professional engineer. Fortunately, by 1805 he had one of the country's most competent ones to hand, William Chapman, the man behind the Muston drainage scheme. With Chapman's help, Cayley set about designing a new kind of engine, essentially a steamless heat engine, one that relied on the expansion of air alone to drive a piston, rather than the expansion and contraction of water and steam through heating and cooling. The advantage of Cayley's new device was primarily its lightness since it required no reservoir of water and no condenser for the steam. A disadvantage was that it generated significantly less power than conventional steam power; another was that no one had ever built one before. This did not deter Cayley building one with Chapman's help and then publishing his results in *Nicholson's Journal of Natural Philosophy, Chemistry and the Arts.*

On September 25, 1807, Cayley wrote the letter to William Nicholson that launched a lifetime in print on the subject of the sciences associated with transportation, as well as a dozen other themes. His first published essay was written in what became the classic Cayley style: a straightforward, honest (sometimes painfully honest) account of his findings and ideas aimed at his fellow amateur, everyman enthusiast. He also knew how to play to the gallery.

Cayley opens his letter with a hint that the French had already taken the lead over Britain in developing the steamless engine, something that may or may not have been true. But it certainly piqued the interest of a patriotic British readership currently at war with France. Cayley then goes on to explain that he'd built such an engine himself but that it didn't really work very well. His candour over its short-comings didn't seem to cause him the slightest check in step as he details at length how it *should* have worked in principle, and about how the design could be improved in any number of ways. Even if Cayley hints at the true purpose behind his endeavours – "the steam engine has hitherto proved too weighty and cumbrous for most purposes of locomotion" – he doesn't seem to be able to bring himself to publicly admit that the reason he wants to build a light prime mover is that he intends to use one to take off and fly.

Less than two months later, in November 1807, Cayley's notebook shows the extent of his continued work in the area of motive power,

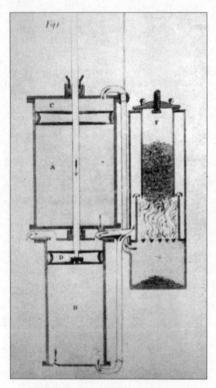

Cayley's caloric "hot-air" engine in *Nicholson's Journal* of 1807.

with his first detailed rendition of his decade-old design for the rather alarming gunpowder engine. This was a fine example of a first-draft idea – all the principal components are there, though all of them are bound within Cayley's own journeyman's level of technical expertise. Two candlewick flames heat the end of a metal spike, which penetrates inside the lower combustion chamber. A small funnel illustrates the means of feeding powder from above into the lower enclosure to allow for an explosive "internal combustion." This action forced up the central piston, which was forced back on the down-stroke by the utilitarian bowstring. A spring might have served the same purpose more elegantly, or better still a counterweighted flywheel, but here we see the early seeds of Cayley's most obvious engineering blind spot: he had something of an irrational fear for engine-related components that rotated.

That his engine designs were created with powered flight in mind is confirmed by the surrounding entries in his notebooks, as his thoughts on the mechanisms of bird flight brought him new insight into the design of the wing itself. During the course of 1808, Cayley, now thirty-five, was in full stride as far as his work on flight was concerned. This year saw him take numerous steps forward by discovering another handful of fundamental principles of flight, followed by a couple of steps sideways with more ornithopter designs, quickly followed by a giant leap with the invention of a new kind of wheel.

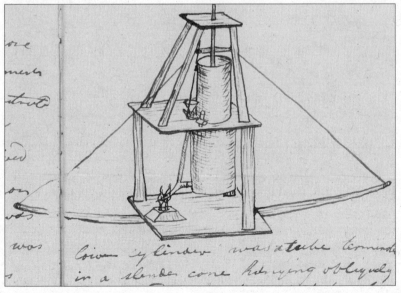

The 1807 gunpowder engine from Cayley's notebook. Typically, the illustrated bow-string return mechanism fails to fit onto a single sheet and so spills over onto the preceding page.

In order to address Chanute's later requirements for the "form, extent . . . of the sustaining surfaces" Cayley required only a dead heron, the sight of a flock of game birds, and an afternoon's deliberation.

> I am apt to think that the more concave the wing to a certain extent the more it gives support, and that for slow flights a long thin wing is necessary, whereas for short quick flights a short broad wing is better adapted, with a constant flutter as the partridge and pheasant.

In spite of Cayley's clear appreciation of the advantages of the long slender wing, he would never adopt this structure for any of his flying vehicles. This contradiction is almost certainly rooted in Cayley's own misgivings concerning the strength of such a wing; he believed it would fail during the rigours of flight. Whatever the

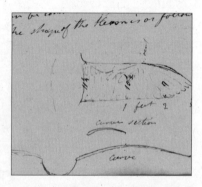

Cayley's sketch of a recently shot heron. Though his notes clearly record his conclusion that a long, slender wing is the best form for sustained gliding flight, he veers away from adopting this high-aspect ratio in most of his subsequent aircraft designs.

An inspired observation concerning the curves of the heron's wing in two dimensions. The curved section (middle) shows the classic airfoil shape for what later became the icon for the lift-generating wing. The lower curve from the head-on view is further confirmation of Cayley's belief in the stabilizing qualities of the "V-shape" dihedral.

cause, his preference for the "short-fat" wing would forever plague his flying machines.

The next few entries in Cayley's notebook show his enthusiasm getting the better of him, and not for the last time. Having calculated the speed at which he was capable of running, and deriving the lifting surfaces needed for manned flight from the wing area of a crow, Cayley designs the first hang-glider. Like the later nineteenth-century fliers

The 1808 wing-assisted ornithopter design, with dihedral wings for lift and roll stability and tailpiece for yaw control (two very good ideas) together with long slender flapping wings for propulsion (perhaps not so good).

who actually constructed and successfully flew such gliders, Cayley realized that the weight and bulk of the pilot-enclosing car might be unnecessary for such low-speed gliders, so he removed it altogether. Unlike later successful aviators, Cayley also decides to add flappers to the machine as the means of pushing it forward through the air. Once more there is no evidence that this particular device was ever built or flown, but it shows Cayley's first attempts as something approaching a working design, even if the method of propulsion distracts the eye from the more practical aspects of the machine.

However ill-conceived his ornithopter idea, Cayley soon improves even this rather Heath Robinson contraption by designing a harness and frame within which the pilot could sit (much as was applied in hang-gliders of the twentieth century). With the addition of a seat and harness, the pilot (who was also the power plant) could now use both feet to push with their full force against the levers driving the propulsive flappers while his cambered, dihedral wings provided the required supporting lift.

This particularly fruitful period for Cayley continued when he returned to considering the advantages of fixed undercarriages for his flying machines. This had come about through his realization that a man running at full tilt while carrying a glider might not prove the most practical idea. But he knew that the aircraft had to gain sufficient flying speed on the ground prior to take-off (meeting Chanute's need for "the method of getting underway") and so Cayley decided to try

> making use of light wheels to preserve the propelling power . . . till
> it accumulates sufficiently to elevate the machine, upon the princi-
> ple of those birds which run themselves up.

However, the problems of weight reoccurred, so Cayley invented a new type of wheel. He came up with the idea of using adjustable cord tensioners to make a light iron hoop as strong as a heavier wheel but without the need for heavy metal or wooden spokes. This same innovation eventually became the "wire tension," or bicycle wheel. The thin cord spokes were tightened to brace against the outer rim, pulling strongly toward the centre of the wheel. This constant and uniform tension all around the lightly built rim makes it rigid and capable of supporting substantial loads; it can bear far more weight than would be the case when not under tension. Cayley illustrates his new wheel with a simple, clear, and carefully drawn sketch that he used in his later attempt to patent it.

Unfortunately Cayley waited until 1827 before seriously considering the commercial possibilities of the invention and by then coach maker Theodor Jones's patent for his own tension-principle coach wheel was already a year old. Jones rigorously protected his rights for the new

wheel's exclusive manufacture and strongly defended his claim as originator. Although Cayley looked into the possibilities of a parallel patent
for his idea, he eventually abandoned it.

Cayley rounded out a remarkable 1808 by designing the first rudimentary biplane as well as finally uncovering how a bird's wing could
generate both lift and thrust on both the up and downbeats – the wing
bends and warps with each stroke to present the appropriate angle to
the air.

Cayley also made a series of key findings on the artificial wing that
spoke directly to Chanute's need for the "construction of the sustaining
surfaces" and "maintenance of the equipoise." Most important was
Cayley's discovery of the concept of the centre of pressure – the point
on the wing at which the upward lifting force acts. In a series of experiments with kites and gliders, Cayley found that the centre of pressure
was not at the centre of the wing but slightly forward of it, toward the
wing's leading edge. Cayley then grasped the significance of his discovery: to balance his flyers while in the air, the weight of the craft (acting

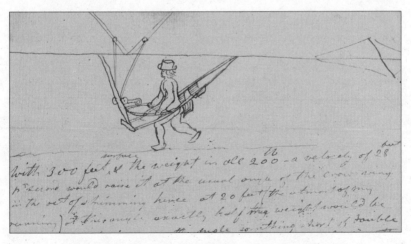

Cayley's modified pilot car for his 1808 wing-assisted ornithopter.

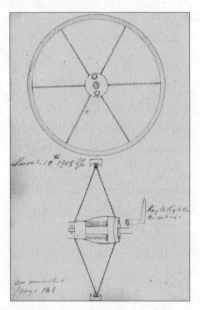

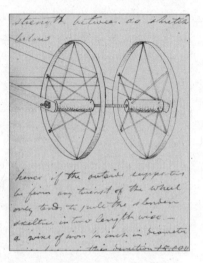

Cayley's idea for the configuration of the new wheel as an aircraft undercarriage bogie (double-wheel).

The 1808 tension cord wheel, carefully dated, signed, and illustrated in detail – Cayley seemed to know he might have a commercial application for them in the future.

down through the centre of gravity) must be aligned with the lifting force of the wings (acting up through the centre of pressure). This would create a naturally balanced vehicle, a plane with "intrinsic stability." Cayley was rediscovering a finding first made in 1550 by the Dutch, who were at the time the world leaders in windmill design. They realized that each arm of a windmill needed to be placed not in the centre of the sail, but toward the front edge, so that the centre of pressure of the wind-driven sail was at the same point as the supporting main spar. What no one realized before Cayley was that exactly the same laws applied to a lift-generating wing.

Cayley then developed the concept of a lightweight frame for the flyer through the use of tubular beams for aircraft construction. He, like early twentieth-century aircraft builders, proposed the use of bamboo. Finally, returning to his more natural studies, he wondered at the elegance of the whirling sycamore chat while explaining how it was that such a simple construction could carry a seed so far from the tree.

One notable absence from Chanute's list of flight-related problems is the need to reduce unwanted air resistance, the drag an object generates when passing through the air. Cayley, however, did not overlook the requirement to streamline as many aspects of a flying machine as possible. In his unpublished essay of 1804, Cayley had coined the phrase "a solid of least resistance" to describe the shape. In July 1809, his notebooks return to the subject by way of a "well fed" trout. Extracting the kernel of nature's solution to such problems, Cayley sketched the proportions of the fish in plan view in order to examine the best shape for avoiding the resisting force of a fluid. The result is a cross-sectional representation of what was later rediscovered as NASA's low-drag airfoil number 63A016. It took the governmental body with the highest budget and largest research team in history some 150 years to catch up with what Cayley had noticed in a nearby stream.

By the end of 1809, Cayley's list of discoveries and inventions was extraordinary. He had realized the need for a small, powerful engine and invented a new lightweight motor. He had recognized the need to separate the lift-generating wing from the thrust-generating flappers. He had documented the benefits of the long slender wings; proposed the use of a strong tubular-construction to build the frame; discovered and applied a design for the dihedral shape for roll stability and the elevator/rudder for control in pitch and yaw; designed the lightweight undercarriage for take-off and landing; considered the strapped harness for the pilot slung beneath and between the wings; and recognized the need for streamlining the whole contraption within a drag-minimizing fuselage.

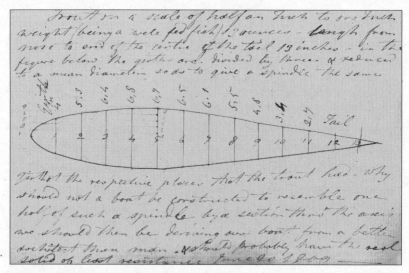

Cayley's "well fed" trout reduced to the function of its plan-view cross-section as a means of illustrating a natural "true solid of least resistance."

As a sideline, just to keep himself occupied, Cayley also published a plan for a new Covent Garden Theatre after the original was destroyed by fire in late September 1808. Cayley's second formal publication, an 1809 article in *Nicholson's Journal*, includes not only safety features such as a fire curtain and outward-opening emergency exits, but an examination of the acoustic properties of the stage and auditorium derived from the ancient Greek theatre. It reveals another developing Cayley characteristic; he simply couldn't keep his ideas to himself, whether he was considered qualified to voice them or not. Architecture was just a fleeting interest, and his thoughts were soon concentrated once more on flight. With almost all the issues associated with practical aviation resolved, it would seem absurd not to put it all together into a single flying machine. Cayley, not a man to disappoint, promptly did just that.

What exactly Cayley built in 1809 is a tantalizing mystery. We can guess from his notebook illustrations and descriptions of all the constituent parts that it was something approaching a full-scale crew-carrying glider, but there is no description of the machine among his surviving notebooks or loose papers. The only reason we know of its existence at all is that Cayley, with a typically offhand flourish, mentions the fact that he'd built a plane while writing the world's first exposition concerning the science of man-made, heavier-than-air flight. The reason Cayley finally chose to push his flying experiments so prominently into the public domain was undoubtedly because he had something significant to report, but as usual it also required some external prod. The catalyst on this occasion was the discovery of a rival in the form of the Swiss flapping flyer.

One of Cayley's more charming quirks was his belief that those involved in the study of flight were as honest, straightforward, and trustworthy as he was. When, through the fog of the continuing continental war, Cayley heard that another aviator had actually succeeded in flying, he was at first intrigued, then spurred into action to ensure that he wouldn't be scooped by some prior publication. The man in question was a Swiss clockmaker named Jacob Degen, who, while living in Vienna, had devised a particularly successful and popular flying act. The thing that seems to have particularly caught Cayley's attention was that Degen had got into the air using an ingenious flapping wing. It was confirmation that Cayley's idea of ignoring the propeller and going with flappers had been right all along. Degen had used an ingenious flap valve, which meant that on the upward beat the wings allowed the air to pass through the wing. These valves closed on the wing's down beat, allowing the pilot to push down against the air, thus pushing himself and the machine upward with some 90 pounds of force. Had Cayley known of this particular figure, he would have realized that something was amiss because 90 pounds of upward thrust is less than half what would be required to get a man and machine (weighing 200 pounds or more) off the ground. The missing piece to the puzzle turned out to be that Degen was actually suspended beneath a hydrogen balloon and used his flappers as an effective and dramatic means of making large bounding leaps above and into the seething crowds who came to see him.

Although there is no evidence that Degen himself attempted any deception, a series of enterprising journalists decided that editing out the rather cumbersome balloon from both illustrations and written descriptions of Degen's exploits made for much more exciting copy – and it was these edited descriptions that had reached Cayley in 1809. Even if he was the largely innocent party, Degen made few attempts to deny the more extraordinary claims made on his behalf – something that later resulted in a particularly disappointed Parisian mob beating him up in 1813. However, Degen's exploits were without doubt instrumental in furthering the progress of aviation, for in the fear of being beaten to the prize by some continental rival, Cayley decided to publish the results of his flying research. Cayley's three papers in *Nicholson's Journal* of 1809 and 1810 are seminal in their contribution to aviation. They are a pure distillation of Cayley's intelligence, frankness, and ability to be brilliantly right and frighteningly wrong in almost alternating sentences.

Placed and dated as "Brompton, Sept. 6, 1809" (though actually published in November), his first paper of the series starts with a thunderclap when Cayley announces the existence of a new branch of science and the beginnings of an industry: "Aerial Navigation." From the outset, Cayley intends to further the development of a practical means of transport with all its associated commercial and social benefits. As a reminder of the historical context, 1809 saw the first *ever* sea-going trial of a steamship by American John Stevens. It was another sixteen years before the world's first steam railway opened. In spite of the absence of a single instance of long-distance, machine-driven mass transportation, on sea or land, anywhere in the world, Cayley goes on to explain how flight was about to become the ideal means of travel for not the distant future, but the immediate one: "We shall be able to transport ourselves and families and their goods and chattels, more securely by air than by water, and with a velocity of from 20 to 100 miles per hour."

Cayley establishes his authority to talk about the subject: "I conceive in stating the fundamental principles of this art, together with a considerable number of facts and practical observations that have arisen in the course of much attention to the subject." He also briefly acknowledges the inspiration for his writing in "the success of the ingenious Mr. Degen. . . ." Cayley's discourse touches on the flapping-winged cliff-jumpers of the past, scorning them as "ridiculous enough, as the pectoral muscles of a bird occupy more than two-thirds of its whole muscular strength whereas in man the muscles . . . would probably not exceed one-tenth," though he cites Degen's success as proof that the mechanical advantage of levers and other related ingenuities will gain some success through that very same method. Then Cayley starts into the meat of the essay – the need for a new prime mover, the propelling force that, combined with a lifting wing, would be the solution to flight. Cayley reviews the performance of the best steam engine on the market and concludes that it must inevitably come up short on power for its weight. After duly noting the assistance of his associate Mr. Chapman, and also that of fellow engineer John Rennie, Cayley discusses a new type of engine, one that would generate the necessary power-bangs for fewer poundage-bucks:

> Probably a much cheaper engine of this sort might be produced by
> a gas-tight apparatus and by firing the flammable air generated with
> due portion of common air under a piston.

Cayley's description of the internal combustion engine could not have been clearer, and though certainly not his idea, he is the first to realize that *this* is the engine that will allow man to fly. However, before coming out and saying any such thing, Cayley explains how it is that a bird can "skim" with apparent effortless ease, accompanying the description with illustrations drawn closely from his earliest triangulated calculations on the acting forces on a wing. He then delivers the first of his "practical observations" by applying his discoveries on bird flight and his newly invented inclined plane to the newly christened aerial navigation. It is one of the most succinct descriptions of powered flight before or since: "The whole problem is confined within these limits, viz. – To make a surface support a given weight by the application of power to the resistance of the air."

Cayley delivers a brief summary of his calculations to date before announcing the magical figure of 37.3[*] feet per second: the speed at which a plane inclined at the ideal six degrees pushes upward at one pound of lift per square foot, the same lift generated by his favourite and much-studied crow.

This "one pound of lift per square foot of wing" is the figure on which Cayley had calculated that manned flight was to be achieved. Using this number, Cayley predicts that an aircraft with 200 square feet of wing area would support 200 pounds of weight if driven with an airspeed of 25 miles an hour. Cayley makes it clear that it is the craft's speed relative to the air, not relative to ground, that is the important point: "It is perfectly indifferent whether the wind blow against the plane, or the plane be driven with equal velocity against the air."

---

[*] This figure is often quoted as 27.3 feet per second as a result of it being the one that appeared in *Nicholson's*. This is a misprint (there were lots of them – Cayley was livid). Cayley's own notes correct the figure to 37.3 feet per second.

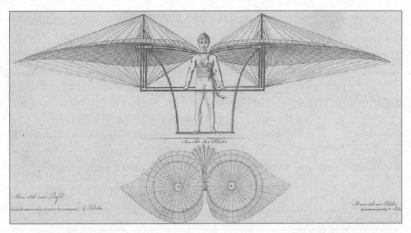

Above: The illustration of Jacob Degen's flying machine that excited so much interest in the world of flight, not least in Cayley, who thought it proof positive that flappers were the answer. Unfortunately, the more accurate rendition of Degen's machine (below) includes the hydrogen balloon beneath which he was suspended to make his flights possible at all.

Another crucial Cayley observation is associated with what is now called "form" and "parasitic" drag – the rearward forces caused by any vehicle as it moves through the air:

In practice the extra resistance of the car and other parts of the machine which consume a considerable portion of the power, will regulate the limits to which this principle, which is the true basis of aerial navigation, can be carried.

Few of the remarkable observations from Cayley's notebook fail to find their way into his published essay, including his suspicion that the concavity of a bird's wing added considerably to the aerodynamic qualities of its flight. From the theory, Cayley then goes on to the practice, and the first indication that he has already built a flying man-carrier.

> I am engaged in making some farther experiments upon a machine I constructed last summer, large enough for aerial navigation, but which I have not had an opportunity to try, excepting as to its proper balance and security. It was beautiful to see this noble white *bird* sail majestically from the top of a hill to any given point of the plane [plain] below it with perfect steadiness, and safety, according to the set of the rudder, merely by its own weight descending in an angle of about 18 degrees to the horizon.

This is the first suggestion that Cayley had built any full-scale version of his flyers, the first hint that he had not just thought about and planned his machines, but built and flown them. This first of three articles rounds off with the almost inevitable return to his fascination with the action of flappers, by way of another reference to his idol, Degen. On the way he describes to the reader, as he had to numerous visitors to his home in Brompton, how to make one of his little helicopter flyers.

Cayley's second essay appeared in *Nicholson's* volume 25, February 1810, three months after part one. Initially, Cayley's new paper appears a little pessimistic in nature, as he decides to tackle the issue of the parachute. Again there is some evidence that Cayley was externally prompted to discuss the subject as in 1808 Jordaki Kurapento became the first person ever to bail out of an aircraft by using a parachute when his hot-air balloon burst into flames. Kurapento was not, however, the first parachutist, for descent by variants of the parachute had been, like ballooning itself, a fair-show attraction for some time. The first parachute jump took place in 1797 when Jacques Garnerin dropped by means of a wicker basket slung beneath what was effectively a large, rigid, inverted cone made from a wooden frame and canvas. Garnerin's first descent was from a height of over two thousand feet in Paris's Parc de Monceau. During his fall, Garnerin experienced a series of violent oscillations, with the basket swinging wildly from side to side throughout. He survived only because the basket was hanging a long way beneath the supporting canopy; had the ropes been shorter, it is likely the whole contraption would have inverted completely, throwing Garnerin to his death. Garnerin had made the first descent in Britain in 1802, and Cayley had either witnessed it himself or, more likely, read reports of the spectacle in the press. Cayley decided that such recklessness was unnecessary, and he illustrates his parachute designs derived from observations of wind-blown seeds and his thoughts concerning the sycamore chat. Cayley points out that the solution is, rather counterintuitively, to use the dihedral form for the parachute canopy – that is, to have the cone pointing downward. This structure allows for a smooth flow of air around the resisting surface and thus prevents the terrible shaking suffered by the hapless Garnerin.

After describing the benefits of the dihedral parachute, Cayley goes on to examine how this and his other discoveries apply to not only falling descents, but flying machines. Addressing Chanute's need for "steering the apparatus," Cayley moves onto the concept of the control surfaces, the means of altering the direction and attitude of his flyers: "To render the machine perfectly steady, and likewise to enable it to ascend and descend in its path, it becomes necessary to add a rudder in a similar position to a bird."

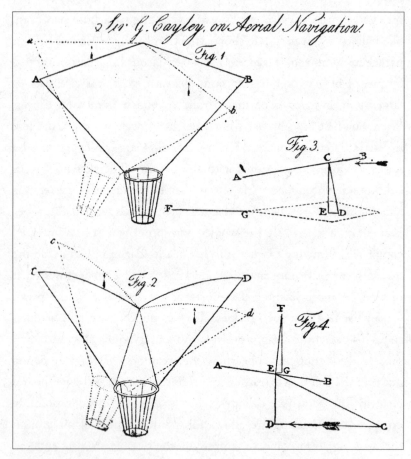

The 1810 parachute description from *Nicholson's Journal*, showing the wrong way (top) and right way (bottom) to design a parachute.

Cayley describes how his experiments have shown the means of landing a machine with his newly designed rudder, and the need to "flare" the machine (raise the nose just prior to landing) "for the purpose of preventing the machine from sinking too much in front." Remarkably, here is the very first "flying 101," a detailed description of what was needed both with regard to the mechanisms of flight, as well as the best practice for flying itself.

Having controlled pitch, Cayley then deals with the need for left-right control through "a vertical sail . . . capable of turning from side to side in addition to other movements, which effects the complete steerage of the vessel." And then comes a more detailed reference to his tried and tested flyers mentioned in his first paper, a machine that embodies most of Cayley's and nearly all of Chanute's attributes for successful flight.

> All these principles upon which the support, steadiness, elevation, depression, and steerage of vessels for aerial navigation depend have been abundantly verified by experiments both upon a large and small scale. Last year I made a machine having a surface [wing] area of 300 square feet, which was accidentally broken before there was an opportunity of trying the effects of the propelling apparatus, but its steerage and steadiness were perfectly proved, and it would sail downwards in any direction according to the set of the rudder. Even in this state, when any person ran forward in it with his full speed, taking advantage of a gentle breeze in front, it would bear upward so strongly as scarcely to allow him to touch the ground, and would frequently lift him up, and convey him several yards altogether.

People had flown in similar ways before, hung underneath kites, clinging to feathered frames and from balloons and parachutes of all shapes and sizes, but this is a first among firsts: a specifically designed winged vehicle, lifting an aviator with sufficient force for him to feel his feet leave the earth and bound skyward, just like Degen. Except this time it was for real, a free-flying airplane: no strings attached. That Cayley should have designed, built, and tested such a machine without leaving any clues as to having done so is at best irritating and at worst suspicious: why no mention of it in his notebooks, only in the formal printed version of his work in *Nicholson's?* A similar claim made by someone who had not so obviously been through the required design loops a dozen times could be more easily dismissed, but Cayley's notebook entries at least corroborate that he *could* have built such a machine, and the detail of the accompanying theory surrounding his claims seems to heavily weigh in Cayley's favour. On balance, it seems that George had gone and done it, he'd made a flying machine – or a hopping device at least – and then tried it out. He was, however, a little optimistic when it came to the summary of his progress to date: "The best mode of producing the propelling power is the only thing that remains yet untried towards the completion of the invention."

Unfortunately, we are then treated to a Cayley diversion into a detailed examination of the process of not only nature's version of bird flight, but Cayley's own version via a flapping wing. Though detailed and carefully thought out, it descends into what a previous biographer has called Cayley's "preoccupation with flapping propulsion." It seems only fair that if we laud his insight when it comes to his aircraft designs and experimental aerodynamics, we must at least sigh a little when it comes to his conclusion that beating the air was the way forward. He just got it wrong, plain and simple.

The third part of Cayley's publication appeared in March 1810 and starts off where he finished part two, with a further examination concerning the wonders of flappers, including a suggestion that Degen's flap valves might be a means of achieving the required propulsive force. There is one pearl among the swine, however, as he applies his experiments with cambered wings to flappers in an attempt to increase their power, as well as applying the advantage of levers to do the same. Cayley identifies a series of principles as they relate to the application of waving wings, as well as a number of methods, some multiply combined, for achieving the desired lifting force. Conscientious though his calculations are, they add little to the science of flight, and detract somewhat from Cayley's scientific credibility. Just when it seems that Cayley will lose his audience's interest, and perhaps patience, he finds the right track once more. After a brief exposition on the use of cables and tubular construction for the frame of his aircraft, a final flourish sees Cayley sally forth with the planet's first-ever examination of the principles of streamlining as it applies to aviation.

> Avoiding direct resistance is the next general principle to be discussed. Let it be remembered, as a maxim, in the art of aerial navigation, that every pound of direct resistance that is done away with will support 30lbs of additional weight without any additional power.

Here Cayley has scored another bull's eye; he realizes that the amount of energy saved from avoiding drag will be paid back more than tenfold; the extra weight of a streamlining car or fuselage could be more than justified by reducing the required forward power. No one had considered this point before Cayley, and making up for his previous lapses, his deliberations on streamlining read like an engineer's primer on the subject.

> It has been found by experiment that the hinder part of the spindle [the body moving through the air] is as of much importance as that of the front, in diminishing resistance. This results from the partial vacuity created behind the obstructing body. If there be no solid to fill up this space, a deficiency in hydrostatic pressure exists within it, and is transferred to the spindle. This is seen distinctly near the rudder of a ship in full sail, where the water is much below the level of the surrounding sea.

Though Cayley has seized keenly on one of the guiding principles of aerodynamic design, he realizes that the complexities involved in the subject were perhaps beyond the scope of his work so far.

I fear however, that the whole of this subject is of such a dark nature, as to be more usefully investigated by experiment, than by reasoning and in the absence of any conclusive evidence from either, the only way that presents itself is to copy nature; accordingly I shall instance the spindles of the trout and woodcock, which, lest the engravings should, in additions to others, occupy too much valuable space in your Journal, must be reserved to a future opportunity.

And that was it. The world's first scientific dissertation on aerial navigation was over, warts and all. The saving grace of Cayley's revelatory insight into so much of the science of aviation might make it possible for us to dismiss or at least forgive his obsession with flappers; unfortunately, it was a precedent that Cayley followed, more or less, for the rest of his life.

Cayley's publication instantly turned him into a public spokesman for the practicality of flight with his position, both societal and financial, allowing him a freedom of expression denied to anyone whose business was reliant on public credulity. Following the circulation of Cayley's first essay, Sir Anthony Carlisle, a surgeon and Fellow of the Royal Society, wrote revealing his own, previously secret interest in the subject, adding that those experiments he had completed "were in private. My profession excludes my taking open measures on a subject so liable to derision and ill-natured remark." On the publication of the final of the three Cayley papers, Carlisle wrote again, saying that serious science could never openly express interest in the subject: "The Wise, the Prudent and the Cunning Classes of Philosophers are too wary to commit themselves on subjects not backed by the cry of the multitude. . . . You escape because you are not in the chain of rival contention, or employed in a mercenary profession." The Royal Society's attitude to aviation continued to be, at best, ambivalent throughout the nineteenth century. The society's standing as an authority on matters scientific would hardly be helped when its president, Lord Kelvin, expressed as late as 1895 his opinion that "heavier-than-air flying machines are impossible" – had the man never seen a bird?

On the other hand, even Cayley was able to recognize the comic potential for his newly declared interest. Shortly after the publication of his triple paper, he arranged an evening's entertainment for Susan and Lt.-Col. William Sibbald, who were stationed at nearby Scarborough. Mrs. Sibbald describes in her memoirs how a traditional evening of dinner followed by musical divertissement veered toward the socially borderline when the subject of whistling was raised; whistling had become something of a fad at the time, especially among young girls. When Mrs. Sibbald announced that she wanted to have a try at it herself, Cayley "bolted the door to prevent interruptions" – especially from Colonel Sibbald who was known not to approve. However, they were forced to open up on the colonel's return, at which point he made it clear that whistling was a social grace his wife could well do without. In order to recover a sticky social impasse, Cayley launched into why he thought that sometimes it was worth having a try at something even if it seemed a little odd. He then explained about his recent attempts at flight and one conspicuous example of failure using "an article in the shape of a large bird with wings that were to flap through the air with the aid of machinery. . . ." Cayley kept his audience "in fits of laughter" as he described how a stable boy had been persuaded to climb into the machine for a test flight and that it had subsequently crashed. Mrs. Sibbald reports that the flight lasted

> only for a short distance, for whether the boy got frightened, and
> did not keep the machinery in motion, or whether the boy was too
> fat and heavier than the bird liked, [Cayley] did not know, but down

the bird and boy came with a plump on the ground – the bird not hurt, but the boy both frightened and hurt but [Cayley] soon found a salve that healed both wounds and fright.

This suggests that Cayley's flyer of 1809 was not only a glider, but a powered one, albeit with the inevitable use of flappers, something that may have contributed in no small part to the problems he had in testing it.

In spite of obvious shortcomings, Cayley's triple paper marked a watershed in the science of flight. Exactly how many people ever read or appreciated it at the time is unknown; *Nicholson's* circulation numbered only in the low thousands. Perhaps the work's greatest impact was as a result of it being reprinted in the U.S. *Aeronautical Annual* of 1895 through the efforts of aviation publicist James Mean. Mean's reprint of Cayley's 1809–10 essays was among the bundle of papers that the Wright brothers received in 1899 following their first tentative approaches to Richard Rathbun at the Smithsonian. Wilbur Wright speaking in 1909, the centennial of Cayley's amazing publication, said, "Cayley carried the science of flying to a point which it had never reached before and which it scarcely reached again during the last century."

Even if the influence of Cayley's first flying papers had to wait a hundred years to be fully appreciated, and though their impact on his immediate social circle was little more than an amusement, there was a more important and immediate outcome. Cayley had pushed his head above the parapet; he had run up his colours and announced to the world that he considered heavier-than-air flight not only possible, but practical and safe. He had also completed the world's first planned wing-borne hop. Not only that, he knew why it went up and why it came back down again. On and off, Cayley spent the next fifty years trying to increase the time between those two events.

Finding the Pieces IV – The Wheels on the Chariots of the Gods

The Wright brothers were aware of Cayley's work, though only those ideas that Cayley published; the rich seam of detailed experimental work contained within Cayley's private notebooks was not rediscovered until the mid-twentieth century. The Wrights' first public declaration of an interest in flight was Wilbur's letter, sent to Richard Rathbun at the Smithsonian Institution in May 1899. The letter begins, "I have been interested in the problem of mechanical and human flight ever since as a boy I constructed a number of bats of various sizes after the style of Cayley's and Pénaud's machines." These machines were variants of Cayley's first flyer, the toy helicopter. The Wright brothers' father, the Reverend Milton Wright, had bought one of these toys as a gift for his two sons in 1878 not knowing just how influential the act would be. Though intrigued by flight from then on, Wilbur and Orville had to work for a living, and what paid their wages and financed their research into flight was their business as bicycle manufacturers and retailers.

The pedal cycle is such a superficially simple machine that it seems almost absurd that it should have taken so long to invent. However, the bike shared with the early airplane the need to be built light enough to be easily propelled but strong enough to support the rider's weight. The requirement for a wheel with these same two characteristics was a considerable engineering challenge; the application of the tension wheel was the breakthrough that made the practical bicycle a possibility.

The Wrights made a solid business out of their bicycle shop, and the skills they acquired through the precision engineering

of bike manufacture could not have been a better apprenticeship for their work designing and building flying machines.
They even acknowledged the fact by naming their most successful aeroplanes the "Flyer" series, a title derived from their
most successful bicycle.

Neither the Wrights nor anyone else at the time knew of
the more subtle way in which Cayley's early nineteenth-
century work on the humble lightweight wheel had contributed
to the Wright brothers' achievements. Who could guess that
Cayley's undercarriage design would end up as the invention
that provided the seed capital for the Wrights' work nearly a
century later?

6

WAR *and* PEACE, POLITICS *and* RELIGION

In many ways the year 1810 marked a transition point for Cayley
and the British nation as a whole. On a personal level, Cayley's
publications were a formal announcement of his interest in flight to a
world that regarded such a hobby as at best fanciful and at worst
deranged. Having thrown his hat into the ring, Cayley became something of a poster boy for the topic of flight and his social position lent
a degree of credibility to it that was, outside of France, unprecedented.
That is not to say that people generally shared Cayley's confidence that
aerial navigation was achievable – in fact, quite the opposite. In a letter
to Viscount Mahon, Cayley himself describes flight as "a subject rather
bordering upon the ludicrous in the public's estimation. . . ." Cayley and
Mahon were regular correspondents in the years following his first
aerial navigation papers, a relationship that seemed to engender considerable mutual support for their respective hopes for a practical form
of flight. Initially, both men retained an undimmed enthusiasm for the
flapping machine developed by Jacob Degen, and they seemed unfortunately to reinforce the other's mistaken belief in its merits. Later
Mahon would hear of the true nature of Degen's success – the use of
a supporting balloon. Cayley, however, always believed that Degen's
flight had been achieved by flapping alone, a fact that proved painfully
influential on all his subsequent work.

As far as his personal interests, it would seem natural that Cayley, having made so many and so exciting a series of discoveries concerning his experiments on flight, would follow them up immediately with further work and publications. In fact, his attention was caught up in the development of his engines, and numerous entries to that effect appear in his notes. But even his ideas on the prime mover would have to wait as he found himself distracted by other issues. During the previous intense period of experimentation and writing, Cayley's domestic life had hardly been standing still: 1806 had seen the birth of his fifth daughter, Frances, and in 1807 the birth of his second son, Digby. In 1812 Sarah gave birth to their eighth child, Catherine, known within the family throughout her life as Kate. Kate inherited her parents' intellectual talents as well as her father's frankness in expressing her opinions, and it is from Kate's personal family history that we get a more candid account of the Cayley family. Cayley himself had reached something of a watershed: his family was established; the line of inheritance was set with two fine sons; and his reputation as a fair but profitable landlord was widely recognized. He had also proven himself both an innovator and leader through his direction of the large-scale land reclamation on his home turf. Kate's account of life at High Hall reveals, however, a more troubled story.

There has been much speculation concerning Cayley's wife, Sarah. There are reports of her "manly" ways in riding astride rather than the more conservative sidesaddle and disapproving talk of her competence with firearms derived from her far from conventional upbringing. These incidents have been used to suggest she was not of the stock normally associated with classical aristocratic womanhood where ladies were expected to march for hours uncomplaining beside their husbands through marsh and mud (rather than take pot shots at the local game themselves). Though unconventional, such behaviour seems hardly the stuff of domestic crisis. More disquieting are the repeated suggestions concerning Sarah's volatile temper and violent tantrums, which were first reported by Cayley in her adolescence. Corroboration of these aspects of her adult character is hard to come by owing to the absence of almost all the correspondence between Sarah and her family members. A suspicious mind might think that such editing of the personal archive was a form of confirmation that something unsavoury was going on, but when it comes to Sarah's personality we have to read between what few lines survive. Writing in her unique style (and making her own rather ill-considered diagnosis), daughter Kate later summed up the relationship between her father and mother saying,

> It was not a happy marriage and the spell of her beauty, her great powers of mind and a moral character of great excellence held him her slave through life. Added to a temper utterly ungoverned (and I should fear latterly ungovernable) there was an entire absence of the feminine qualities on which domestic happiness depends. This was her misfortune not her fault. The conformation of her brain was entirely masculine.

A further cause of domestic stress (or perhaps its result) was the increasing presence of Miss Philadelphia, whose involvement in the up-bringing of the Cayley children became more frequent as time went by. Miss Phil was a close confidant to the children, and a regular corre-spondent and close friend to Cayley himself. Once more the record of their letters is pitifully small and almost exclusively made up of the friendly, playful but innocent notes from Cayley to his cousin. Kate was obviously close to Miss Phil, and her descriptions of the inter-action between her mother and Phil give an indication of some kind of friction in the family:

I for my part was exceedingly attached to her [Phil]: she was very clever with a strong turn for sentiment! Her one attachment in life was for my father and it was purely platonic. Her sympathy with him was intense. I feel certain that if my mother had allowed her conduct and made her husbands happiness her study, none would have rejoiced more than poor Phil Cayley.... My father was the last man to willfully cause unhappiness to any living person, much less to his wife, but she withdrew her affection from him. The misery of his life doubtless found solace in the devotion of his cousin.

What is known is that as Cayley's family grew, so did the involvement of Miss Phil in their daily lives. It might have acted as a calming influence, even if all the underlying motives for her doing so would never be known. It did not, however, ease the tension in a household in which socializing was a central activity with a constant stream of visitors and house guests at the High Hall. One of Cayley's notebook entries includes another less than typical example of an evening's dinner conversation:

Dec 6th 1812. The Baron de Roget De La Garde informs me that he is the only survivor of a party of French Nobility who hid a very considerable treasure of money and jewels in the wall of a well where the stones had been hollowed out on purpose and replaced by the party in the night with the treasure. The house is now standing and the well entrance and likely to remain so – It is easily known being at the time belonging to Mon^S Le Baron De Sweff at Mentz province De Loraine.

It is uncertain whether Cayley ever followed up this intriguing lead, though doing so at the time would have been complicated. Even if Napoleon was busy conquering the ashes of Moscow when the baron revealed the whereabouts of his treasure trove, travel to France was impossible at the time with the European wars in full swing throughout the continent. Thus the Baron de Roget De La Garde's story could not be verified by Cayley or by anyone else as far as we know. The anecdote's presence in Cayley's notebook seems to indicate that Cayley believed it, though this might be another illustration of his charming reliance on the honesty of others. To the jaded twenty-first-century observer, the combination of the unverifiable nature of the baron's story due to chaos of the war, the extended name-dropping, the "only survivor" detail, the (now worthless) cash, and (perpetually valuable) jewels makes it sound more like a con game than the sincere recollections of a displaced French noble. It should be remembered that under the pre-Revolutionary ancien régime, almost one in ten of the population claimed to be an aristocrat of one kind or another, so being one was neither a mark of particular distinction nor an indication of the likely honesty in the incumbent. Early nineteenth-century Britain was awash with displaced and impoverished continentals, and perhaps some of them felt the need to sing for their supper.

Cayley's notebook closed out 1812 with another exquisite little sketch of "a very ingenious contrivance," a rope-making machine he observed in a visit to a Liverpool factory. This entry was the last for nearly three years as Cayley's life took a turn for the worse.

In 1813 Sarah gave birth to another son, their third, whom they named after Cayley's father, Thomas. Baby Thomas would never be strong or healthy, and during an epidemic of the measles that swept the area during the autumn Thomas died. On top of one tragedy came another; Thomas's ten-year-old brother George, the Cayley heir, also caught the dangerous disease and died, leaving Digby the only male offspring to survive. There is no formal documentation of the events beyond the barest fact in the parish records. No letters concerning the painful event are found in the Cayley archive, but there are hints at

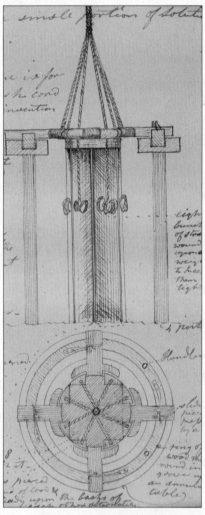

"This engine is for plaiting tress from chord and is the invention of a poor man of the name of Watt at the Blind Asylum Liverpool...."

the impact it had on Cayley himself. Shortly after these deaths, Cayley made another and rather morbid contribution to *Nicholson's Journal*. It was his commentary on a drowned man found under the ice of a frozen lake in London. Though Cayley's interests and publications were varied to say the least, he seems to have been pressed this time to comment on a subject emotionally close to home. Two years later, when making out one of his regular updates to his will, Cayley rendered the document null and void by inadvertently entering as his heir the name of his deceased son George, rather than that of surviving son Digby. Although life in eighteenth-century Britain involved, even for the wealthy, the repeated and close personal experience of losing loved ones, the loss of his son and namesake had a lasting impression on Cayley. In time, he looked to a second George Cayley junior for the continuance of his legacy.

The unusual weather that caused exceptionally low temperatures in Britain, with consequential effects on almost everybody's health, had begun in 1812. The persistently poor weather of the early 1810s resulted in correspondingly low harvests, exacerbating the shortages in Britain as a result of the wartime blockade. The civil reaction was evident in more rioting and general discontent but the immediate fears of a popular British uprising were temporarily forgotten in early 1814 with the abdication and imprisonment of Napoleon following his defeat by the British allies, who entered Paris in March. Britain and the continent's relief was short-lived, however, for Napoleon escaped from exile on the island of Elba in 1815 and embarked on his "glorious 100 days." Napoleon's reign ended with his final and irrevocable defeat at Waterloo at the hands of the Duke of Wellington and the mad Prussian Marshall Blücher (the latter thought he was pregnant with an elephant, fathered by a Frenchman, no less). Sandwiched in between these man-made catastrophes was a natural one that claimed even more lives. In April 1815, Mount Tambora on the Indonesian island of Sumbawa exploded in a series of volcanic eruptions that removed the top 4,000 feet from its summit and ejected over 200 billion tons of rock, lava, ash, and dust into the atmosphere. The estimated 10,000 deaths from the eruption itself, and a further 82,000 from the resulting tsunami, were dwarfed by the global effects of the ash and dust, which removed an entire growing season from the agricultural calendar in 1816: "the year without a summer." Crops failed all over the planet but the most severely affected were eastern North America and northern Europe.

The British government's response to the rising crisis was swift and decisive. They introduced the Corn Laws to prevent the price of British grain from plummeting as a result of the lifting of the continental blockade. On top of a series of terrible harvests, and almost none at all in 1816, cheap imported grain was effectively banned; the profits from agriculture therefore remained both stable and artificially high. This was of course good news for those whose income depended on it, namely the tenant farmers and landowners who had supported the reactionary Tory Lord Liverpool, now the country's prime minister. As if what amounted to a tax on bread wasn't bad enough, 1816 also saw the introduction of the Game Act, making the pheasants, partridges, hares, and rabbits that lived on a given piece of land the property of the landowner. The Game Act was a natural progression of hundreds of Enclosure Acts that were passed in the eighteenth and nineteenth centuries, laws that made common land previously accessible to everyone now part of the private estates of local landlords. Following this legislation, there was no common grazing pasture and the previously legal act of catching game to supplement an already meagre diet was now regarded as poaching. In response to the upwelling of popular discontent over food prices, iniquitous law-making, and a flailing economy, Lord Liverpool applied the true and tested mechanism of suspending the right to trial, allowing for the imprisonment without charge of those who opposed his policies. In order to silence the growing criticisms in the press, he introduced a "tax on knowledge" through a levy on newspapers. These events once more spurred Cayley into direct political action, but first domestic matters required his attention.

During this chaotic period, Lady Sarah gave birth to her tenth and last child, Mary Agnes, in April 1815. As befitted a child born into such times, this youngest daughter eventually outstripped all her siblings put together in her ability to bring drama to the Cayleys. The birth of George and Sarah's final child, when they were both forty-one years of age, marked the beginning of a new period in their relationship, with the needs of adult, teenage, and infant children becoming an increasingly dominant influence on the Cayley household. This additional source of stress was one with which Sarah in particular had problems. Her angry outbursts became something of a fixture of the domestic scene, with their frequency and intensity becoming ever greater as time went on. It could have been hoped that the second and perhaps most enduringly significant woman in Cayley's early life, his mother Lady Isabella, would have provided a controversy-free oasis for her son. Unfortunately, even from this quarter there was trouble. This time the cause was religion.

Although Isabella probably converted to Methodism during the 1790s, the first formal record of her transfer of theological allegiance appears in the family archive in the pivotal year of 1810. Isabella took well to her new responsibilities in providing succour, as well as evangelical zeal, to the poor and infirm of the parish. She set aside three hours a day for her work among what she regarded as her flock, writing that "I bless God for my title. I do not pride myself on being called Lady Cayley, but it is a key that opens every door in this and parishes adjoining. . . . I can lift the latch of the cottage . . . and talk to the people of the Saviour's love." Like many other conservative parishes, Brompton's reaction to Methodism had not been welcoming. Cayley's eldest daughter, Anne, recalls in her diary how her great-grandfather (the less than affable first Sir George) had turned out a certain Thomas and Frances Allin from their cottage solely on the basis of their following the Methodist faith. The homeless couple had knelt in the street and "prayed that Heaven would one day send a Cayley to restore Methodism to Brompton." Isabella sought to fulfil that role following a revelatory experience while attending a local dance: "I was convinced of sin in an assembly room where everything in an instance appeared madness and folly, and where the faultiness of my whole life was brought to my recollection. . . . I resolved on an entire change of life, to read the Bible and pray." From that moment, Isabella was a force for the new faith throughout the area.

Cayley, like everyone else, knew of Isabella's religious work; it was hard not to as the Methodism applied by his mother was as outdoor, outspoken, and evangelical as the Wesleyan pioneers could have hoped. Cayley's own close association with the Unitarianism of his youth had been gradually but completely exchanged for the more conventional ministries of the mainstream Church of England. The depth of his convictions was defined by an honest personal faith in the Anglican Church, a faith that was constantly reinforced by his social position. Having reached middle age, with over half of his event-filled years spent as "Sir George 6th Bart," he had an obligation to see the authority of his Church go unchallenged. However, "challenged" describes exactly the state of the church at the time.

The Anglican Church of late eighteenth and early nineteenth centuries was unresponsive and apathetic to the radical social changes going on around it. The Church was largely rural, populated by a social and intellectual elite, and wholly tied to the most conservative institutions of the nation. In contrast, a huge shift in population had taken place, as people moved from the country into the towns as industrialization grew and the profits from agriculture sank through the floor. This movement combined with a population explosion and the emergence of the new and loud middle class to produce an increasing proportion of the British people without traditional ties to land or landlord. Neither Church nor Parliament had followed the shift in demographics well, leaving a large proportion of both new and old segments of society as disenfranchised from the parliamentary process as they were isolated from the mother Church. Into the secular vacuum flooded everything from moderate reformism to outright revolution; the theological gap was filled by nonconformist faiths, and one of the most successful was Methodism. The Methodist Society replaced the distant and often snooty religious hierarchy of Anglicanism with a flattened and immediately accessible "connexion," the Methodist term for the ruling council of their group. Every Methodist was part of the ministry as the division between clergy and congregation was blurred to the point of non-existence. As the "age of reason" matured, reason itself was celebrated as the means by which Methodists could examine, explore, and celebrate the scriptures. Methodism was vibrant, popular, all-inclusive, and for a woman of Isabella's fortitude and talents it provided an outlet for her energies, a vehicle for her intellect, and a focus for her devotions. However she, her fellow Methodists, and Methodism itself presented a serious threat to the Anglican Church, and as its local representative Cayley felt that although he could not stop the religion, he would not encourage it. The most effective means of slowing down the local spread of Methodism was to ensure that there was no focal point for it, such as a local chapel. However, one of the strengths of the Methodist Society was its minimalist nature, requiring little in the way of money, material, or even parishioners to sustain it. Methodists would meet, pray, and celebrate their religion in houses or rented space, with congregations being anything from two upward. As Isabella and a small enclave of Cayley servants accompanied the group of Methodist Brompton villagers to nearby Snainton and Ruston to join "the communion of saints," the subject of a more local meeting place became a hot topic. But if they were to do anything within the 6th Baronet's sphere of influence, it would have to wait until Cayley himself was safely out of the way.

In 1816, during one of Cayley's extended absences in London on business, Lady Isabella quickly acquired a plot of land within the village and had a rudimentary Methodist chapel built. When Cayley heard the news on his return home, he was apoplectic at what he saw as a clear deceit on behalf of his tenants and, more shockingly, his own mother. He quickly drafted his own "Cayleyan Bull," which he dramatically nailed to the door of Brompton's Anglican and, as far as Cayley was concerned, Brompton's *only* parish church. Some days later he arranged for a slightly more tempered version to be printed up and circulated within the village. It was another example of Cayley's fearless confidence in publicly declaring his beliefs, as well as of his miserly use of the period.

To my tenants of the Methodist Persuasion in Brompton. My friends, you have hitherto found that I have dealt with you upon exactly the same footing as my other tenants, and with an equal hand I have distributed the advantages in my power, even to such of your persuasion as were not previously connected with me, you had free exercise of your religion in your own homes, and in a subscription-room, space more than sufficient to hold all the Methodists of *this* village: but in the pride of your sect you have called to the aid of it's public purse, to establish a meeting-house for the reception of Methodists from the surrounding parishes; thus taking unfair advantage of the liberality, with which you have *here* been tolerated.

I admit a full right of the individual judgement in matters of religion; and I have no objection to my tenants professing whatever religion they please, provided it does not prevent that wholesome and natural dependence of one rank of society upon another, which has hitherto so firmly sustained the fabric of British strength, and raised it to the first class among nations. It is the leading fault in your doctrine that it tends to undermine this natural compact between the higher and the lower ranks of society; in which under Providence, the latter have ever found their greatest protection, and the former their best field for exercising the endearing charities of life. No sooner does an uneducated man imagine he had become, if I may use your own language, "a chosen vessel" than he looks upon all who he thinks not so chosen, as his inferiors: the succession of fostering hands, which for generations perhaps may have administered to the wants and comforts of their forefathers and themselves, are forgotten; and the natural allegiance due to such a connexion, is transferred to some petty leader of a band, not qualified either by education to direct, or by property to sustain him under the contingencies of advancing life. – It was with this view that I wished to oppose the farther introduction of Methodism among my tenants and neighbours, which the erecting a more public meeting-house was calculated to effect, your disregard of my remonstrations upon this occasion, is a proof of the very result of your doctrine which I have pointed out; and I fear that the worldly parade, which you have taken such pains to excite, has in it more spiritual pride than of Christian meekness and devotion. Neither do I approve of the mode in which this building had it's origin, more than that of it's completion.

During my absence for a few days, a piece of land was purchased for this building, by two or three individuals. Amongst these was a tenant of mine, to whom I applied, for the purpose of knowing why so serious a step, involving the highest interest of the inhabitants of the village, has been taken without acquainting me previously; I was informed, that it was their intention to have consulted me; but that my being from home prevented it. In direct contradiction to this statement, another of these persons declared, that this subject had frequently, in a concealed manner, been talked over by them, so far as respected the communication of this project to myself; and that it had been determined, on his suggestion, to build a meeting-house without acquainting me, as the most effectual way of getting it accomplished. Had my assent been previously solicited, I should have replied that "if the Methodists of this township could afford to build a meeting-house, I should not object to it, but that I must object to it's being erected, merely for the accommodation of the Methodists of other villages, whose inhabitants have no pretence to interfere with the affairs of Brompton."

You are now in full possession of my sentiments upon this occasion, which I have thus fully stated, in order to show that it is not the religion you profess, but the insubordination and ill conduct, to which it inevitably gives birth, that I object, George Cayley, Brompton, July 1816.

P.S. As the original address was written in great haste by myself, and copied in still greater haste by another, without any opportunity for revision, and as it was not permitted to remain upon the Church longer than a day or two, I have printed a few corrected copies, that every tenant of mine may see my sentiments upon this subject.

This is classic Cayley, a man who never allowed grammar to get in the way of a sentence in full flow. There are one or two issues raised by his announcement, not least whether either one of the "tenants" mentioned happened to be his own mother. Perhaps Lady Isabella had been the snitch who admitted that they had been planning the whole thing for months. We also see the revolutionary zeal of his teenage years in full retreat, now requiring "that wholesome and natural dependence of one rank of society upon another." The now lost original and apparently less restrained version of his bulletin must have been a shocker.

Perhaps more revealing is the emergence of Cayley's need to equate wealth with the personal attributes of those who possessed it; he seems unable to disassociate political and managerial savvy from social position. That Cayley took his responsibilities for maintaining the local peace seriously is beyond doubt, but his illiberal sentiments regarding the proposed Methodist Chapel have to be seen in context to be fully understood. In an age when there was no police force anywhere outside the larger cities and where the voluntary, amateur, and unpaid peacekeeping machinery of the provinces had remained essentially unchanged for over two hundred years, the local landowner was the only effective authority short of military law with its frightening methods. Anything that disturbed the balance of power was seen as a threat, and there had been too many recent examples of civil unrest for even the smallest revolutionary act to go unchallenged. From a distance of nearly two hundred years, Cayley's opinions seem at best unendearing and probably more like downright offensive. The same bloody-mindedness that led Cayley to publish his thoughts on flight and damn the consequences caused him to do the same when it came to what he regarded as his paternalistic responsibilities in Brompton. His attitude approaches dictatorship, but these were revolutionary times. What's more, there were examples of rebellion even on the Brompton doorstep.

Thirteen Luddites (the paramilitary group of anti-industrial sabo-teurs) had recently been hanged in nearby York, with dozens more transported to Australia, for destroying industrial machinery. The Luddites sought to overturn the early and unpopular effects of indus-trialization, though their ire was aimed at more than just the change in working practice. Following a huge rise in unemployment, not helped by 300,000 soldiers and sailors returning from the Napoleonic Wars, the icon for these unwelcome changes became change itself, and in par-ticular the newfangled machines and the owners of the factories housing them. The Luddite movement had spread from Nottingham throughout the industrial heartland of Britain, including the textile industry of West Yorkshire. The government's response had been typically harsh, making machine-breaking an offence punishable by hanging, thus helping to bring the number of crimes attracting the death penalty to over two hundred. With riots over the cost of food and low wages, riots over the change in lifestyle engendered by mech-anization, unrest over the lack of electoral reform, and more discontent still over the established Church's failure to provide a moral lead to a changing congregation, Cayley was trying to do his best to hold together his own little corner of England.

In the aftermath of the religious fallout in his own backyard, as well as the volatile political climate, Cayley typically sought an outlet for his concerns in positive action, which crystallized into his formally entering the political arena. One of his first acts was to support the establishment of a York Whig Party in 1817. His involvement in overt politics, and his more subtle manoeuvrings for political advantage, continued until he was in his eighties. Cayley acted as a general moderating influence on those around him, something that was sorely needed in a political climate that was nothing short of frenzied.

British politicians had been for the years preceding 1817 broadly aligned with either the Whigs or the Tories. Typifying the dirty-pool tactics of the day, even the labels applied to the parties were derived from insults: "Whig" ("whiggamor") was a name for a cattle driver, "Tory" was Irish slang for an armed thug. Though neither group was an organized political party in the modern sense of the word, the Tories were generally associated with the Royal patronage and the Church of England, while Whigs were more associated with the moneyed class and religious dissent. Many Whigs of Cayley's era saw themselves as middle-of-the-road politicians. Similarly, Cayley described his views as a compromise between "two violent and pernicious factions – the courtiers, who are for arbitrary power – and the democrats, who are for revolution and republicanism." Such polarization was coloured by the considerable length of time the Whigs had spent out of power – once they returned to office, they would find themselves compelled to use many of the methods they had so vocally deplored the Tories having applied. That Cayley saw himself as a Whig had more to do with the huge political spectrum bracketed by the party than with the appeal of a specific set of Whig electoral goals – especially as at the time they didn't have many. Whiggery in general seemed to align well with Cayley's own sympathies for the idea of some moderate electoral reform while retaining the structures he felt embodied Britain: the Crown and Parliament, both the Commons and the Lords. During 1817 and 1818, Cayley considered what it was specifically he could do, and as he did little better than putting his views down on paper and then into the public domain, the result was another publication. The product was a political pamphlet in the form of an open letter to the mentor from his teenage years in London, Major John Cartwright, "the father of reform." Cayley had been a recent and critical correspondent with Cartwright, and if Cayley had once been the political pupil, he now took up the more paternal voice of restraint, fearing the consequences of too rapid a rate of change.

The length of time he spent musing on his publication was as a result of another near revolution in 1817 over the worsening economy and its direct effects on the poorest workers, mainly those in agriculture. Cayley's letter attempted to address both the economic and social ills of the day. To say that his 1818 political debut rambles on a little would be an understatement. Though he had something of a gift in extracting key principles from the morass of obscuring details in the field of mechanics, his political writing has a tendency to do the exact reverse: inspiring oratory would never be one of his fortes. In essence, Cayley's lengthy letter declares a need for change, though only very gradually and within much prescribed limits. That it takes a six-page introduction and a twenty-three-page main body to explain his analysis might have been because of a wide-ranging and penetrating series of insights, but unfortunately it isn't. He does, however, clearly say what he is against:

> There have gone forth throughout the kingdom two diametrically opposite, and I conceive, equally false opinions . . . universal suffrage as the only cure for political evils . . . [alternatively] . . . supporting ministers in every encroachment on the rights and liberties of commoners to enable us to stem what they conceive to be the popular tide towards revolution.

What Cayley is *for* is both the contemporary equivalent of motherhood and apple pie ("Let wisdom govern") and the rather contentious re-expression of his ideas about who the wise governors might be: "Property implies independence and education, and these are the two chief ingredients to constitute an efficient elector under a free government."

It would be hard to argue with the suggestion that the electorate should be independent and educated. It seems somewhat reactionary, however, that the only means of proving you had the required qualities for office was by exhibiting independent financial means and owning property of value. Although this view may appear short-sighted, high-handed, and even repressive, the all-too-obvious alternative seemed to be either the continuance of the repressive regime of the Tories or descent into a civil war. Cayley knew that such an outcome could cost more lives than the countless thousands who died in France – with most of the casualties being among the very citizens the revolution was designed to liberate and then protect. It would be unfair to label Cayley's opinions as blinkered, for he admits that the future may hold a radically different political system: "I make no doubt that that universal suffrage, nay even republicanism, will have it's day. . . ." But his line is one of "jam tomorrow" with the menu in the short term offering only bread and butter (for those who could afford it). His overall tone is restrained, concerned, and above all sympathetic even if some of his analogies border on the hackneyed:

> We must not forcibly unravel the opening bud of human society, and leave those ripening glories to wither in the early chill of spring, which were designed to develope themselves under the full sunshine of a maturity yet unborn.

Cayley voices his opposition to the present administration, and then aligns himself with the common goals of both his fellow moderates and Cartwright's radical reformers: "The truth is, that we both see a fault in the present order of things, of so great a magnitude, that some remedy must be had or the liberty of the land is gone. . . ." His discourse goes by way of the national debt to the economics of the recent war with France and the dangers to his grandchildren of having to fund it through higher taxation. He even includes a less than veiled threat, saying that a moneyed man's interests "are not so interwoven with the soil of Britain, but that he can transfer them to any part of the globe he pleases."

What Cayley does advocate is a moderate increase in the number of M.P.s, "an hundred disinterested country gentlemen," as a means of diluting the power of the current reactionary government. In a final monstrous analogy, Cayley asserts that the path of moderation is the only one that would avoid "the howling scylla of revolution on the one hand, or the no less fatal charybdis of despotism on the other."

In his conclusion, Cayley seems to admit he's perhaps extended his welcome as a correspondent, though he feels the need to round off with one last pun: "I feel almost ashamed of having harped on so long upon the string of caution." Whether there was any formal response from Cartwright is unknown, but Cayley's sentiments at least captured the mood of many moderates at the time. Politically, things in Britain got a lot worse before they got better.

On Sunday August 16, 1819, seventy thousand people gathered in St. Peter's Field, in Manchester, northern England. Essentially, this was a peaceful gathering, although many political banners called for the repeal of the Corn Laws, voting by secret ballot, universal suffrage, and yearly elections. The political leaders of the reform movement were expected later in the afternoon; the aging Major Cartwright had been invited, though it was unclear if he would come. At 1:30 p.m. the crowd was formally "read the Riot Act" by a local magistrate but they refused to budge, even though failing to comply was just one of more than two hundred crimes warranting legal execution. Instead, some sixty amateur Yeomen (essentially partly-trained local militia) were sent in to arrest the ringleaders and remove the offending placards.

The crowd reacted by linking arms to stop the Yeomen, and fighting broke out. The local military commander promptly sent in the professional cavalry, in the form of the 15th Hussars, who cleared the crowds within minutes. Ten demonstrators, including a woman and a child, were killed, and four hundred people were seriously injured. One Yeoman lost his life. There were accusations of the militiamen being drunk and violent and counterclaims of the crowd being malevolent and violent – not to mention illegal. The use of sabre-wielding troops to quell a peaceful demonstration by civilians dressed in their Sunday clothes was compared to the tactics applied in the closing battle of the Napoleonic Wars, and the incident became known as Peterloo. That the death of fewer than a dozen people could be labelled a massacre and go on to become the focal point for socialist theory for nearly two hundred years probably says more about British politics than anything else; a natural tendency to accept the status quo seemed instilled from birth. Nevertheless, at the time the effect on an already troubled country was electrifying. As Britain teetered once more on the edge of open revolt, the government responded with the Six Acts, bringing Britain closer to a permanent state of dictatorship. Local magistrates could now search premises at their discretion; meetings of fifty of more people were illegal, as was meeting outside of your local parish bounds; the penalty for the loosely defined "sedition" was increased to fourteen years transportation (in effect a life sentence); access to bail was further restricted; and a tax on newspapers was extended to anyone publishing so much as an opinion. In effect, the right to due legal process, the right of association, and the right to freely express opinion were removed from British law. Cayley's worst fears had been realized.

That Britain did not implode into civil war in 1819 has always been something of a mystery to historians – the same fate did not escape Spain, Portugal, and Italy the following year. Britain was awash with discontent at every level: the labourer over food and unemployment, the middle class over the absence of representation in Parliament, the manufacturers over restrictions to trade, and the wealthy over low agricultural income. One commentator put the absence of a war, or at least a change in government, down to simple chance: "It was just that not everyone was angry at the same time." Another factor may have been the presence of so many political activists out there stirring up apathy. If Cayley's York Whig Party declaration of 1819 is anything to go by, it may be that getting all revolutionary just wasn't something the British tended to do. Though the Whig announcement boldly advocates "RADICAL REFORM in the House of Commons," they quickly qualify their stance by adding, "We mean nothing tending towards *Turbulence*, or dangerous to the established *Authorities*." They further hedge their bets as to what exactly they do advocate:

As to *Specific* Modes of *Reform*, we deem all Observations, on our part, at this time premature: – Whatever Reform shall at once rectify Public Grievances, and leave uninjured the Fabric of our Constitution, will to us be satisfactory.

Though not the stuff that sends blood coursing through the veins, its non-specific hand-wringing was much in line with Whig sentiments at the time: change was needed, but no two Whigs seemed able to agree on exactly what it was that needed changing. The feebleness of the document may have been because the York Whigs needed to ensure that their declarations did not fall foul of the law. As it happened, their pamphlet just preceded the Six Acts; if it had not, then even so timid a declaration could have been labelled "an overt act of treasonable conspiracy" with serious repercussion for its signatories. As a new decade dawned, the public's rage at the machine of government calmed a little, but the process of even moderate reform was another eighteen years in coming. When it did, Cayley would have a front seat.

7

THE PUBLIC *and* PRIVATE AVIATOR

The ten years following the triple *Nicholson* papers in 1809 and 1810 were dominated by domestic and political matters. Nevertheless, Cayley still made an occasional notebook entry concerning his thoughts on flight and published a series of articles that followed up a selected number of themes. Following the death of William Nicholson (and closure of his magazine), Cayley turned to *Tilloch's Philosophical Magazine* as another outlet for the ideas he wished to share with the public. There now appears a clear divergence between what Cayley would publicly put his name to compared to his thoughts in private. When going to press, Cayley now exclusively sought to stimulate debate (and try to drum up cash for) the mainstream subject of lighter-than-air machines: "fire" (hot air) and hydrogen balloons. This change reflected Cayley's need to develop a more conservative reputation. If his emerging political persona was to be taken seriously, he would need to keep his more radical ideas on flight to himself. His correspondence and notebooks, however, show him typically unconstrained and with flappers firmly on his mind.

In Cayley's notebook entry for 1815, we see his design for a "tandem" flyer, incorporating two pairs of wings and an enlarged rudder (elevator) toward the rear. Each of the four wings is composed of flapping tips to generate thrust with the wing portions nearest the aircraft centre being used to generate lift – though his design fell short of the elegance of bird flight in that his flappers generated thrust only on the downbeat. Cayley's idea was that diagonally opposite wings would beat together so that there would always be a down-beating wing to push the plane through the air. Cayley uses a Degen "flap-valve" as the means of generating thrust on the downbeat, the valves opening on the upbeat to allow the air to pass through. This design joins what is becoming a lengthy list of "thought of, but never built" flyers from his most vivid imaginings. The following year Cayley progresses even farther down the beating route by experimenting with a set of flappers specifically designed for vertical flight – once more along the lines of his hero Degen. The flappers generate an impressive 92 pounds of downward force. However, as the combined weight of the apparatus plus Cayley was 222 pounds, the machine is really going nowhere.

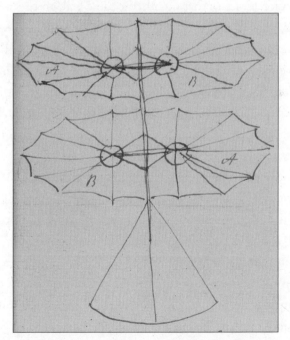

The 1815 "tandem" flyer, inspired by a dragonfly.

As his private ideas followed their own distinctive paths, Cayley realized there might be something gained from joining the mainstream of contemporary aviation, and he made his first contribution to lighter-than-air flight the following year. As usual, Cayley was called to the fray by someone else encroaching on his aerial navigation patch.

Although ballooning had never really gone away since its inception in 1783, there had been precious little progress in development since the time of the Montgolfiers. Experiments in ballooning had, like almost everything else, taken something of a back seat over the last twenty years due to what amounted to a world war. However, the military application of an "eye in the sky" had not been lost on the country with the lead in aviation – post-revolutionary France. The first military use of balloons took place in June 1794 during the French victory over the Austrian-Dutch forces at Maubeuge, where a balloon was used to spy out the opposition forces. Later that month, the same balloon became the first airborne command and control centre, remaining almost permanently aloft while messages were dropped down guide ropes to the troops below during the decisive victory by the French at Fleurus. This was the high point in French military ballooning. The low point came four years later when the Napoleonic "Balloon Corps" were wiped out, along with Napoleon's naval expeditionary force to Egypt. French military ballooning did not re-emerge for another half-century.

The saving grace for lighter-than-air flight arose out of the French Revolutionary Council's view that science was the most ideologically appropriate outlet for central government-funded work. In general the (no longer Royal) Académie des Sciences proved a catalyst for scientific investigation during this period – they even allowed the completion of the ancien régime's work on the meticulous triangulation of France to calculate the metre (set as the length equal to one ten-millionth of the distance from the North Pole to the equator via Paris). In this spirit of scientific endeavour, small-scale experiments with balloons also continued in France, particularly as they represented the most obvious high point in Gallic accomplishment and were a welcome distraction for the increasingly restless masses. In 1804, physicist Joseph-Louis Gay-Lussac and mathematician Jean-Baptiste Biot reached an altitude of 23,000 feet while investigating the composition of the upper atmosphere. Of the components absent at such heights, warmth and oxygen were the most noticeably lacking, and the Académie promptly forbade further high-altitude experimentation as the effects of cold and anoxia threatened to kill off their most famous academics.

Though ballooning as an active recreation and passive spectacle persisted throughout the nineteenth century, pioneering aeronauts realized that to make it a practical mode of transport the balloon should be *dirigible* – capable of being steered. This called for three aspects of design: an aerodynamic shape, to make the balloon's passage through the air more efficient; rudders and elevators to point the balloon in the right direction; and a motive force to drive it along the path required.

A Frenchman had been the first to address the shape required of a dirigible balloon: Lieutenant Jean-Baptiste Meusnier realized that an ellipsoidal (blimp-shaped) balloon was needed. Unfortunately, Meusnier's contribution to flight was cut short when he was killed in action in 1793; the collapse of French military interest in ballooning occurred shortly afterwards following the Egyptian disaster of 1798. It was left up to the interested individual to develop the technology further, and one such up-and-coming inventor was to be found in England. Cayley's first public contribution to ballooning appeared in response to an 1815 article by John Evans in *Tilloch's Philosophical Magazine*. Evans addressed the need for powering a balloon by suggesting the use of a huge inclined plane to drive a balloon forward as it rose, reversing the plane's inclination on its descent to achieve the same forward motion. This principle, later termed "dynamic lift," was utilized in airships of the early twentieth century. The resulting roller-coaster progression wasn't elegant, but it was at least a feasible method of propulsion.

Cayley responded to Evans's proposition by placing his own thoughts in *Tilloch's* with a letter dated December 24, 1815. Cayley opens his article with the customary nod to previous work on the subject and then continues with a typically homespun analogy concerning the future importance of flight:

> This subject is of great importance to mankind, and is worthy of more attention than is bestowed upon it. An uninterrupted navigable ocean, that comes to the threshold of everyman's door, ought not to be neglected as a source of human gratification and advantage.

Cayley goes on to point out that an elongated shape offers considerable benefits in allowing a balloon of large volume to present a relatively small resisting surface area to the air. Though this repeats Meusnier's work (albeit unknowingly), Cayley proceeds in rapid succession to advance balloon design toward what was later termed an airship: a practical vehicle for lighter-than-air flight. First Cayley details the need for semi-rigidity and how his design is "kept to its shape by light poles." Then he addresses the importance of scale, realizing that the larger the vehicle, the more lift it would generate, ending up with a balloon of huge proportions, "15 yards in elevation, 30 in width and a 100 in length." The balloon itself would be formed by two independent envelopes (in case one punctures) fed by an oval (streamlined) chimney "furnished with three wire nets to prevent sparks from passing up."

Left-right motion would be controlled by "a sail or rudder," though Cayley seems to have discarded his rather clever elevator designs from his airplane drawings for pitch control. Cayley decides that Evans may be on to something with his roller-coaster forward motion, but suggests

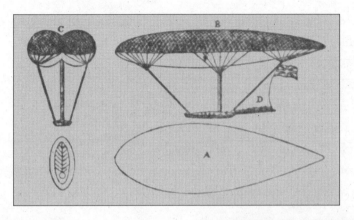

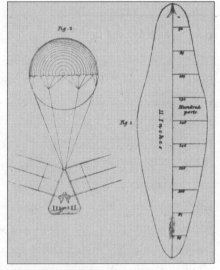

The rapid progression in Cayley's airship design: December 1815 (top), May 1816 (centre), and May 1817 (bottom).

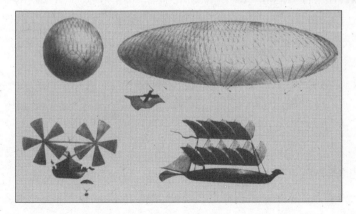

that this can be better achieved by raising and lowering the nose of the balloon by hauling on the ropes fore and aft. Cayley clearly sees this as an experimental vehicle and realizes that without a group effort (and serious financial input) a design on this scale would be a non-starter; he certainly does not propose funding the exercise from his own pocket. He continues his essay with estimates of the fuel consumption – "about 100 pounds of fuel will be expended for every mile of conveyance" – but can't help suggesting his favoured motive force as a by-the-by "sails wafted by the steam engine at a less expense of fuel."

As usual Cayley has hit a few bull's eyes (the streamlined shape, the twin envelope, the semi-rigid structure) and then misses the mark with the inevitable preference for flappers. However, he quickly follows up his first paper with a second in May 1816, and as far as flappers are concerned, he has the bit between his teeth. His second publication, with a streamlined balloon inspired from "the body of a woodcock," now has envelopes filled with hydrogen rather than hot air. It also boasts no fewer than six huge flappers arranged in two tiers of three and weighing a frightening one thousand pounds. Though the flappers' primary purpose is propulsion, Cayley hopes that they could also act as gliding wings should the now highly flammable hydrogen balloon catch fire, requiring the gondola to be cut free. Though his gliding experiments might give him some optimism to expect that the flapper-cum-wing-equipped car would glide to earth and "permit a safe descent," we assume that he intends to test this before it is ever applied. Although his balloon is now a mere 210 feet long, he calculates it will lift up to 50 tons, though a large proportion of this weight would be the heavy steam engine, water, fuel, and crew. In spite of the weight, he estimates the balloon will "convey 500 men during one hour, 410 men during 12 hours, 290 men for 24 hours and 50 men for 48 hours without fresh supplies of fuel or water."

A month later, a letter from Cayley appears once more in *Tilloch's*, noting the news that two foreign émigrés had decided to independently fund a large-scale dirigible design in Britain. John Pauly and Durs Egg, gunsmiths, set about building a ninety-foot airship in Knightsbridge, London. The exercise proved to be both too complex and too costly – Pauly died before its completion, and Egg abandoned the project after having spent the better part of £10,000 of his own money on the project. This first attempt to build an airship in Britain seemed ample evidence that the cost of any large-scale machine would need some form of central funding, but so fanciful and risky an activity attracted neither private investors nor public subsidy. This setback did not stop Cayley attempting to garner public interest in the subject, but in the near-revolutionary times of 1816 the British government and the population in general had other priorities.

Cayley continued his public pronouncements on flight with a brief correspondence on airships via the pages of *Tilloch's* magazine. Unfortunately, Cayley comes off the worse, as Evans's letter, commenting on Cayley's second design, homes unerringly toward the Cayley Achilles heel – flappers. Evans points out, in the most polite of terms, that there might be a better idea.

> I would therefore beg leave to suggest that a large wheel with oblique vanes . . . be substituted, which by revolving continually in one direction would attain the desired object, with no more waste of power than would arise from the additional machinery to obtain a rotary motion from the steam-engine.

It seems strange that this idea should not have come from Cayley himself, especially as his own doodled design for a propeller-driven balloon appears in his schoolbook from 1793. Cayley's reply to Evans, contained in his fourth publication in *Tilloch's* in 1817, admits, "This reasoning against reciprocating [flapping] movements is in general perfectly correct, but in this case the maxim does not hold good."

Cayley's argument then disappears into a ball of mechanical gobbledegook that seems to rest on his design being "properly contrived" without explaining exactly what the proper contrivance was. To further confuse the issue, Cayley's paper includes two further airship illustrations, one of which has two huge five-bladed propellers, the other being equipped with two tiers of flappers. Bearing in mind the bright future of the former proposal and the dead end of the second, it beggars understanding why Cayley would not just do the experiments and the math to compare the two methods of propulsion and make up his mind based on the results. Aviation historian Gibbs-Smith, one of Cayley's ardent admirers and most honest evaluators, was similarly perplexed by Cayley's airship publication.

> One cannot avoid the conclusion that Cayley includes the airscrew alternative in his illustration as a direct result of Evans' letter, and in order to defend himself against any implication that he had not considered such an alternative.

That Cayley *had* considered propeller-driven balloons twenty-four years previously makes his views difficult to follow. His hobby of building those helicopter toys that so clearly demonstrate the practical application of an airscrew makes Cayley's propeller phobia doubly incomprehensible.

This latest Cayley article in *Tilloch's* includes the usual plethora of calculations, this time concerning the effect of winds on the safety of the airships and another plea for a subscription to be raised for experiments on balloon flight in general. Tucked in at the end of his article is a re-introduction of the need for an elevator and rudder for steerage, though both had been excluded from his illustrations because they "would have made the drawing confused."

As a result of these publications, Cayley and Lord Mahon exchanged a further series of letters during 1817, which include Mahon's revelation that he had visited Degen and discovered the supporting balloon. In spite of this news and in line with Cayley's persistent belief in flapping technology, Cayley suggests that perhaps Degen's original experiments were achieved without a balloon, but with wafting alone. The eye of faith (and the closed mind as far as flappers were concerned) seems to once more be driving Cayley away from the more profitable pursuit of propeller propulsion.

This being Cayley's private communication, he does not feel confined to speaking only of balloon flight but also of the wider implications of aviation in general. Included in the correspondence and reflecting the deep concerns for the unstable nature of Britain at the time, Stanhope voices his anxiety over the military and social implications should aerial navigation ever be achieved,

> by multiplying the means of annoyance whether between nations or between individuals, while the means of self-defence would remain very imperfect by creating general insecurity, by rendering still more difficult than at present the detection and apprehension of criminals . . .

Cayley responds with a prudent estimation of the length of time it would take to perfect aviation: "It appears to me that there is more likelihood of its never being accomplished at all in our age." Cayley also recognized the action-reaction effects of the application of technology to conflict. "Your Lordship seems to think that the means of conveyance will be increased whilst the means of defence remains the same: surely the defendant may use the same instruments as the assailant." Cayley realizes that the inevitable military use of aviation will result in measure and countermeasure. His observation seems a prophetic one as the first aerial conflicts of World War 1, almost exactly a century later, so horrifically demonstrated.

Another distinguished Cayley correspondent, Lord John Campbell, was prompted by Cayley's airship publications to reveal his own secret interest in flight. Responding to Lord Campbell's letter of January 1818 Cayley includes a summary of his *Nicholson's* triple paper, as well as a sketch of his latest gliding model, which reveals a further innovation that proved crucial in the development of twentieth-century monoplane designs. Cayley explains how "the balance and steering of aerial vehicles is perfectly ascertained, the sheet [the cloth forming the wing] should be extended like the letter V in its cross section and the weight below it at the vertex." The means by which the V-shaped wings are made rigid is through using a central king post, against which the tensioning wires attached to the wing struts are braced. This king-post structure made the earliest single-winged aircraft possible, including that of Louis Blériot, the first man to cross the English Channel by plane in 1909. It was another Cayley first, though like all of his heavier-than-air discoveries of the time, it remained out of the public gaze and would be rediscovered only after aviation had already leapfrogged ahead of Cayley's hidden insights.

Cayley's interest in balloons extended beyond simply designing them in the abstract, as is revealed in his continuing correspondence with Lord Campbell. Both men began actively experimenting with airship models, as well as powered ornithopters, their shared belief in the wafting wing bonding them ever closer in their clandestine experiments. In a letter dated 1818, Campbell, referring to his own model testing, reports that "the wings in London were far too powerful for the force applied to them, and could not, by the strength of the spring tried, move with sufficient velocity to raise a greater weight than 28 pounds." Campbell even used a pair of real-life (though dead) heron's wings in an experiment powered by a Stirling Air Engine, a variant of the same machine first designed by Cayley himself in 1807. By 1820, both Cayley and Campbell were also experimenting with crudely powered model airships and apparently having similar problems. "Your account of the state in which you find the balloon amused me very much," Campbell wrote, "because I have one here precisely in the same predicament. I had made it out of double silk varnished on both sides. . . . It was too heavy and was of course thrown aside and came into the glutinous state you describe yours to have been."

Cayley went on to conduct more experiments on small-scale gliders and make further developments on his earlier whirling arm in order to more accurately measure the lift and propulsion forces generated by simple inclined planes and flapping wings. However, nearly twenty years elapsed before he found the time to publish on the subject of flight again. In the 1820s, Cayley's focus of interest shifted, as the needs of his growing family once more took precedence.

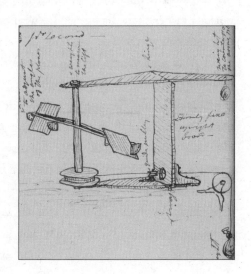

Cayley's whirling arm Mk III of 1818: "I tried on a very delicate but firm and large instrument the resistance of the air to two surfaces containing 2 square feet each. . . ."

8

RELATIVE MOTION

Cayley's family, including relatives both close and distant, was a central part of his life. In part this stemmed from the traditional familiarity within the aristocracy and the pre-eminence of the family unit in the society of the time. In the case of the Cayleys in particular, this bond was strengthened by an inclination toward the romantic. Many family members were aspiring poets and artists, and Cayley was a little of both, though the quality of each was at best uneven. A family anecdote tells of an absent-minded Cayley mistakenly giving his visiting doctor a peppermint wrapped in paper (from his left waistcoat pocket) rather than the guinea fee wrapped in paper (from his right). On being politely informed of his error, Cayley dispatched the required sovereign and shilling coins with an attached note: "The fee was sweet, thanks for the hint, these are as sweet, they've both been through the mint." Similar ditties appear here and there in the family papers, to his wife, to friends and family, and to Miss Phil. They all exhibit a similar level of sentimentality and are executed with that same journeyman's level of expertise that defines his sketches. They are another illustration of Cayley's lack of inhibitions when it came to expressing how he felt, and the unique way in which he expressed it.

Another strand of Cayley life that bonded the family closer was their habit of producing large numbers of offspring and the tendency to keep marriage ties pretty close to home. As if that were not enough, the religious devotions of all of them made for a continuing reinforcement of their communal links. Even during the time when his earlier work away from the domestic scene had been the most conspicuous focus for Cayley's energies, his family had still remained pivotal. The period between 1822 and 1831 was dominated by family concerns, and during this time Sir George and Lady Sarah saw all but two of their children married. Cayley's other works – in science, politics, and patronage – were, to a large extent, squeezed somewhere in between.

By 1820, Cayley and his wife, Sarah, were both forty-six and had been married twenty-five years. They shared their lives with eight children, of whom seven were daughters ranging in age from Anne at twenty-three years, through Isabella (Bell), Emma, Sarah Philadelphia, Frances (Fanny), Kate, and Mary Agnes aged four. They had one surviving son, Digby, now aged twelve. Cayley's mother, Isabella, was probably in her mid-seventies; she remained remarkably sprightly however, possibly because of the invigorating power of her much disapproved Methodism. Miss Phil was forty-four, unmarried, a constant companion to the children, and a close family friend and supporter to Cayley himself. Daughter Kate relates how the strained relationship between her father and mother, and the increasing distance between mother and children, made the role of Miss Phil all the more important in Cayley's life: "As years passed on and his unhappy domestic life continued so did his reliance on Phil Cayley."

Whether Philadelphia's intimacy with Cayley and his children was a cause or a symptom of Sarah's increasing withdrawal from both her husband and many of her children is not really known. Kate writes that the family had strong and mixed feelings for their mother from early in their adolescence until adulthood:

I have been asked by my surviving sister Sarah Lady Worsley and her daughters to say a little more about my mother. They all consider her to have had more tenderness of nature than I gave her credit for. They remember her showing this to her daughter Emma . . . who was gentle in disposition and who perhaps being less irritated by her mother's temper than the rest of her family, was able to feel more affection for her.

With the family now spanning infants to adults, Cayley had the further worry of making plans for their future, most particularly the future of his daughters, who faced life in an increasingly unstable social climate. Even if the Brompton finances were on a solid footing, any major change in the makeup of the ruling classes would mean a less than rosy outlook for the offspring of the aristocracy – and Britain's political situation remained dangerously precarious. Although post-Napoleonic Britain had not experienced the much-predicted revolution, it had come frighteningly close. One of the more dramatic turns came in 1820, when a group known as the Cato Street Conspirators took advantage of the turmoil resulting from the death of Mad King George III. They planned on gatecrashing one of the regular (and publicly advertised) cabinet dinners with a serving of revolvers and grenades. Though unsuccessful, the plot illustrates the deep level of resentment over the iniquitous political system in place at the time. In contrast to the problems at home, Britain, rather surprisingly, was officially not at war with any of her European neighbours. It was a revolutionary situation all of its own and one that Cayley fully intended to turn to the advantage of his children.

Cayley was increasingly concerned with the wider educational needs of his daughters and son. Like his own mother, Cayley saw the necessity of expanding their horizons beyond socializing with their peers in cozy country estates or frenetic townhouse parties. Though Europe was still reverberating from a dozen uprisings and rebellions, there had hardly been a time in history when it hadn't, so Cayley seized the opportunity offered by the absence of all-out war to gather up his family for that fine aristocratic tradition: the Grand European Tour.

The practice of packing off well-heeled youngsters for a lengthy continental adventure was a well-established British tradition. The idea was to endow emerging adults with a grounding in classical art and architecture, to broaden the mind, and to make them more versed in the conversational topics of the better off. For the aristocratic daughter, it was also seen as both a useful asset for and active aid in finding a suitable husband. Marrying off one's daughters could be a lengthy and highly costly enterprise for an aristocrat because a heavy financial commitment was involved. Luckily for Cayley, having a son and male heir meant it wasn't as bad as it could have been, because providing for an "heiress" was a tricky business. The term heiress, one that litters the pedigrees of the nobility, indicates the absence of a male heir to the family fortune, which would instead be split among the daughters and then passed on to their respective spouses. The much more marketable "sole heiress" was a woman with exclusive claims to her family estate, so the man selected as her husband would benefit from a large injection of liquid assets. However, every noble daughter was required to provide something to the marriage bond, and this practice manifested itself in the age-old dowry gift to the newly married male. The simple dowry payments of medieval custom had, by the nineteenth century, evolved into the much more complicated "marriage settlement" – an agreement between the husband-to-be and his wife's family, covering the conditions by which a daughter's future was to be secured. In many cases, it all boiled down to little more than horse-trading over the financial terms. A settlement included a series of legal safeguards aimed at explicitly agreeing on the rights and obligations of man and wife; the transfer of substantial monies made it a legally binding contract. For the less financially endowed husband, marrying well was a springboard to gaining the contacts and cash he needed to establish a dynasty of his own. Even the wealthy male could always use fresh funds, as well as fresh blood to expand estates and family. Although Cayley's daughters were encouraged to be strong-willed and ambitious, one of the few outlets for this intellectual energy was through the social circle a woman could create for herself by marrying wisely. A good marriage could result in a woman gaining influence and status as well as financial security. Marrying the right kind of man (or the right amount of money) could mean the kind of independence rarely achieved by even relatively wealthy males. As she matured, the aristocratic daughter had to plan for her marriage and consider the process to achieve a satisfactory union. An extended trip abroad to see the sights and to mingle with like-minded, eligible men was a means of both raising her profile and widening her choice of suitor.

In the late autumn of 1820 the Cayley nuclear family accompanied their father and mother on their first trip back to their ancestral homeland of France. They planned a journey of more than two years and had revelled in the excitement that first-time foreign travel brings. What it brought first of all was tragedy, as revealed in Cayley's letter home.

> Paris, Jan 24th 1821. My dearest mother, I write to communicate an event which altho' it was never to say unexpected in our family, yet has, at very short notice, thrown us into affliction. Our dear sweet Frances died this morning a few hours ago without a struggle from the mass want of proper circulation of the blood – She was only ill two days and one of these was scarcely to be called a day of illness. She was surrounded by all her best friends and in skilful hands as to medicine but it was a case when no aid could avail. . . . She has been the happiest child I ever saw from her birth to her death and

a purer or kinder heart never existed – you must tell Phil and our Brompton friends of this event....

Frances, sixteen at the time of her death, had been in poor health for some years. A weak heart valve had been diagnosed in her infancy and few had expected her to live long. She was buried later that week in the cemetery of Père-Lachaise in Paris. The only record we have of Frances's death is Cayley's letter to his mother, though years later while visiting Père-Lachaise, daughter Anne sent a portion of vine found growing on Frances's grave to her father as a keepsake.

If the family had thoughts of abandoning their journey, they did not act upon them. After the winter weather abated, they continued to venture even further afield. They spent some six months in and around Paris and then went on to summer in Switzerland. At some point over this period, their travels produced at least one positive outcome, as Cayley writes again to his mother announcing that his second eldest daughter, Bell, has become engaged to "a very agreeable man – Sir Charles Style who has become extremely attached to her and who is equally beloved by Bell." The couple married in Florence, Italy, in October 1822. As would be the pattern for the Cayleys of this generation, their life would be far from straightforward.

Bell was described by her sister Kate as being a woman of "good health excepting the pull upon her nervous system caused by her mother's temper" and was the chief inheritor of her grandmother Isabella's artistic talents as well as her name. Bell's husband, Sir (Thomas) Charles Style, 8th Baronet of Wateringbury, Kent, descended from a line even older than the Cayleys. The original Style baronet, the first in a long line of Sir Thomases, gained his coronet from James I in 1621. The newlywed Charles and Bell eventually settled in Ireland, where they had considerable estates at Stranorlar, County

Donegal. Here they set about improving the quality of their land and the lot of their tenants, though their attempts to stamp out the local practice of distilling *poitín*, the famous and illegal Irish spirit, was neither successful nor popular. Their only daughter, Emma (named after Bell's favourite sister), was born in 1827 but died of meningitis only seven years later while they were travelling abroad. The Style and Cayley families became closer in 1837 when Sir Charles became member of Parliament for Scarborough. However, on losing the Scarborough seat in 1841, Charles suffered a depressive episode that led to him "amicably separating" from Bell for the next nineteen years. He lived in Lausanne, Switzerland, where the couple had first met and where his beloved daughter, Emma, was buried. Finally Bell and Charles reconciled and lived together for twenty more years until Charles's death in 1879. Bell died two years later, aged eighty-four.

Two years after the marriage of Bell and Charles, and following the family's return to Britain from their holiday abroad, Cayley's daughter Emma was married in the grand tradition to Edward Stillingfleet Cayley. Edward was simultaneously Emma's second cousin and fifth cousin once removed, depending on which route through the labyrinthine family tree one prefers to follow. Edward Stillingfleet hailed from the very local village of Wydale, his middle name preserving the surname of his great-great-grandfather Edward Stillingfleet, Bishop of Worcester. Edward the younger was a man of considerable intellect and talents: a doctor of law, Justice of the Peace, and another Cayley son-in-law destined to become a member of Parliament. Edward acted as confidant and legal adviser to the Cayleys up until and even after Sir George's death. Emma and Edward produced three equally talented sons: Edward Stillingfleet (the even younger), who followed his father in his career as a barrister and as a local magistrate; George John, named after his grandfather; and a third son, Charles Digby, who died at sea off Scotland, aged seventeen during service in the Royal Navy.

Aunt Kate noted that "there was a strong vein of eccentricity in both Edward and George John," and it was George John, the middle brother, who inherited Cayley's great interest in mechanics and flight. Though he temporarily joined the Bar of the Inner Temple in London as a solicitor like his elder brother and father, George John was at heart and in action an adventurer and a poet; he later re-emerged in the Cayley story of flight in the most dramatic way.

By 1827, a third Cayley daughter was married, once more into the local aristocracy when Sarah Philadelphia tied the knot with yet another relative, this time a first cousin, William Worsley, later *Sir* William Worsley, 1st Baronet of Hovingham, making his wife another Lady Sarah. They had eight children, and their eldest daughter, Catherine, married back into the Cayley clan once more, this time to *her* own first cousin, George Allanson Cayley (Sir George's grandson), making her Lady Cayley when George Allanson became 8th Baronet of Brompton in 1881.

As with his daughters, Cayley also thought to the future of his son, in whom his baronetcy was now solely invested. In this case, the apple had fallen a little farther from the tree. Though Cayley was a keen shot and talented fly fisherman, he tended to indulge each pursuit as a means of putting dinner on the table or, more likely, into the laboratory. Cayley was not the caricature "huntin' shootin' fishin'" country gentleman of his day. Perhaps in rebellion against the assumption that he would grow to be the son of his father, Digby seemed to positively shun education and the pursuit of science. His sister Kate wrote of him, "He grew up totally different to any of his family and I do not think that his parents quite understood him." Though no sluggard when it came to intellect, Digby seemed to find little interest in technology. Instead he was fascinated by traditional country lore and country pursuits: riding to hounds and the pleasantries of being both a generous host and a charming guest. In an attempt to stir activity from the eyebrows up, Cayley enrolled the eighteen-year-old Digby in a series of lectures concerning the latest scientific discoveries at Edinburgh University when the family wintered in Scotland during 1826. Digby seemed less than enthralled by the subject matter and refused to attend. Rather than losing out on the educational opportunity (and wasting his money), Cayley simply took Digby's seat in the lecture room. That Digby had the wherewithal to manage the farming aspects of the estate seemed in little doubt; he took over elements of their control during his very early twenties. He would not, however, be seeking to extend the intellectual work of his father, and he looked on Cayley's experiments into flight with considerable embarrassment. One area in which Digby did excel was in his ability to attract ready cash into the family business. In 1830, he married Dorothy Allanson from the exotic-sounding Middleton Quernhow – in fact, a Yorkshire village not far from Brompton. Dorothy's marriage settlement brought considerable funds into the family business, as well as the Llannerch Estate around Colwyn Bay in Wales. Dorothy hailed from the kind of conservative tradition that made her feel a little out of place in the frantic world of the Cayley family, though she found her niche eventually, becoming something of a moderating influence on the household, a factor that further separated her and Digby from the less-than-conventional Sir George. The contrast in temperament and interests of father and son was made all the clearer by their proximity; Digby and Dorothy took up residence in one wing of busy High Hall shortly after their marriage.

An even greater boon to the family coffers came in a roundabout though typically Cayley fashion when Digby's first cousin (once removed), the Reverend and notoriously tight-fisted Arthur Cayley, died, leaving the rump of his estate to Digby in 1848. The Reverend Cayley had married his own first cousin, Lucy Cayley, daughter of Sir George's uncle Digby Cayley (senior), who had come into a considerable fortune on marrying the sole heiress Elizabeth Robinson of Wellburn in 1783. Through this incestuous route, Digby (junior) ended up with a windfall which amounted to the large fortune of £70,000 in cash, and land generating the small fortune of £600 per year in rents. These events, along with the sale of the Cayley estates in Lincolnshire, brought the family accounts to an all-time high. There was never a better time (financially) to be a Cayley, and Digby subsequently set about redistributing his funds by purchasing additional estates. These were in the nearby villages of Ebberston and Allerston on the Pickering to Scarborough road. The former property includes the curious Ebberston Hall, known as "England's smallest stately home," a house built by a Scarborough M.P., William Thompson, in 1718 for his mistress, who apparently hated the sight of it and refused to ever live there. The village of Allerston retains a more obvious link to the Cayleys, as the village pub displays a crest, lion (tongue), and other heraldic symbols and boasts the name "The Cayley Arms." Another of Digby's investments is found in his passion for horse racing and his occasional laying of wagers at the racetracks of York and Doncaster. As Digby's income outstripped expenditure, he really didn't have to worry about such extravagances but later Brompton baronets turned that equation on its head with disastrous results.

In 1831, at the age of nineteen, the fifth Cayley daughter, Kate, married Henry Beaumont. Beaumont was the fifth son of yet another Yorkshire member of Parliament, the untitled Thomas Richard Beaumont of Bretton Hall. The negotiations over Kate's dowry were both protracted and complex, with even Cayley's patience being tested during the process. The final figure hammered out was a sizeable £10,000 to be paid in instalments, a deal that led Cayley's son-in-law and legal adviser Edward Stillingfleet Cayley to voice his concern over "the suspicious character HB!" However the prenuptials were agreed, they married, and the couple went on to produce four children who survived to adulthood – though only one turned out to be a Yorkshire M.P. Sadly, Henry died in 1838 though the dowry payments continued to his executors as a result of Henry having used the promise of the payments as a security for loans. This left Kate, aged twenty-six, an indebted widow with four small children. Cayley provided for them until 1845 when Kate remarried into another local family, this time the Legards. Her second husband was Captain James Anlaby Legard (Royal Navy) whose great-great-grandfather's second wife was the daughter of Sir William Cayley, 2nd Baronet of Brompton. This allowed two branches of the Cayley bloodline to co-mingle yet again when Kate and James produced two strapping sons: James Digby and Allayne Beaumont. Both later helped enlarge the British African Empire (by stealing elements of the Zulu one) and then went on to become authors. Allayne produced one of the first detailed descriptions of the state of Colorado; the then *Sir* James penned the family history in *The Legards of Anlaby and Ganton*, a book that adds another intriguing piece to the Cayley legend.

As the process of establishing his family continued, Cayley still travelled abroad with his children when he could. The Cayleys holidayed again in France in 1827. This time, as a result of his growing reputation, Sir George was hailed as something of a celebrity and he met with both Parisian scholars and arctic explorer Sir John Franklin. While in Paris, Cayley and his family were hosted by the fantastically named André Étienne Just Paschal Joseph Francois d'Aubedard Baron de Ferussac. André (for short) was the editor of the *Bulletin Universel*, a leading French scientific journal of its day. Cayley was an early investor in the journal, and the returns had entirely covered the expenses for his first continental trip seven years before.

These excursions had not been successful in finding a partner for Cayley's remaining unmarried daughters, with his eldest, Anne, being of particular concern. As early as 1822, toward the end of the Cayleys' first European expedition, Cayley wrote to his mother concerning the trials of extended travel and his unease over Anne's future: "I hate the eternal rattle of wheels – and company – but I feel I make the sacrifice in conformity with my duty to my family. . . . I want to get up a husband for Anne, which I could never do at home." Exactly why Cayley had given up looking locally for a suitable partner is unclear, though among the qualities included in sister Kate's description of Anne are some that are less than endearing: "She was selfish, sensual & illtempered. Interested in politics, had a fine voice and sang well with much taste. . . . Her general conduct was marked by selfishness, but on great occasions she could rise and act a kind and self denying part." Despite been engaged a reputed five times, Anne had problems deciding on one for keeps, an issue not helped by Cayley having turned away at least two additional suitors as being unsuitable. By the late 1820s, with the unmarried Anne an unfashionably thirty-something, she began to lose interest in the idea of marrying well or even at all. Eventually she settled into single life in Brompton with a house filled with dogs and enjoyed a relatively quiet life until her death, aged seventy-seven.

This leaves only one young Cayley unaccounted for: the last-born, Mary Agnes. Though vivacious and popular, particularly among "selfish, unscrupulous men," Mary Agnes did not marry until 1846, when she was thirty and her parents seventy-two. The consequences of her ill-considered matrimony even found their way into Cayley's last will and testament through what became known as "The Alexander Affair."

Cayley's family and its future dominated much of this decade but he still found time to invest in his thoughts on invention, though his energies became diffused by their very breadth. Cayley's interests, influenced as ever by the events swirling around him, settled on a number of emerging themes. Some had echoes of his earlier fascinations; others foreshadowed his later work.

Cayley's concerns over the average worker's lack of education was an issue he decided to do something about, and the changing times presented the ideal opportunity for his input to have a practical result. The demographic shift toward urbanization and a cultural shift away from a previously London-obsessed Britain meant that the provinces began, at last, to establish their own social agendas. The late eighteenth and early nineteenth centuries saw a boom in adult education, an interest that gave birth to a series of public clubs dedicated to the pres-entation and discussion of the new sciences and a new-found interest in the arts. The list of municipalities forming literary and philosophi-cal societies echoed the spread of wealth to the cities that formed the heartland of the industrial revolution. The first of these societies was founded in the manufacturing centre of Manchester in 1781, with George Walker at its helm. The coal and steel centres of Derby and Newcastle followed in 1783 and 1793 respectively. The British Midlands, with its textile and later engineering business, was repre-sented by Birmingham's society, founded in 1800. The great ports of Glasgow, Liverpool, and Plymouth formed their societies in 1802, 1811, and 1812. Yorkshire's coal and ironwork interests helped fund their learned societies' formation for Leeds in 1818 and Sheffield in 1822. This same year, the Yorkshire port of Hull founded its first group dedicated to public lectures on science, and a year later the mighty southern port of Bristol joined the learning club. In 1821, Cayley helped establish the Yorkshire Philosophical Society in the rather quainter county town of York by joining others and pledging a large subscription for the founding fund. Cayley became a life member and was later vice-president; he remained a behind-the-scenes influence who encouraged and supported the institution, leaving the business of lecturing and the day-to-day management of the process to the more ambitious younger members. A decade later, Cayley helped create a second such society on a smaller scale in local Scarborough.

These societies were dedicated to providing instruction, demonstrations, and discussions of the hot topics of the day, with science and the revolutionary effects of its advances being in the forefront of debate. Paralleling Cayley's interests, the study of machines and their commercial application was the catalyst for the most revolutionary phase of British history. Most importantly, these institutions, which held lectures on the underlying science and demonstrated the new technologies, were accessible to anyone willing to pay the modest fees required to attend. For the first time, knowledge itself became celebrated by the general population, and its possession changed from being a social asset to a business necessity. Suddenly the scantily educated worker couldn't get enough of it.

Even as his involvement in education widened, Cayley continued to tinker with his ideas on engines, particularly his "hot-air" engine. However, as an active participant in the discussion of technology, he appreciated that the rapid development of the well-established steam engine had leapfrogged his earlier ideas on hot-air power. Cayley realized that steam was leading the way, for land-based transport at least. The twenty-seven-mile Stockton and Darlington railway opened in 1825, with an increasing proportion of the coal and passengers pulled over the sophisticated iron railways by George and son Robert Stephenson's brand-new steam locomotives. As the reliability of engines improved, they began to consistently outperform the traditional horse-drawn wagons, which shared the burden of hauling passengers and coal. The railway became a vivid demonstration of the economic advantage of machine power over brute force. However, the benefits of the newfangled locomotion came at a cost, and some did not regard the development as a transportation panacea. Some detractors were genuinely skeptical of the reliability of the engines or feared for the safety of the workers and passengers; others were motivated by the threat to their monopolies in coach transport. The prospect of an even bigger and exclusively steam-driven railway brought the arguments to a head. During the fierce debate over the proposed Manchester-Liverpool Railway, a huge venture requiring a significant piece of parliamentary legislation, George Stephenson, attempting to promote the benefits of the railway, predicted he could transport goods and passengers at an incredible twenty miles per hour. A spokesman for the anti-railway faction managed to convince the editor of the popular *Quarterly Review* to express a not uncommonly held concern of the time:

> What can be more palpably absurd and ridiculous, than the prospect held out of locomotives travelling twice as fast as stage coaches? We would as soon expect the people of Woolwich to suffer themselves to be fired off upon one of Congreve's ricochet-rockets, as trust themselves to the mercy of such a machine going at such a rate.

Ironically, though his motivation was much more benign, Cayley had a similar concern. He became a vociferous proponent for safety on public transportation.

In considering the problems of cross-country travel in general, Cayley also developed his own ideas and, not surprisingly, they were a little more revolutionary than most. In 1809, Cayley and George Walker had developed a crude version of the caterpillar track. The idea of the caterpillar had been around even before Cayley. One of the early pioneers was Richard Lovell Edgeworth, an associate of George Walker and member of the "learned insane" group of aristocrats known as the Lunar Society. The often-stated claim that Edgeworth's eight-legged, wall-climbing, wooden mechanical horse was the "first crude caterpillar track" is a little short of the mark – it climbed up nothing and never worked (unlike his excellent mechanical turnip cutter, which worked rather well). By 1826, Cayley had developed the original concept into a detailed and near-practical design that he then patented, promoted, and published in a commercial booklet dedicated to the subject of invention and ideas: *Mechanics' Magazine, museum, register, journal and gazette.* What stymied "Sir George Cayley's Patent Universal Railway" was the very stumbling block for the development of all contemporary means of transportation (flight included): the absence of an engine powerful enough to drive it. Cayley's massive tractor, though originally designed to be horse-drawn, really needed a suitable power plant for it to independently cross roughened terrain. A more efficient steam engine and finally the internal combustion engine almost a hundred years later made tracked vehicles a practical proposition. Cayley's invention languished in the patent office, unapplied and forgotten. It was re-invented in either 1901 by the American wood-logger Alvin Lombard, or, if you are British, in 1905 by David Roberts of R. Hornsby & Sons, Lincolnshire.

Cayley rounded out the decade with a publication in 1829 on his estimate for absolute zero, the temperature at which molecular motion ceases. This new line of thought, published in his academic journal of choice, *Tilloch's Philosophical Magazine*, was inspired by Cayley's time among the Parisian scientific community two years previously. His estimate for absolute zero is close enough to suggest that he was on the right lines: he suggested -480° F rather than the more recognized -459.4° F, though he did not specifically follow up this new line of his research.

These two publications bracketed an event that marked the end of an era in Cayley family life, the death of Lady Isabella. In a letter dated April 1828, Cayley writes to his mother saying,

> I am glad Phil attends so kindly to you, as to your increase of illness [it can] furnish an excuse for requesting me to put off all idea of a trip to Ireland so I shall not feel uneasy about you.

Cayley has written on the letter, "To my mother, Last letter 1828." Isabella's health then entered a rapid decline, though with typical

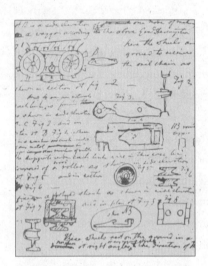

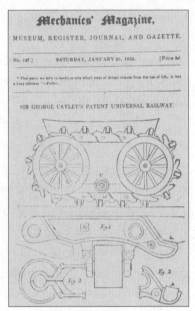

Cayley's notebook entry for his "universal railway" . . .

. . . and his article in the *Mechanic's Magazine*.

stubbornness she lived another four months before dying on July 30. The Lady Isabella had outlived her husband, Sir Thomas, by an impressive thirty-five years, and in spite of her rebellious religion and strong character (or perhaps because of it), Cayley had been devoted to her. An earlier letter of those that formed the final series of correspondence between mother and son includes details of Isabella's concern over leaving Cayley in debt over the finances of The Green. Cayley's reply is categorical: "I shall never consent to any plan that would inconvenience you residing at the Green – that is your only natural abode." With Isabella's parting, Digby, now just in his majority at twenty-one, took over the management of the Green Farm and continued his interests in all things agricultural.

The next stage of Cayley's life would be another variation on already established lines. As both the age of steam locomotion and parliamentary reform beckoned, Cayley began to make his contribution to each.

9

POWER THROUGH *the* ACTION *of* STEAM
and HOT AIR

Cayley had nailed his political colours to the masthead as a Whig in 1820, though the term "Whig" covered opinion ranging from radical, through reformist, past those uninterested in change, and on to those positively against it. Throughout the decade, Lord Liverpool, the Tory prime minister, ruled with an iron fist clenched hard within an iron glove. Liverpool's exit from politics resulted from his suffering a massive stroke in 1828 and, as often happens after the extended tenure of a strong-arm rule, his departure threw the subsequent leadership race into turmoil. Three different prime ministers served in a single year. Even the steady hand of the venerable Duke of Wellington at the tiller was not enough to see the nation settled. Wellington's ability to form an effective coalition from the wide range of views of his fellow parliamentarians, many fervently wishing to change the political process root and branch, was not helped by his suggestion that Britain's "existing system of representation was as near perfection as possible."

Discontent at every level yet again boiled over into violence during the "Swing Riots" of 1829 and 1830. These riots were reminiscent of the earlier Luddite Rebellion, with a mysterious Captain Swing (who was almost certainly a complete fiction) replacing the earlier (and equally invented) King Lud as the proclaimed leader of what was really a series of violent and destructive acts of sabotage. Cayley's response to the turmoil was measured, forthright, and personal: he addressed a village meeting of Brompton in an attempt to explain the economic basis for the country's low wages, high food costs, and increasing unemployment. He followed up the meeting with an essay sent to his tenants to iron out any residual queries. Cayley recalled his gift of "an acre of tillage land to every labourer in the township capable of cultivating it" from a quarter of a century before and reassured them that things would turn for the better eventually. At least his efforts showed an attempt by a local landlord to appease tenants reeling from the economic effects of the Corn and Game Laws. Cayley concluded his treatise with a now much more liberal reference to his belief in the social position enjoyed by his tenants and workers: "Let us cheerfully support each other in the cases of individual distress, and live our lives as fellow countrymen, looking forward with humble confidence to a better order of national affairs." Cayley's optimism for the country as a whole was, however, another triumph of hope over experience.

The political upheavals at a national level came to a head with the death of George IV in 1830, and in many ways the event resolved a number of thorny issues that had infuriated some and scandalized many. As Prince Regent, George's extravagance had been a source of outrage for both rich and poor. His coronation in 1820 cost a staggering £943,000, and he continually appealed to Parliament to service the growing debts that resulted from his lavish lifestyle. As the effective head of state since his father's insanity certification in 1811, George had not exactly gone out of his way to make himself popular; on top of his outrageous personal life, his politics approached intransigence. He had steadfastly refused to support Catholic emancipation in Britain despite the fact that he had married, in secret, the Catholic Maria Anne Fitzherbert in 1795, a union that was effectively illegal as British constitutional law forbade an heir to the throne marrying into any religion other than Anglicanism. One of King George's final political acts, after a series of dithering reversals, had been to finally agree to the Catholic Emancipation Act in 1829 on the understanding that anything less would result in the revolutionary loss of Ireland. King George's death even drew little in the way of sympathy from so revered a newspaper as *The Times*:

> There never was an individual less regretted by his fellow creatures than this deceased king. What eye has wept for him? What heart has heaved one throb of unmercenary sorrow? . . . If he ever had a friend – a devoted friend in any rank of life – we protest that the name of him or her never reached us.

As a result of Parliament's monarch-dominated protocol, the most significant effect of the King's passing was that it required an election be called. The outcome was an increase in seats for the opposition Whigs, though the Tory Wellington retained the authority to form the government until his defeat in a parliamentary confidence vote in the autumn. The influx of new M.P.s and the presence of the more liberal King William IV (George's younger brother) heralded the premiership of the aging Whig, Lord Grey. Earl Grey became one of the most influential parliamentarians of his generation, even if his lasting fame has less to do with his legacy of reform than the success of his preferred blend of bergamot orange-flavoured tea. The embattled Grey had to fight both Parliament and the Lords and call snap elections in 1831 and 1832 before he finally got his reforming legislation onto the statute books. The resultant changes to the electoral process and consequent shift in parliamentary membership provided an opportunity for Cayley to make his mark at a national level. But Cayley was not entering politics for its own sake, he needed to find a cause to promote and another new-found interest dominated Cayley's short parliamentary career.

In the autumn of 1830, one of the key events in British industrial history occurred: the completion of the world's first exclusively steam-powered railway. The new line joined the west coast port of Liverpool with the manufacturing powerhouse of Manchester. The engineering achievement of its age, the line had been designed by its chief proponent, George Stephenson, along with the equally talented engineer Joseph Locke. Present at the opening were a wealth of local dignitaries, including Sir George Cayley. Also attending were the somewhat unfortunate Duke of Wellington (he was booed and jeered by the locals) and the very unfortunate William Huskisson, who marred the celebrations by becoming the world's first steam railway fatality on its very first day of operation. Huskisson, a retired politician in failing health, had left the train as it stood to take on water and was conversing through the open window of Wellington's carriage in an attempt to cheer up the rather crestfallen Duke. As Stephenson's famous *Rocket* locomotive appeared on the opposite line, Huskisson, a man not known for fleetness of foot, stumbled, and his left leg was crushed by the oncoming train. Despite being rushed by train to a local town (thus becoming the world's first rail-evacuated casualty), he died of his terrible injuries later that day. The event had a profound influence on Cayley, who was shocked by the accident and concerned about the safety of the travelling public.

Cayley had briefly published on the subject of the railways earlier that same year, suggesting wooden tires for a locomotive's iron wheels as a safety measure to improve traction and braking efficiency. Shortly after the Huskisson incident, Cayley once more published his thoughts on the practicality and safety of rail travel, though his suggestions seemed neither very practical nor particularly safe. His complicated "cow-catcher" was, as even he admitted, "by no means so easy a matter to prescribe" and his suggestion of a passenger "scoop," which would allow rail travellers to get on board without the train actually stopping, was probably a joke – even if a similar idea was later implemented as a means of getting bags of letters and parcels off and onto speeding trains. These publications reveal the new focus of Cayley's attention, but he knew that for his ideas to have any real impact, they needed to be placed before an audience of decision makers. Early in 1831, Cayley announced that his previous involvement in local politics might require him to take the next step, to Parliament itself. "It is possible I may have some claim for offering myself as one of its representatives in the future," he said at a local meeting of Whigs. First, he had to get elected.

Cayley's willingness to stand for Parliament and the likelihood of his success were considerably enhanced by the first major reform in the English electoral process since the sixteenth century, when Lord Grey finally forced through his Bill of Reform in 1832. Though the bill passed easily in the Whig-dominated Houses of Commons, the House of Lords consistently refused to pass it. Their lordships saw the extension of the vote to all male property owners as an open assault on their carefully cultivated and expensively procured strength in the Commons – younger sons of the aristocracy were often offered safe seats in local constituencies to mirror their fathers' position in the House of Lords. The legislation's success was secured only after the threat that King William would, albeit reluctantly, flood the upper house with newly ennobled Whig peers to swamp the opposition. The Reform Bill was a watershed in British politics. Fifty-six of the most rotten of boroughs were abolished, including the delightful constituency of Dunwich in Suffolk, which had exactly sixteen voters per M.P. as a result of most of the town having recently fallen into the North Sea. However, many pocket boroughs – constituencies "in the pocket" of either local nobles or equally unelected borough burgesses – remained intact, and because votes were still cast by public proclamation, bribery and coercion continued to openly influence elections for another fifty years. Nevertheless, the 1832 Reform Act acquired the prefix "great," and it opened the door for a new election in December of that year. Cayley allowed his name to be added to the list of candidates.

Cayley's opening for his nomination speech, given on the steps of the Scarborough Town Hall on a dank and dismal evening, was appropriately light: "On the present occasion I am almost compelled to break the first law of politeness by speaking of myself." He followed up with a brief autobiography, which starts with an intriguing reference to his birthplace: "I had the honour to be born fifty-eight years ago, within a hundred yards of this spot." Then he speaks of his early exposure to the French revolution, his teenage associations with the reformers Tooke and Cartwright, and his conclusion that Lord Grey would in every way be the country's preferred first minister over the Duke of Wellington: "As a prime minister, in my opinion, we cannot have a worse – as a general officer, we cannot have a better." This was no jingoistic crowd-pleaser at work. Cayley thought the hero of Waterloo was a disastrous politician and wasn't afraid to say so. He also had harsh words for the sinecure-ridden system of government and its tendency to borrow now and pay later: "We find ourselves as a nation ruined by that extravagance."

Though Cayley was really an independent by nature, his close association with the country's swing to Whiggism secured him victory, and he was duly elected as the member for Scarborough. Though no stranger to London, his interests now shifted to the country's capital and the *realpolitik* of government. The purchase of a townhouse in fashionable Mayfair marked a formal division in Cayley's civic duties as both a rural Yorkshire squire and Westminster politician. Cayley's grand Georgian residence at 20 Hertford Street was situated conveniently close to the Houses of Parliament and was a second family home for over thirty years. (Coincidentally, the Royal Aeronautical Society later took up residence just two hundred yards around the corner in Hamilton Place.)

Bearing in mind the scale of changes the new Parliament both represented and went on to enact, Cayley's contribution was relatively modest. As a parliamentary neophyte he was hardly likely to be consulted on the monumental matters of state being thrashed out at the time. Instead, Cayley took his more familiar role as personal representative of the people and spokesperson for causes to which he was emotionally committed. In 1834, Cayley presented a petition on behalf of Scarborough's ship owners but his most notable intervention came about by a combination of his interest in transport technology and his well-established belief in fair play, particularly when it came to a friend and fellow inventor, in this case the magnificently named Goldsworthy Gurney.

Gurney was a man after Cayley's own heart. Twenty years junior to the now sixty-year-old baronet, Gurney was the highly educated son of a well-connected family from Cornwall. He had gained his wonderful forename from his godmother, who was a maid of honour to Queen Charlotte, the devoted and long-suffering wife of George III. Though trained as a physician, young Gurney had become familiar with the pioneering work of fellow Cornishman Richard Trevithick, whose steam-driven pumps were used in the local tin mines. Gurney's fascination with the new power had led to his spending some five years and £30,000 of his own money developing a road-based, steam-powered carriage, the first of which was patented in 1825. By 1830, Gurney had established manufacturing premises in London and began the first commercial passenger service on the toll road between Gloucester and Cheltenham. His machine maintained an average of ten miles per hour and his engines performed with remarkable reliability; the novelty of the ride adding to the economic success of the service. As the possibilities of powered road travel became apparent, Parliament was deluged by petitions seeking a toll to be applied to all powered vehicles on the road. Fifty private bills were submitted in 1831 alone, all from parties with financial interests in horse-drawn coaching, supported by the landowners through whose estates the new steam-powered contraption travelled. Eventually the tolls forced Gurney out of business, and without a reduction in what amounted to a punitive levy, he was going to stay that way. Cayley's longest recorded speech in Parliament (it may have been his *only* speech) occurred in 1834 and was in support of his good friend Mr. Gurney. The account of Cayley's oration runs to only a few hundred words and it is a little gem.

After a brief apology for occupying the House's time, Cayley introduces Gurney's case by opening with a gag: "I only wish he would invent steam power for speech as effective as his steam carriage; for then the business of the House could be dispatched at a rate much more agreeable both to members and the public [laughter in the Chamber]." Cayley goes on to lightly scold but also reassure the farming interest that the introduction of steam power would not cause the price of (horse-fuelling) oats to tumble and their landed interest to be diminished. He closed with an appeal to the nature of the new Commons:

> It is true that but too many instances have occurred of national ingratitude and neglect towards the creators of inventions of public importance. . . . But Sir these instances occurred in the time of the *unreformed* Parliament. . . . The real representatives of the people who now sit in the House will, I am sure, on the contrary press their abhorrence of such treatment of the men of science, by acknowledging and rewarding, to the full extent their merits, all public benefactors like Mr. Gurney, for they will be aware that at the same time they are doing an act of individual justice, they are serving the best interests of the country. I cordially support the prayer of the Petition.

They were putty in his hands, and after much hear-hearing and a series of similarly supportive speakers, the Commons voted Gurney a grant to cover his out-of-pocket expenses and a revocation of all toll-related impediments. Unfortunately, the oats-obsessed House of Lords would have nothing of it, and the bill was thrown out on its ear – so much for the will of the people.

In spite of Cayley's failure to further Gurney's case, the two men continued as lifelong friends and collaborators, even making a formal agreement whereby profits from Cayley's heat engine would be split in return for Gurney's assistance in perfecting the design. Nothing commercial ever came of it, however. As the years progressed, Gurney enjoyed a roller-coaster career as inventor. He followed up on his initial discovery of "limelight" (which would brighten the stage) with the development of a new form of illumination, the oxygen forced-fed "Bude Light." With this invention, the Gurney–Cayley friendship finally bore financial fruit. Cayley was on the committee investigating which lighting should be used for the newly reconstructed Palace of Westminster (which had been largely destroyed by fire in 1834), and Cayley's unsurprising recommendation was that the new Bude lighting system was required. Eventually, Gurney became superintendent of heating, lighting, and ventilating for Parliament and receive a knighthood for his efforts, thanks in part to a certain Edward Stillingfleet Cayley, M.P., who sang Gurney's praises during a parliamentary investigation into the new Westminster ventilation system. The mutual support between Gurney and Cayley remained undimmed for another twenty-five years; as late as 1853, Gurney was still vociferously championing Cayley as the originator of the air engine in a meeting of the Institution of Civil Engineers.

Cayley was neither a great politician nor a notable parliamentarian. In part it may have been his oratorical powers that failed him – he could address any man as his peer, but he rarely seemed to stir much emotional response from his audiences, perhaps deliberately. Common sense, fact, and practicality are what drove him but he shunned the back-scratching and -stabbing necessary to become a powerful figure in the party and the Commons. Cayley's head remained well below the political parapet and his voice largely unheard. That neither fairness nor wisdom seemed to be the guiding principles in Parliament must surely not have come as a shock to a man of Cayley's experience, but it was with less than wholehearted commitment that he pressed himself into his second election campaign in January 1835. One factor in his reluctance was the manner in which the election had finally come about.

After a historic session of Parliament that had seen Lord Grey's administration finally abolish slavery throughout the British Empire and begin the process of establishing workers' rights via the Factories Act, the government eventually fell over a classic political cock-up. Following a morass of accusation and counter-accusation concerning broken promises dealing with the Coercion Bill for Ireland, Earl Grey followed through on his oft-repeated threat and resigned to leave them to it. In truth, Grey had had enough of politics, and many Whigs had had enough of the increasingly conservative Grey. The country headed to its fifth election in ten years, and Cayley was forced to the hustings once more.

Although there is no doubt concerning Cayley's dedication to democracy, he certainly saw no good coming out of electioneering, something he said could only "perpetuate the political ferment ... and keep up agitation during those intervals of repose from party feeling which are so conducive to the general harmony of Society." Unfortunately, the Tories of Scarborough decided to import a candidate who was a little more proactive in his pursuit of the newly enfranchised electorate. With there now being 412 registered voters – a whopping five per cent of Scarborough's population – many of them first-timers, an enthusiastic and moneyed candidate had the opportunity to turn the election around. The considerable weight of Colonel Sir Frederic William Trench (Knight of the Holy Cross) did just that. In spite of the concerns over Sir Frederic's generosity at the polls and his scandalously unfounded accusations of corruption against Earl Grey, Cayley resigned his candidacy before the final result was even counted. Scarborough would be represented by one Tory and one Whig candidate for the next two years, and neither of them was from Brompton. It was some small consolation that Cayley's son-in-law, Sir Charles Style, would retake the constituency in the 1837 election, but all in all Cayley had had enough of bellying up to the Westminster trough. His brief political career behind him, Cayley looked elsewhere to apply his energies.

Finding the Pieces V – Making Your Mark at the Public Ballot

Voting in secret during British elections had to wait until the 1881 reforms of what was by then the Liberal Party of the mighty William Gladstone (the man whom Queen Victoria accused of addressing her like a public meeting). Until then there was a public right to know who voted how, so your decision could have serious personal repercussions. However, democracy's loss is the researcher's gain for the results of Cayley's 1835 election are printed in minutia under the pithily titled "Bye's list of voters who polled during the contested election for two representatives to serve in parliament for the Borough of Scarboro' in the Town Hall on Wednesday 7th 1835."

Any publisher can tell you that the market for a bare list of names and crosses is a small one, so J. Bye, Printer Bookseller Etc., of Newbro' Street Scarborough quickly realized that the naked facts alone would need a little spice to drum up the necessary sales. Because of this, his publication is less an objective matter of record and more an undisguised pillory of the scoundrels who failed to vote Cayley back in as their M.P.

It may be purely coincidental that the same printer secured the business to publish Cayley's hustings speech of 1832 and just chance that Cayley's public announcement of withdrawal from the 1835 election was entrusted into the same inky hands – surely Mr. Bye would not allow profit to sully his testimony to the democratic process? As it turns out, the resulting document is a fascinating record of not only votes but voters, their trades, and even their relationship to the candidates.

Bye's listed professions included the obvious – gentleman, farmer, shoemaker, schoolmaster, ship builder, butcher, cabinet maker (and two hair-dressers) – as well as the more obscure – carrier, brazier, scavenger, twine-maker, cork cutter, and two whitesmiths. It lists those who did vote, those who didn't, and even one who tried to vote and failed – though what James Flemming did to warrant the memorandum "vote tendered but refused" remains a mystery.

Any residual doubt concerning the political leanings of Mr. Bye are eradicated in his closing "remarks," which note:

> Let those Electors who have, at this time, so shamelessly made their franchise a matter of profit and loss, remember for the future, that they are Electors, not *only for themselves*, but for every *poor man* in the town who has not a vote to give. . . . What would be thought of a man who, appointed trustee under a will, were to seek to administer that trust the most in accordance with his own private interests, instead of that of the widow or the orphans, or the relatives of the deceased. He would be pronounced a knave; and perhaps a mercenary wretch. . . . Every individual of common feelings would be shocked by such an atrocity . . .

Having accused the voters for Colonel Trench of the political equivalent of grave robbing, Bye finishes his note exclaiming, "No less than 35 individuals, who on Wednesday polled for COL. TRENCH are said to have pledged themselves to SIR GEORGE CAYLEY!!!"

10

LEARNING, LOCOMOTIVES, *and the* MAN-MADE HAND

C ayley's memorandum to himself, found on a loose sheet in the family archive, expresses his personal doctrine concerning the acquisition of knowledge.

> Inform myself of the useful branches of human learning – history, philosophy, political economy, political creed, practical acts, works of taste and genius. Apply knowledge in acting wisely, and with energy, in favour of Ones Country, ones family, ones self and of the general welfare of the human race, and others, the inferior creatures in man's care.

As if he had not already illustrated his commitment to the spread of learning in a country shamefully unforthcoming with public funds for public education, Cayley now used the period following his brief parliamentary career to redouble his efforts. He had become a well-connected and well-liked public figure with his easy-going celebrity peppering a cluster of social groups: the residents of Scarborough and Brompton; his extensive social and family circle; the curious and intellectually active of Yorkshire's Philosophical Society (and York's Mechanic's Institute, of which he also became president); and the national readership of popular philosophy and mechanics. He also moved among the better educated aristocrats in Britain and France and a representative sample of those involved in the activities that were the precursors to the industrial revolution. Cayley revelled in the company of the scientific enthusiast and, though he would rarely rein in his interests, the next decade saw him home in on two general themes: the development of commercial mass transit and the welfare of those masses on the move. Each of these topics had its antecedents in his earlier work.

Cayley interleaved his major interests within a wealth of sundry correspondence on subjects near and far, and the breadth of his interests seemed almost unbounded. Letters to and from Cayley ranged from those on electromagnetism through to galveno-magnetism (and the use of magnets for propulsion of trains) to the "undulatory (wave) theory of light"; from the popular mesmerism (hypnosis) to the development of a nine-inch exploding shell; from the mathematics of fluid flow as applied to drainage schemes to the development of rocket power as rudders for balloons; from an expansion of his invention of a dibbling machine (a kind of seed drill) to his design for a steam-powered plough; from his self-righting, unsinkable lifeboat to improving the method for tanning leather. Other topics related more directly to his ongoing interests, including the best varnish for finishing airship balloons and the continuing work on his air engine and new steam boilers with Goldsworthy Gurney. Around and between these interests he found time to become elected as an associate member of the Institution for Civil Engineers and publish on a variety of subjects, including why a truly upright image on the retina appeared inverted, echoing another of the cartoon illustrations from his schoolboy notebook. Cayley's correspondence also extended his knowledge of his home and landed interests: the best practice for forestry plantation and management, developing methods for timber preservation, and a new kind of chimney sweeping brush. By the wayside fell his ideas on a new type of steel pen nib (his patent had been anticipated).

Together with a tidy cross-section of inventors on the fringe of legit-
imacy (and some well beyond it), Cayley's correspondents included
many prominent men of what was soon to be Victorian Britain. Charles
Babbage, the inventor of the first programmable, mechanical computer
and vocal critic of the cronyism involved in the Royal Society, traded a
number of letters with Cayley about learned bodies, invention, and
science. Babbage, like Cayley and other prominent voices, bemoaned the
stinginess of government when it came to supporting invention and
innovation, though Babbage's unhealthy obsession with questioning
the back-story of beggars he encountered in the street (he spent days
personally verifying their tales of woe) suggests a certain lack of personal
generosity on his part. Dr. Peter Roget, sitting in the opposite corner to
Babbage when it came to the Royal Society (being as Roget was its secretary), discussed at length Cayley's conundrums concerning magnetism
and electricity, while at the same time completing his most lasting work,
his thesaurus. Another Cayley pen-pal was Henry Bessemer, a prolific
fellow inventor best remembered for the Bessemer process, a means of
industrializing the production of ductile steel to replace the more brittle
irons. Cayley and Bessemer traded friendly enough words over one of
Cayley's suggestions for railway safety that the man of steel seemed to
think might infringe one of his patents.

A fourth renowned confidante was George Rennie from the
famous Scottish family of engineers responsible for building London's
Waterloo and Southwark bridges (and infamous for their refusal to
work with George Stephenson because they thought that "he wasn't
a proper engineer"). This correspondence raises a specific puzzle
because Rennie, having proved to be a mediocre locomotive engineer,
turned his hand to designing the practical means of propelling ships.
His invention of the conoidal propeller was a major breakthrough in
screw design and marked the beginning of the end of the paddle
steamer. So here we have Cayley, champion of flapping propulsion,

talking with the leading propeller designer of the day, and yet Cayley
still remained attached to his Degen-style wafters even through to his
very final aircraft. In another of those hindsights, we can't help won-
dering how Cayley could snatch the poorest engineering solution
from the jaws of the superior one. His appetite for learning was insatiable but when it came to propellers, his mind was like a trap: once
it was closed, nothing would open it.

Education, both for himself and anyone within earshot, was more a
vocation than a mere hobby for Cayley. His daughter reports him
saying, "A day passed without acquiring a new idea, was a day wasted."
Cayley's formal involvement in the promotion of learning stemmed
from the founding of the Yorkshire Philosophical Society in 1821.
This had been one of the first steps in his attempt to encourage those
interested in basking in the warm glow of the developing technology.
A secretary of the Yorkshire Philosophical Society was John Philips,
who had helped establish it as one of the country's most celebrated
forums for scientific debate, before going on to become president of the
Geological Society. By coincidence, Philips was the nephew of William
Smith, the founding father of geology and maker of "the map that
changed the world." During the shameful period of Smith's enforced
obscurity in the 1820s (after his groundbreaking geological map had
been stolen by jealous rivals), he had resided in North Yorkshire's
Harkness Hall, just a stone's throw (or three) north of Brompton. The
soon-to-be-rediscovered (and duly honoured) geologist spent years
under the protection of the local squire, Sir John Vanden Bempde
Johnstone, the second of the two M.P.s for Scarborough and the man
who joined Cayley as a freshman parliamentarian in 1832. During his
time under Sir John's protection, William Smith designed the unique
Scarborough Rotunda to exhibit the area's equally unique fossil. In
keeping with Smith finding Yorkshire something of an intellectual
refuge, the county had perhaps more than its fair share of amateur

scientists and its county town of York became a focus for a revolution in British science all of its own.

The clamour for reform in the early decades of the 1800s in Britain was not restricted to the political and social arenas. The industrialization of the economy had caused an increasing rift between the rarefied pursuit of science for its own sake (by men of independent means) and the need for the applied sciences that would fuel industrial development. This rift was most keenly exhibited by the contrasting presence of the Royal Society with the emergence of numerous local and specialized societies populated by enthusiastic amateurs and science professionals alike. The Royal Society was more like an exclusive intellectual club for the well-connected than a powerhouse for change. Its entry requirements followed along the lines of "you can't go there unless you've been there before," with a prospective Fellow having to be nominated by fellow Fellows to stand a chance of joining. The Royal Society's readiness to embrace change had been considerably suppressed throughout the unprecedented forty-two-year presidency of Sir Joseph Banks, a man whose intellectual prowess as a botanist was matched only by his entrenched conservatism. Banks maintained that the Royal Society was the *only* suitable organization to champion each and every branch of intellectualism, and it was only as Banks's influence waned and those reform- and independence-minded specialists gained prominence that the Royal Society lost its British monopoly on serious thought. As other disciplines sought to free themselves from the restrictions of centralization, there was a flood of new institutions: the Geological Society (1807); the Institution of Civil Engineers (1818); the Astronomical Society (1820); the Zoological Society (1826); the Geographical Society (1830). Other groups for law, literature, and culture sprang up as well. In spite of the presence of these bodies, the Royal Society retained that most elusive and sought-after position; it held the ear of the only real source of funding – the government. The arguments concerning the role of the Royal Society in promoting scientific study simmered gently within academia until Charles Babbage published his acidic (and probably libellous) *Reflections on the Decline of Science and some of its Causes.* His timing was impeccable. It hit the streets in the summer of 1830 while the country reeled from riots in the north and uproar in the soon-to-be-reformed Parliament. The publication's title even created a new proper noun, as Declinists sought a forum that would sidestep the Royal Society and actively push science forward. Two of the leading figures in what was little more than a general feeling of malcontent were Sir David Brewster and William Vernon Harcourt. These two individuals galvanized a disparate assemblage of free-thinking and reform-minded gentlemen scientists into a slightly more organized, wandering band of free-thinking and reform-minded gentlemen scientists. The two men had between them the combination of talents and connections to make a new group viable. Brewster had the reputation: he was a researcher into optics and inventor of the kaleidoscope, but more importantly he was a leading member of the Royal Society, being the winner of its prestigious Rumford and Copley medals. Harcourt had the people skills, political savvy, and right connections. He was the younger son of the Archbishop of York and shamelessly invited potential members of their new group to stay with him and his father in the riverside palace in Bishopthorpe. Harcourt was also the first president of the influential Yorkshire Philosophical Society. Brewster and Harcourt knew that if a new organization was to flourish, it would need to attract the right kind of members, and Brewster, writing to Babbage in 1830, recognized who the right kind were: "A few influential noblemen and M.P.s would give great help in forwarding such an object."

Cayley, though at the time still only a prospective M.P., seemed to fit the bill quite nicely.

In September of 1831, under the auspices of the hosting Yorkshire Philosophical Society, a group of scientists met in York for a vaguely defined purpose of reversing a decline in science that many blamed on the Royal Society. That reversal was the primary aim of what became the British Association for the Advancement of Science, an organization whose name was later rather unkindly abbreviated to "The British Ass." The organization would even be satirized as "The Mudfog Association for the Advancement of Everything" by a highly unsympathetic Charles Dickens.

In spite of widespread advertising and personal entreaties from Brewster and Harcourt, out of the 353 (paying) attendees, only a few aristocrats attended that first meeting, among them Cayley. At that formative meeting Cayley made his presence felt by leading the objectors to the proposal that to become a committee member of the new association the appointee must have a paper published through an approved Philosophical Society – what was wrong with the *Mechanic's Magazine* or *Tilloch's Philosophical Magazine* as an outlet for the scientific musings of the interested man? Cayley became a regular attendee in meetings of the British Association (BA), which cycled annually through major industrial cities of Britain, though carefully avoiding the home of the Royal Society in London. The peripatetic BA returned to its birthplace in York in 1844, by which time it boasted over 1,800 life members, including the ever enthusiastic Cayley and his rather less enthusiastic son, Digby. Ironically, the association's lasting claim to fame was its recommendation *against* funding Charles Babbage's development of his analytical engine, thus helping deprive Britain of perhaps the greatest single advance in computing it would ever have. The organization survives to this day as one seeking to make science accessible to everyone – though it never achieved the position of Britain's primary scientific lobbyist. That role, if it lies anywhere outside of academia, remains solidly with the Royal Society. As with his membership in many other professional bodies, Cayley acted more as a catalyst than an active manager in the workings of the British Association. He could always be relied on to attend its annual meeting and subtly promote its ideals through his widespread connections within Britain's scientific and intellectual movers and shakers. Cayley simply did not have the resources to dedicate much more than a small proportion of his time to any one of the dozen such groups to which he belonged. The singular exception to this rule, however, concerned what Cayley came to refer to as his adopted youngest daughter, whom he named "Poly."

Having helped encourage the formation of an organization at the most rarefied end of the intellectual spectrum, Cayley then set his sights on a point a couple of rungs below. In 1835, there was little Cayley could do to change the entrenched establishments of England's only three universities even if Scotland proudly boasted having four such institutions (for a brief period there were as many universities in Aberdeen as there were in England). Oxford, Cambridge, and the brand-new Durham universities remained the dominant influence on England's educational culture until the "red-brick" universities of the provincial cities were formed at the end of the nineteenth century. So instead of dreaming spires, Cayley looked to providing access to education and practical science to those most like himself: the self-educated amateur.

Cayley's first brush with encouraging the uptake of intellectual pursuits for the everyman had been back in 1830, but it had not been a success. The Adelaide Gallery in the Strand, London, abandoned the twenty-minute lectures and demonstrations of models in favour of "amusement and dancing" soon after opening; it had to make a profit after all. The manager of the Adelaide was Charles Payne, who on resigning his position in 1835 sought to establish a new institution with the primary aim of providing access to the most modern technology and learning (and the barely secondary aim of yielding a financial return). In order to make the scheme work, Payne needed investment capital and a high-profile name to attract both investors and the paying public. A large proportion of the money came initially from William Mountford Nurse, a speculative builder who saw the profit side of the endeavour. The requirement for a well-known front man was met when Cayley agreed to become the chairman of the board which drew up the new institute's prospectus for shareholders. The investment prospectus clearly shows the hand of Cayley's ever widening interests, with the new institute aiming to provide "a practical knowledge of the various arts and branches of science connected with Manufactures, Mining Operations, and Rural Economy." An impressive property in Cavendish Square (just around the corner from Cayley's Mayfair home) was secured to house the new institute, with the building forming "extensive premises in perfect repair, with commanding frontage." The competing demands of revenue generation and accessible education became a constant stress within the organization, and although Cayley's head appreciated the demands of the balance sheet, his heart was differently driven. He wanted the institute to be where "scientific discoveries were thrown off hot from the brain before they became public property by publication. . . . We want a good scientific board confined by no aristoc-racy of orthodox men who sit like an incubus on all rising talent which is not of their own shop. . . . Freedom is the essence of improvement in science." With Cayley at the helm, the founding fund eventually reached the point that allowed the extensions to the Cavendish premises to be completed, including the building of a Great Hall for exhibitions and the provision of a second entrance on the much more fashionable Regent Street. The multi-faceted Polytechnic Institute open its doors on August 6, 1838, by which time Cayley had been appointed director of the governing board. Poly was formally recog-nized as an educational establishment in 1839 when it received its charter of incorporation, setting out its goals and responsibilities as a business and a school.

The Regent Street entrance of the   The Polytechnic Institute Great Hall.
Polytechnic Institute.

The nearest modern equivalent of the polytechnic is probably a popular science museum, with exhibits and hands-on experiences available to the paying public. The Great Hall had two canals for ship models and a highly popular diving bell, which allowed visitors to be submerged into the twelve-foot-deep reservoir. In and around the model waterways were a miscellany of working exhibits, scientific instruments, cased objects, and just about anything else that could pique the interest of the paying customer. Below stairs were a chemical and physics laboratory, an engineering workshop, and working demonstrations of industrial steam engines. A lecture room held academic and popular science presentations. It was here that Lewis Carroll's *Alice in Wonderland* received its first public presentation, the lecture room also being the venue for demonstrations of theatrical and special effects for the amusement and delectation of the curious Londoner. Cayley insisted that as well as amusements, the institute provide practical classes and lectures in basic physics and chemistry. The personalized experience of experimentation that had formed his own education was something he was determined on providing for his new clientele. Another direct influence of Cayley's interests was the inclusion of aviation exhibits and lectures. In 1840, the famous British balloonist Charles Green ("over 500 ascents made and 2,900 miles traversed") used the Polytechnic to promote his ideas concerning his proposed transatlantic crossing. His design included a propeller-driven and rudder-guided balloon, which could take on and offload ballast (to maintain a constant altitude) by dragging a series of rope-strung buckets through the sea as it went. To support his ideas, Green provided a clockwork model of the balloon, which took London's chattering classes by storm. Prudence eventually prevailed, and Green did not attempt his estimated three-month-long flight, though his hardly less spectacular flight later acted as the inspiration for yet another Cayley publication.

In 1841, the institute began self-applying the prefix Royal to its name through the tacit approval of Prince Albert, the modern-minded and enthusiastic husband ·of Queen Victoria. However, the Royal Polytechnic Institute (RPI) remained at the mercy of its financial status, and there was a constant battle for it to remain commercially viable, not helped when the major investor, William Nurse, demanded a better return on his money and threatened legal action. Cayley retained his position as director up until his death, and it remained one of his proudest achievements. In many ways the RPI's series of events and exhibitions characterized the widespread, sometimes almost random interests of Cayley himself. Having seen to the safe delivery of his latest offspring, Cayley's mind turned once more to another of his causes of the past. The reason for the change was driven, as always, by contemporary events for, like the rest of the country, Cayley found himself gripped by a railwaymania.

The world's first railway season ticket was sold in 1832 for the 5 3/8-mile-long journey between the historic Archbishop's city of Canterbury and the small fishing town of Whitstable on the Kentish coast. The commercialization of the Canterbury and Whitstable Railway (known locally as the "Crab and Winkle Line") marked the beginning of a frantic race between the engineers developing the technology, the venture capitalists raising the money, and Parliament trying to control an investment frenzy that puts the dot-com bubble of the 1990s to shame. By the mid-1840s more than 1,000 new proposals for railways lines had been put forward. Some of these railways were short goods lines directly connecting commercial sites to their marketplaces, but most were mixed cargo and commuter lines connecting harbours, towns, and cities. In 1830, 157 miles of railways were in existence, but by 1845 over 2,000 miles of track had been laid. In 1825, the swiftest coach took thirty hours to travel between London and Yorkshire's port of Hull. In 1845, the same journey took less than eight hours. Now fresh goods could find a marketplace almost anywhere in the country; similarly a London newspaper could sell in Edinburgh before the news was stale. Britain, a nation that already benefited from being a small island with few internal barriers to communication, essentially halved in size within a decade: every major town was connected to each and every other population centre through less than a day's travel. The rate of social and economic change had shifted up a gear, and the call from every quarter was "make it even faster." In the middle of it all was the humble rail passenger, and there seemed to be little thought for how the competing economic imperatives were likely to affect the safety of those paying the fare. Cayley took up voice of caution by publishing his concerns in the November 1840 edition of the *Mechanic's Magazine.*

Cayley starts by bringing the effects of a rail crash to life with a typical domestic analogy, whereby a collision in a train travelling at twenty-one miles per hour "has a tolerable parallel in what might be expected should the drawing room floor give way and precipitate its inmates onto that of the dining room beneath." Cayley's solution was a dedicated car to be placed at the front of the train fitted with a huge pneumatic buffer. In a sporadic series of five publications over the next seven years, Cayley included designs for automatic braking systems and a mechanism for controlling the distance between carriages, as well as padding for the internal walls of second- and third-class passenger cars like those for first-class passengers, though "in a coarser but not less efficient way." An additional suggestion was for each passenger

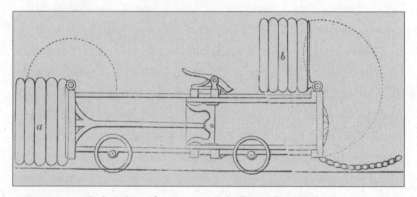

Cayley's design for an automatic "buffer car" for rail safety.

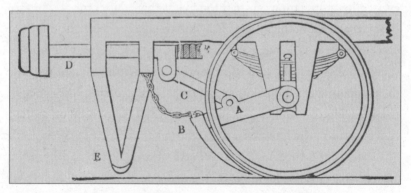

Cayley's buffer-activated automatic braking system.

to wear a safety belt, though he admitted, "How John Bull may relish this sort of straight waistcoat I do not know."

Concern over the swiftness of trains was a regular theme in his publications, something that led him to suggest both mechanical and regulatory mechanisms for restricting their speed. One of his most prescient designs was his proposal for preventing trains entering one stretch of track before the preceding train had left – this became "block signalling" in later railways. Following a horrific rail accident near Paris in 1842, he vigorously blamed the government's hands-off approach to the railway boom as being in part responsible for the lack of safety. By 1847, his frustration at both the railway and the government's inaction led him to the most gruesome of parallels:

> Let me add that the present method of placing second and third class carriages at the rear, to serve by being "smashed up" with the bones of their passengers as buffers to those in first class, is most disgraceful and inhuman.

During the period in which Cayley's concerns over the safety of the travelling public dominated his publishing output, he had been quietly involved in a small local tragedy that resulted in yet another expression of his ingenuity. In 1837, George Douseland, the adult son of one of Cayley's tenants, had caught his hand in the belting of the village watermill. The horrific crushing injury resulted in Douseland's right hand being amputated just above the wrist. Genuinely moved by Douseland's plight, Cayley designed a prosthetic replacement, but the stump had proved so tender that Douseland found it impractical and he eventually moved away from the village, leaving Cayley's partially complete invention behind. In early 1845, Douseland returned to Brompton, and Cayley set about completing and fitting the artificial hand. This one was not merely an aesthetic replacement, but one capable of considerable strength. The device allowed Douseland to "lift the weight of five stone [70 pounds]."

Involved in this and almost all of Cayley's mechanical endeavours of the time was one of the unsung heroes of the Cayley story: Thomas Vick. Vick was Cayley's resident engineer, the man who helped turn many of those fanciful contrivances into reality. We know very little about Vick beyond that he was born in Scarborough around 1803 and that he, his wife, and two daughters lived at "number 87 Brompton" until shortly after Cayley's death. From what we do know, he was a versatile and dogged fabricator whose loyalty to Cayley had an equally canine quality. There are references to Vick in many of Cayley's letters, and it is certain that the mechanical hand was to a large extent the product of Vick's talents and application.

The artificial hand was formed by a harness fitted over the upper and lower arm, with the stump held within a loop. This allowed the full leverage of the remaining lower arm to be applied through the linkages that closed the mechanical "fingers and thumb" of the cork and leather hand that fitted on the end of a third, lower strut. This mechanically ingenious but rather mediaeval-looking contraption caused Douseland and his hand to become something of an exhibition, and eventually they become a regular feature of lectures at the Royal Polytechnic Institution. Later, Douseland made an appearance at the home of Lord Northampton, president of the Royal Society, who was entertaining no less than Prince Albert and the aging Duke of Wellington. The praise heaped on Cayley by all and sundry was genuine and spontaneous, sentiments echoed in Cayley's stated reasons for publishing details of his device in the *Mechanic's Magazine* of 1845:

> I hope by thus publishing it to prevent its being pirated and
> patented, as it is quite misfortune enough to lose a hand, without
> being obliged to forego the use of even so humble a substitute, for

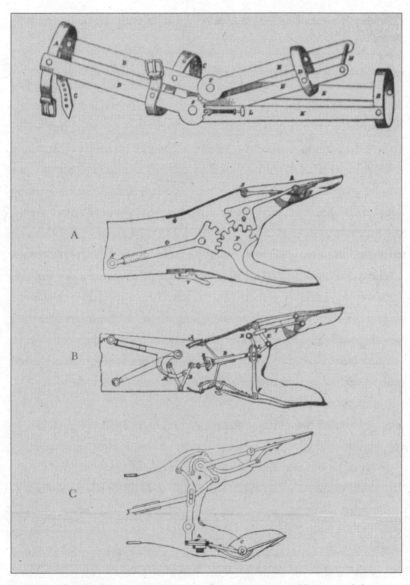

Cayley's artificial hand: topmost is the harness fitting over upper and lower arm; below are three designs of increasing sophistication for the "gripping hand" (a) showing the original mechanism, (b) a development allowing the wrist to pivot, and (c) the inclusion of an artificial thumb joint for better grasping – the idea of Cayley's grandson Edward Stillingfleet Cayley.

want of means to purchase it or otherwise to procure it at an exor-
bitant price.

Unfortunately, none of this august company seemed aware, including
rather shamefully the medical Dr. Roget, that Douseland increasingly
felt himself to be the object of an intellectually well-meaning but nevertheless demeaning freak show. In effect, Cayley's device left Douseland
with three arms: one natural, one an obvious stump, and a third one
wholly artificial. As has become better understood in the intervening
years, the stigma of disfigurement often outweighs the trauma of practical incapacity associated with losing a limb. Many people prefer an
effective disguise over a working but obviously false replacement.
Eventually, Douseland rebelled against his regular appearances and disappeared for good. A certain Mr. Buckingham, a mechanic at the RPI
with more than half an eye to the potential profit from manufacturing
similar prosthetics, wrote in high dudgeon to Cayley shortly afterwards.
It was a letter devoid of any apparent compassion for Douseland's decision to decline further opportunities to be a public spectacle.

> Since he left town I have had persons come in and make complaints
> of his conduct while wearing the apparatus at the Institution.
> When he was asked questions about its use, he would maintain a
> sullen silence, which conduct has made people doubt there was not
> jugglery about it.

The whole Douseland affair reveals Cayley (and others) being
swept up in the momentum of invention while unfortunately leaving
their sensitivity at the door. Enthusiasm and an appreciation of
mechanics may form the ideal basis for effective engineering, but they
don't make for a sympathetic bedside manner, no matter how sincere
the intentions and generous the spirit.

The 1830s and early 1840s were a period during which Cayley's reputation, previously confined to closet aviators and personal associates, blossomed to encompass a knowledge of and appreciation by a considerable proportion of the major technological and learned societies of the day. As Cayley approached his eighth decade, it could have been expected that he would perhaps slow a little. His speed would, if anything, increase, though the sureness of his step was less in evidence.

Finding the Pieces VI – Cayley: Man of Letters

Location: The British Library, Manuscripts Salon, St. Pancras, London, England.
Wednesday 23rd Feb 2005, 10.30 a.m. (GMT)

I'm here to research Cayley's correspondence with the great and the good; correspondence lovingly preserved in Britain's most extensive and auspicious archive.

It's busy in the manuscripts reading room today with most of the desks occupied. I'm still not quite used to the rarefied atmosphere and the moderno-classical decor: the furniture is fashioned in light oak and green leather styled after the old British Museum (BM) Reading Room, which was abandoned when the British Library moved to the spanking new St. Pancras building in 1998. The move was prompted by the need to consolidate nearly a dozen sites scattered around the capital that the library had previously occupied. I worked for the British Library for twelve years, but this is the first time I'd ever seen the inside of the new Manuscripts Salon. It has to be said it's rather grand.

On top of every desk are the original nineteenth-century BM bound folio holders: huge, dark oak and leather book rests that you use to support the bound volumes of manuscripts. The room is low ceilinged and, though subtle, the lighting still glares off the magnifying glass I had to borrow from the readers' desk. I'd wanted to buy my own glass before I left home, in true Sherlock Holmes fashion, but I'd forgotten. It turns out Manuscripts have a private supply of their own suitably embossed with "MSS" in large red letters.

I enquire whether the items I ordered might be ready, and a really large book appears. I leaf sequentially through literally hundreds of other pieces of correspondence before I get to the one I want. The only helpful annotation to the reams of letters carefully pasted onto every page is attached to one that some conscientious British Museum curator had marked as being from "Dr. James Walters" – the note being necessary because the nineteenth-century doctor's handwriting was simply illegible (some truths are eternal).

And suddenly, there it is. Folio number 323, in Peel's papers, general correspondence, volume CCCXCII, 6–23rd August 1845. Sir Robert Peel, British prime minister (1834–1835; 1841–1846) and inventor of the modern police force (kind of), had a lot of personal correspondents. One of them was Sir George Cayley, who was writing from Brompton on August 20, 1845 (he was seventy-one). This is the first time I've seen a Cayley original; the microfilm and reproductions just don't do him justice. It's a tiny letter, but I recognize the script, and certainly the signature. So off Cayley goes with an opening sentence that actually makes no grammatical sense whatsoever.

> Sir,
> Altho' I do not have the Honour of your acquaintance I take the liberty of placing before you, during the recess, some observations on the prevention of Railway accidents, in which I trust you will think me justified by the series of Commendable inquiries that have lately Been caused by The want of proper precautions in the use of Railways.

Two causes seem to have led to the increased number of accidents, first the intrusion of Railway lines with greater rapidity than they can be supplied with experienced Officers which will in time work its own course. Secondly, the insatiable demand of the Public for a more dangerous degree of speed –

Before a velocity, exceeding forty miles per hour, be permitted in a case where the traveller has no choice in the means of conveyance, the Legislature has a clear right to enforce the adoption of every sound moral & mechanical means to counteract the risk, *found practically to be excessive* and to placate cost of such measures, as in from deduction from the interest received by the Shareholders –

The enclosed essay is merely proposed as pointing out some of the leading objects of enquiry on the mechanical part of the subject, but does not enter into the moral and precautionary part of it, which is of equal, if not still greater importance –

The subject seems to demand the attention of the Best practical engineering Authorities acting under the Auspices of a parliamentary Committee of enquiry –

This essay was printed in 1841, But is equally applicable to these later, as to the former series of accidents –

Again apologising for having thus addressed you. I have the Honour to be,

Sir,

Your most obedient Servt

Geo Cayley

The Right Honble

Sir Robert Peel

x x x

Handwritten in Cayley's compressed script, the letter is just about exactly the dimensions of my handprint and it is a classic. You can see that he means well and wants to get things done, but there's more than a hint of self-promotion here, plus an almost cavalier disregard for the basic rules of sentence structure. I catch the attention of a passing Manuscripts curator and ask first what the procedure is for getting reproductions of the letters (she hands me some forms and a scary price list). Then I ask her for an opinion . . .

"Are those *kisses* Sir George Cayley has put on the end of his letter to the British prime minister?"

"Oh, I don't think that's likely . . ." she replies, looking over my shoulder. Then she adds, ". . . though they do *look* like kisses, don't they? Actually I'm a curator of mediaeval manuscripts so maybe you should ask the afternoon curator, I think he's nineteenth century."

I'm sure he is.

———————————————————————

It's now 2:00 p.m. and I still haven't gone for lunch. I just want to find the letter from Cayley to Charles Babbage. Babbage's correspondence volume XIX is another weighty tome but I find the one I'm after fairly quickly. As usual it's on the hand-sized paper; this time dated "Tuesday Morning."

> Dear Babbage,
> I wish you would come and dine with us on Monday 19th
> at a quarter to seven – you will meet Sydney Smith, prob-
> ably Jeffrey & a few chatty fellows. Suggest Lady Cayley
> will be in town by that time to welcome you also –
> Yours sincerely,
> Geo Cayley.

Not sure there's much I can glean from that except Babbage and Cayley seem to be on pretty chummy terms, though Babbage was a notoriously over-social character who loved a dinner party just as long as he was the centre of attention. The reference to Lady Cayley suggests, despite her temper and unpopularity with her children, that she is an active part in Cayley's entertaining at his London home in Hertford Street at the time (whenever that time might have been). There are other Cayley letters to Babbage, though none of them seems to shed much additional light on their relationship so I move on to another topic.

—————————————————————

Now it's 4:00 p.m., and lunch is an unhappily forgotten memory as I'm in the Humanities Reading Room to pick up the copies of the *Mechanic's Magazine* I ordered. Humanities Reading Room (No. 2) is a little more parochial than the rarefied MSS Salon; it has a similar decor, though now a muddy blue colour replaces the British Racing Green I have become accustomed to at *my* desk across the corridor in the Manuscripts Salon. Karl Marx used to have a favourite seat in the old British Museum Reading Room but I doubt whether my presence will ever register on the radar here.

There are maybe two hundred seats here. The place is pretty full, maybe 150 people or more. The only reading room that gets regularly full on a weekday is in Philatelic. This is largely because there *is* only one reader's seat in Philately, meaning you get the 8,252,724 stamps, covers, and water-marks all to yourself.

I sit down with my stack of ordered items at a cubicle conveniently close to the issuing desk.

I sort through my requested items and start down to business. Then I realize why a desk in such a prime spot had been left unoccupied. The man opposite is researching the history of Kensington Gardens, a fact I and everyone else knows because both his lips and his vocal chords work as he reads. I try to concentrate on my stuff.

Mechanic's Magazine, Saturday August 30, 1832, price 3d (three pennies in old money). Page one is dominated by a eulogy on James Watt, steam engine designer and inventor of work, if my schoolboy memory for physics serves me accurately. A quick bio of the great man is followed by a description of a diving bell and then, on just page nine, bingo! Research simply isn't this easy, I've done it before, so I know. Page nine is entitled "Flying in the air," recalling Eilmer of Malmesbury who foresaw the Norman invasion in 1066 but was not so canny about predicting the consequences for himself of jumping from a lofty belfry with man-made wings. The article is not signed, but do I sense the hand of Cayley here? He was on the brink of entering politics at the time so perhaps he had to keep his eccentric views on the possibility of flight as anonymous as he could.

I read it through and decide this *could* have been Cayley – it finishes off with a description of Degen, the Swiss watchmaker famed for his flapping flight. As far as we can tell, Cayley always believed Degen to have built a successful ornithopter, so it could be that what we have here is an undiscovered Cayley recapitulation of aviation to date. However, the lack of any reference to Cayley's own 1809 publications in *Nicholson's Journal* is maybe the giveaway – I'm sure Cayley would have cited it. The article does conclude with Cayley's favourite phrase, "aerial navigation," though by this time it had entered into general vocabulary. Ah well, I think we may never know who wrote it. But I continue reading.

. . . a cure for the common cold ("boil hoarhound in two quarts of water"), a test to see if your linen tablecloth has been lime-bleached by some nefarious manufacturer ("add several spoonfulls of good vinegar . . . if the linen contains lime the acid will excite considerable effervescence"), how to carry fire in your hand ("line it with ashes"), how to build a cup that never overflows . . . to detect cotton mixed with wool . . . avoid foul air in wells . . . all these among the highlights. Finally a poem about a blacksmith's birthday and a letter from the editor.

This closing editorial commentary explains that as every other educated country on the planet (by which I assume he means France, Italy, and Hanover) has a weekly bulletin on how to cook your carrots without spoiling the stove, the lack of such a work in England would be nothing short of a national scandal. For only 3d, every person "within 150 miles of the metropolis" will be able to build a steam engine; fly; never get a cold or be sold dud linen; carry fire; explore deep wells; and harbour a deep appreciation for the honest labour of the noble smithy – sounds like a bargain. Next week the editorial promises an article on Spitalfields' Weavers from "an eminent economist." The time machine of retrospect allows me to check this for you and I can indeed confirm that this is no idle boast; the next issue contains the most detailed examination of Spitalfields' business prospects before or since.

The concluding italicised text of the publication invites

communications from Intelligent Mechanics and all others who
may take an interest in the diffusion of useful information on any
of the subjects embraced by this work. . . .

which has to encompass every subject on the face of the
planet. Such communications should be *"addressed to the Editor,*
and post-paid to the care of the publisher."

There is no publisher's address, though there is the
printer's:

T. C. Hansard, Peterborough Court, Fleet Street, London.

Could this be the same Thomas Curson Hansard who published the proceedings of the British Parliament? That would
be too good to be true . . . I just bought a book on Hansard!

II

HARD TIMES

In 1837, the same year in which Cayley began work on the Douseland artificial limb, Britain greeted a new monarch and a new era. Victoria ascended the throne at the age of eighteen, following the death of her uncle, William IV. Victoria's accession came as the result of William's only two legitimate children having died in their infancy, though his ten illegitimate offspring by his mistress, the actress Dorothea Bland, flourished under the surname FitzClarence, for generations. The young and vibrant new queen was soon matched by an even more energetic husband when she continued the now century-old tradition of the British monarch choosing a spouse from the Germanic nations. In this case, it was the handsome and modern-minded Albert of Coburg (Bavaria), a man who just happened to be Victoria's first cousin. Unlike many Cayley-cousin marriages, however, this union introduced a change in surname for the British Royals. The relatively straightforward "House of Hanover" became the rather more of a mouthful Saxe-Coburg-Gotha until it was hurriedly exchanged for Windsor at the outbreak of World War I.

With the beginning of the Victorian age, Cayley broke his nearly twenty-year drought in publications concerning flight. Precedent dictated that entering the public domain required an external impetus, and in this case it was the flight of the balloonist Charles Green, not across the Atlantic (as he had proposed at the Royal Polytechnic) but across the still significant North Sea, landing in the tiny Duchy of Nassau (an area that is now the Luxembourg–German border). The exact timing of Cayley's public commentary on flight may also have been influenced by his decision to end his days of over-the-counter politicking, leaving him unfettered by what the average voter might feel about the subject. Cayley's 1837 paper, his fourth on airships, was titled "Practical Remarks on Aerial Navigation" and appeared in the journal with which Cayley was beginning to form a close relationship: the *Mechanic's Magazine*. Cayley's choice of subject matter for his article shows his keen sense of the public's taste; he knows that his audience wants an essay on ballooning, and so an essay on ballooning is what he delivers. The self-imposed publication ban has left Cayley bursting with new ideas on flight, ideas he had been discussing and experimenting on privately, out of the public's gaze. Now that he has an audience once more, he just lets himself go. His paper starts with a recap of the principles of dirigible flight followed by what has been described as "an astonishingly prophetic footnote." Cayley predicts that for an airship to balance the needs for large scale, strength, and lightness "they will probably be made of thin metallic sheets." Sixty years later, just such a design was implemented by the Croatian engineer David Schwarz, using aluminum strips to form the airship body and the same metal to form the internal structure. Schwarz died at the age of forty-five from a heart attack the day before the first successful flight of his craft – some say as the direct result of his excitement over the news of imminent government funding for the project. Subsequently, a highly under-qualified aristocratic aviation enthusiast named Ferdinand von Zeppelin would steal many of Schwarz's technical drawings before going on to produce the famous airships that bore his name.

Cayley's paper continues with a reiteration of his findings on the need to streamline the front and rear of the airship. Following his customary source of flying inspiration, Cayley suggests the airship mimic nature's solution for passing easily through a fluid by having a shape like "a cod's head and a mackerel's tail." Cayley then veers off at 90 degrees from the right track by describing and then illustrating his thoughts on the use of an inclined plane and a double balloon as a means of achieving steerable flight – echoing the idea for a similar design by John Evans that had sparked Cayley's first ballooning publications back in 1815.

Cayley then swings back nearer to the right line with a detailed calculation of the weights, lifting potential, and propulsion power requirements for a balloon some twenty-five times the size of the *Great Balloon of Nassau*, which Charles Green had recently used to cross to the continent. Cayley's calculations conclude with the need for a massive 60 horse-power engine if the ship were to be capable of the required 14 miles an hour.

And so, with some degree of trepidation, we get to Cayley's ideas on the subject of what means of propulsion he recommends. At first he edges toward his scary ideas on "waftage," but this is just a fake and he quickly sidesteps back toward a variant of the propeller. Cayley doesn't suggest the standard airscrew (as he did in his paper of 1817) but instead pairs of counter-rotating screws with cambered, sectional blades "reversing, as it were the action of the sails of a windmill." Cayley then performs his customary redemption, this time by adding the simply inspired suggestion that the propellers should be mounted on multidirectional swivels to allow them to power, steer, and control the altitude of the airship. The alternation of gutter balls and strikes continues as he considers, then discards, fan-generated, jet-powered steerage and then reiterates the excellent suggestions that the internal gas bag for the airship should be split into a number of individually sealed units for safety and ease of filling. Cayley concludes with a second unsuccessful attempt to establish the Society for Promoting Aerial Navigation.

Gibbs-Smith describes this publication as Cayley's "most curious and most distrait" – it does seem to be the least *dirigible* of Cayley's papers. Perhaps the oversupply of ideas on aviation, built up over the previous twenty years, suffered from the lack of any editorial pruning. Not that that was likely to happen – the *Mechanic's Magazine* uncritically published anything and everything the now famous baronet sent their way. This was Cayley's last publication devoted to airships (though not his final commentary on the subject) and acts as the curtain-raiser to a final series of papers that defined his golden age of aviation work. This same age brought the bouquet title "father of aerial navigation" as well as actions that warrant the brickbat accusation of wanton plagiarism. The cause of both accolade and censure stems from Cayley's role as the era's clearing house for ideas on flight. One reason that he chose this time to throw himself so passionately into his research, and so uncharacteristically failed to meet his own exacting moral standards when he did so, was the increasing stresses of his family life.

Lady Sarah's mental health had been declining steadily for some years but it was becoming a cause for acute concern. The Cayley archive contains none of her rumoured correspondence, reported as being rude to the point of scandal. What exists are hints and in some instances more than hints as to Sarah's state of mind. By 1840, daughter Emma is compelled to raise the issue with her father:

> I wish Anne had more particularly informed us of poor Mamas
> state but I understand that she is now pronounced to be decidedly
> insane. . . . The thing now to be done is to cure mama and comfort
> those who have so long suffered her insane litany which for her own
> sake must no longer be allowed to exist.

Sarah is often bed-bound and Cayley even enters into correspondence with a Mr. A. Wilson concerning the development of a "liquid bed" to ease her sores; her mental state and temper remained largely untreatable. The loving but clearly forceful Emma even writes directly to her mother in an attempt to address the problem head on:

> I feel most deeply the torment of your heart. It is impossible not to lament and grieve and turn over any means of remedying the present wretchedness of your life. I am your daughter and as such I have the right to advise. . . . Can I tell you that in my judgement the wretchedness you suffer from is *more* than partly of your own creation. You expect from human beings what can never be found, that they will behave to us like angels and you resent instead of submitting. . . . Are you conscious that your temper is bad? That you have this fault I believe you are partially aware. It is very trying to all who live with you.

Sarah's physical health sustained her for another decade and more, but her mental illness continued as an emotionally draining downward spiral for all those around her. This hidden pressure had its own peculiar impact on Cayley's conduct.

Cayley's reputation as a centre for all things aerial brought him correspondence from across the country and beyond. One of the most curious incidents occurred in July 1842 when he received a letter from a mysterious Robert B. Taylor, who had recently arrived from the United States with perhaps the most ingenious suggestion thus far for heavier-than-air flight. Taylor, by way of introduction in his letter, hints that his own father, "Doct. Taylor," formerly from nearby Bolton in Lancashire, may have met Cayley before emigrating to the United States in 1819. It appears that Dr. Taylor had either read or knew of Cayley's triple papers of 1809–10 and had developed a belief in the possibility of heavier-than-air flight. Taylor Sr. had passed to his son,

Robert, "a firm conviction of the practicability of traveling thro' the air by mechanical means, without inflation."

Taylor then reveals to Cayley his own idea on how flight might be achieved. Taylor illustrates and explains in detail how two propellers ("sets of vanes") mounted one above the other would provide the necessary lift with each blade counter-rotating to ensure that the passenger isn't counter-spun into delirium. Once airborne, these same vanes then

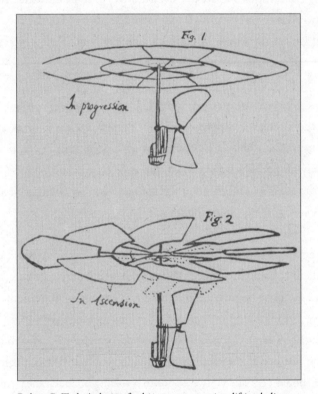

Robert B. Taylor's design for his counter-rotating, lifting helicopter (figure 2), whose interlocking blades form a single lifting plane that is then driven forward by the smaller, secondary propeller (figure 1).

interlock to form a tilted wing surface, at which point a third driving propeller takes over to push it through the air. With regard to the resulting inclined plane, Taylor acknowledges, "The lateral movement of a large plane surface edgewise, to attain and retain altitude is, I conceive, your original invention or idea," seeming to confirm knowledge of Cayley's earliest papers. Unlike Cayley, Taylor hasn't understood the weight problems associated with the suggested power plant ("The power I contemplate is steam, eventually") but in all other respects the naturalized American's idea is nothing short of inspired.

As if uncannily aware of Cayley's Achilles heel, Taylor even articulates *why* propellers are the way forward:

> Nature cannot use rotary motion! The wheel and axle is prohibited to the animate creations of nature. Bones, sinews, muscles and joints are incapable of producing, or even permitting, a continued rotary motion of relative parts of the same animal; and yet it is only by the use of this motion that on land and water we outstrip Nature in speed, and excel her endurance.

By return post Cayley responds to Taylor's letter. After a lengthy preamble in which Cayley goes through the necessary social exchanges, he suddenly comes out with the most extraordinary statement:

> Long ago I came to the same conclusion as you have done, as to the main features of the mechanical aerial locomotive; that is, the first rise should be made by two opposite revolving oblique vanes which should when required become the simple inclined planes, or part of them, for progressive motion, by any other propelling apparatus. . . .

Now we have to pause here for a moment. Cayley is saying that Taylor's idea of the propeller flattening to become a wing was something

he'd thought of years ago, an assertion that, to put it mildly, is questionable. To put it more candidly Cayley's claim is unsupported by a
single line in any publication, any note in his private journal, or any
statement recorded as being uttered or written by Cayley on the
subject. A far more likely explanation is that Cayley was simply aghast
that this Johnny-come-lately could have derived what amounts to a
brilliant solution to the triple problems of getting airborne, moving
forward through the air, and landing again. That some literal unknown
from a country younger than he could pull the rug out from under
Cayley's aviation feet must have come as something of a shock for a man
in his seventieth year, but even this is no excuse, never mind a justification, for what Cayley did next.

Continuing his reply, Cayley helpfully points out the major fault
of Taylor's (and everyone else's) winged-flight designs: that the power
of the steam engine came at a weight cost that would leave it on the
ground, "hence I have been at work within the last 30 years at many
sorts of first movers of a lighter description, and have constructed
several engines worked by the expansion of air by heat."

Then Cayley comes to the bottom line:

> You seem to wish to patent the reverse revolving flyers [propellers],
> and thus you would in fact, if the air engine be brought fully to
> succeed, or any other light mover be discovered, tie up my engine or
> the means of its application to the purposes for which I intended it,
> and have been labouring so long.

Taylor has made no mention of patenting his idea in Britain or anywhere else. In fact, his intentions seem to be quite the opposite. His
frank and detailed disclosure of his idea to the man acclaimed as the
leading expert in the field would be the very last thing a man would do
if he were intending to capture the exclusive intellectual rights to his

invention. Having let out what could be described as a rather shrill cry of complaint, Cayley then seems to return to a more familiarly avuncular tone suggesting that

> there is plenty of room however for the energies of both of us, and if you will come over here, as you propose, we can probably arrange matters so as to be fair to each other: and you will find in the Miss Lawrences, who are with us, some old friends of your father.

Despite Cayley's seeming hospitality, even this friendly invitation appears a little creepy after the preceding list of what at are best half-truths and at worst an attempt to falsely claim prior discovery of Taylor's ideas. Cayley's letter concludes with further suggestions that he has been thinking about this for decades, even stating that he had thought of related ideas as far back as 1792. Certainly his schoolbook designs from this time include rotary flyers and propeller-driven balloons, but there is no evidence that these were designed to fold into a lift-generating wing, a facet that lies at the heart of Taylor's ingenious design. Emphasizing his claim to originality, Cayley includes his reply with a sketch of his helicopter model from his teens and encloses a copy of his previous publication on ballooning.

Taylor's second letter is dated but a day after Cayley's reply and begins by thanking Cayley for his pamphlet but adding that he may not be able to visit as his travel schedule is so hectic. Acknowledging Cayley's insight concerning the use of steam power, Taylor then throws a second curve ball, which edges his invention over the science/fiction boundary:

> I further have reason to believe that in about a year or two a power will be in general use – derived from *electro-magnetism* – from which can be obtained five to ten horse power in the space of an ordinary lady's band box. Some friends of mine in the U.S. were only waiting

to hear from Germany before taking out their patent when I left Washington, and I firmly believe in their success.

Taylor then pays respects to the "Miss Lawrences," promises to write again, and promptly disappears forever.

Six days after the exchange of letters between Cayley and Taylor, a related note arrived in Brompton from Mr. J.C. Robertson, a man who seems to be a character stepping straight out from the darkest imaginings of Charles Dickens's Britain. In his letter, Robertson, an editor in *Mechanic's Magazine*'s Patent and Design Registration Office, states that there is no record of R.B. Taylor having taken out any relevant patents in Britain and that

> it would be a thousand pities were a stranger to step in to reap the harvest of your long and arduous labours in this department; or even to thwart or impede the consummation of your views in the least. In anything which I can do to protect your interests you may of course at all times freely command me.

Even without Robertson adding how "terribly, terribly 'umble" he might have been, there are echoes here of what could be called the worst clichés of Victorian dialogue if only it weren't genuine. However, before he deals further with Robert B. Taylor, another aviation upstart would be on the receiving end of Cayley's uncharacteristically disingenuous backhands.

William Samuel Henson was born in 1812 and had followed his father into a highly successful business of lace-making in Somerset, southwestern England. William had a gift for engineering and a passion for innovation, the two prerequisites for any early flying pioneer. Along with his technical expertise, he also realized that it would cost a small fortune to develop a heavier-than-air vehicle and that the best way forward would be to secure considerable funding upfront before he started, a view that seemed almost universal among early aviation enthusiasts with the ironic exception of those who actually *did* develop successful flyers. In order to progress his ideas in the most economically viable way, Henson first set about securing a patent, then, in March 1843, he sponsored a bill through Parliament to incorporate a business and raise funds to pay for the development of the flying machine itself and the resulting new method of transportation via the Ariel Transit Company. By the time Henson had his patent in hand, he had singularly failed to secure funding capital owing to some fairly prudent skepticism on the part of potential investors. At this point, the power of marketing was felt in the person of Frederick Marriott, who commissioned a series of widely distributed prints depicting the imaginary sight of Henson's airplane sailing over the major landmarks of the world. These images caused a sensation, with some newspapers wrongly reporting the pictures as illustrating actual events, rather than an artist's impression of them for the purpose of drumming up cash.

Barely three days after his patent was granted, a description of the Ariel Steam Carriage appeared in *Mechanic's Magazine,* where a broadly supportive review of the machine was penned by technical correspondent John Chapman. Looking back at Henson's design, it was a revelation. With the benefit of 150 years of hindsight, we can see that conceptually the vehicle exhibited just about everything you could hope for in an early monoplane. It had the long thin wing (which Cayley had already noted as being the ideal form, though he had subsequently avoided it like the plague). The wing was kept rigid by bracing wires mounted through king posts (another abandoned Cayley idea). The wing was formed by two separate surfaces of canvas stretched over an inner lightweight frame made of hollowed wooden poles. It was propelled using twin counter-rotating airscrews. It had a single, enclosed,

An "artist's illustration" of the Henson and Stringfellow "Ariel" over Britain.

streamlined fuselage containing the steam power unit, crew, passengers, and cargo. The tricycle formation wire-tension wheels formed a strong and light undercarriage. It had a rear elevator for pitch control and a (downward-pointing) rudder for control in yaw. Essentially it was a compendium of all the most successful principles of heavier-than-air flight, most of which were derived directly from Cayley's published work, just leaving out his worst ideas and adding in a couple of really good ones. At the end of the review, which was both balanced and upbeat, the editor of *Mechanic's Magazine* himself took over the discussion of the vehicle via the inclusion of an essay-length footnote. In contrast to Chapman's earlier commentary, this appendix was less than even-handed; in fact, it crossed from the sunlit foothills of impartiality to enter the gloom of vested interest, where it pulled out the rhetorical equivalent of a baseball bat, dropped its shoulder, and leaned into the pitch:

> While we agree with him [Chapman] generally in his views, and
> admit most freely that Mr. Henson's is a step in the right direction
> ... the truth is that we can discover nothing of importance in the
> present scheme which has not been proposed, and even tried before;
> with perhaps the exception of the steam boiler; and even that seems
> to be rather a combination of various known contrivances....

The footnote continues by referencing Cayley "the philosophical
baronet" and, with some merit, points out that many of the ideas
incorporated by Henson derived directly from Cayley's published
research. The editor follows this up by placing an article by Cayley
himself immediately after the Henson review. Cayley seems to have
retained the dark mood that had dominated his correspondence with
and subsequent actions regarding Robert Taylor.

Cayley begins by suggesting that the blaze of publicity surrounding
Henson's machine might lead "others to reject it as a visionary hoax on
public credulity," a comment that, though unkind, is not actually that
unfair. Cayley continues with a concise review of his own work, including the reliable basis upon which gliders and powered aircraft might be
designed, then he loses it completely by including his own footnote
that Degen had done it all years ago. Cayley then repeats his highly
pertinent points concerning steam engine *weight* making steam engine
power unfeasible for flight. Cayley adds a note on the need for some
means to prevent heavier-than-air machines from rolling uncontrol-
lably, a definite failing of the Henson design, and something nobody
would fully resolve until the Wright brothers. Then, out of the blue
(except it wasn't), Cayley reveals his plans for a machine that would
rise vertically using lift propellers, "which when not employed in this
way, are so made to become flat," forming the inclined plane required
for sustained forward flight. This is Taylor's idea plain and simple, and

Cayley singularly fails to say so. Cayley has committed the scientific equivalent of original sin, and there doesn't seem to be much to obviously mitigate the behaviour. Instead, Cayley compounds his crime in the most spectacular way.

The following week, on April 8, 1843, Cayley publishes his most original, most complex, most intricate design for a flying machine. It was a marvel to behold, and only Robert B. Taylor of New York would have known that it was not Cayley's idea – except by now Taylor was back in the United States and well outside the 150-mile radius of London that defined the circulation footprint of *Mechanic's Magazine*. It has to be said that what Cayley does with Taylor's plans is to turn a concept into a design – something older engineers have done to their younger protégés since the dawn of time. It was something Cayley seemed to achieve with panache, and not a little relish.

Any doubt over the provenance of Cayley's new design is quickly removed by the illustration: the basis of the machine has clearly been lifted from Taylor's original note. Further evidence of *Mechanic's Magazine*'s collusion in promoting Cayley above all others is clear from the title they apply to Cayley's paper: "Sir George Cayley's Aerial Carriage" is an obvious trumping of "Henson's Aerial Carriage" from their issue of only a week before.

Cayley's article follows the well-trodden path of his previous works in being wide-ranging, wildly inconsistent, and occasionally brilliant. It also includes a pinch of vitriol absent from his previous papers; perhaps he feels the nip of young pups at his heels and is inclined to show them who's boss. In spite of the negative tone, his paper includes yet another startling idea – one that eventually provided the most singularly important design concept in early aviation and the one idea that allowed practical powered flight to be finally realized. But first Cayley lays into Henson.

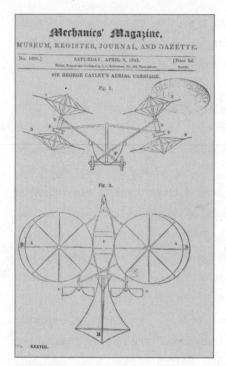

Cayley's 1843 Aerial Carriage – the most innovative design ever to come out of the Cayley
aviation stables – inspired, but unattributed
as such, by Robert B. Taylor.

Cayley's criticism centres on the scale of the Henson machine: "the magnitude of the proposed vehicle will, I fear, militate against its success. . . . There appears to be a limit in nature to the convenient application of winged sur-faces. . . ." We can perhaps forgive Cayley from reaching this conclusion as it relates to nature because the fossils of the giant pterosaur flying rep-tiles were at the time largely misclassified as being sea-dwelling rather than land-based animals capable of flight, and the mighty forty-foot-wingspan *Quetzalcoatlus* was not unearthed until 1917. It is harder to reconcile Cayley's pessimism over the practicality of a large-scale machine with his own thoughts and calculations in his notebook of 1795: "hence it is demonstrated that when the plain is large enough and the angle small enough 1lb [of thrust] might support a million – 2 million or any number whatever. . . ."

And yet, though consciously unaware of his own previous consider-ation of the subject, Cayley's phobic concern over the strength of a long, slender wing once more dominates his thoughts:

The atmosphere, even in moderately calm weather, near the earth is subject to eddies; and the weight of the engine and cargo etc., in the central part of this vast extent of surface, would, in the case of any sudden check, operate with enormous power to break the slender fabric.

Cayley seems to have brought aviation to a juddering halt once again, just as he had nearly fifty years before. Apparently the whole endeavour is doomed to failure on account of man's inability to fabricate the light, strong, flexible limbs of a bird and couple such a structure with the efficiencies of a lightweight power source. Then, as if he glimpses the darkest moment of the night and checks his pocket watch for dawn's approach, Cayley announces the solution to the whole conundrum with a seemingly effortless flourish: "In order to obtain a sufficient quantity of surface to sustain great weights in the air, the extension ought not to be made in one plane but in parallel planes one above the other. . . ."

And so Cayley's long-pondered biplane was sprung upon the world. In fact, Cayley goes a step further, suggesting a triplane as being the best solution: "a *three decker*, each deck being 8 or 10 feet from the other, to give room for the passage of air between them. . . ."

Cayley's paper then continues by suggesting that Henson's wings should form the dihedral V-shape in order to give it some means of preventing it rolling in the air, a point in which he is undoubtedly right: even Henson's patent application paid scant regard to the actual aerodynamic qualities of his aircraft. Another of Henson's suggestions had been to achieve take-off speed by descending a ramp (the Wright brothers later used a falling weight, pulley, and a tow rope to achieve the same effect). Ramp assistance is something Cayley takes issue with because it seems to impractically limit where the craft could take off and land, which is a valid point as well as a lead-in to his own ideas for his vertical take-off and landing machine (a considerably less supportable one). Along the way, Cayley includes his most ardent statement on the future of aviation so far: "There can be no doubt that the inclined plane, with a horizontal propelling apparatus, is the true principle of aerial navigation by mechanical means," an observation followed not long afterwards by a half-reversal that once again illustrates Cayley's driving fear for safety in larger vehicles: "Hence, on a great scale, balloon flotage offers the most ready, efficient and safe means of aerial navigation."

Via a brief passage concerning the familiar theme of requirements for engine power (obviously to push flappers up and down), Cayley then doubles back again in favour of heavier-than-air flight and on to his brand-new, ingenious, and undeniably stolen ideas of a new helicopter/airplane, a device Gibbs-Smith christens Cayley's "convertiplane." Cayley had taken Taylor's idea and very nearly made it fly. Instead of a single pair of counter-rotating propellers above a seat for the pilot, Cayley now has two pairs, arranged to form the more stable dihedral configuration mounted either side of a fuselage fitted with driving propellers, rudder, elevator, and eagle figurehead. On achieving the necessary altitude, the propeller blades interlock to form his favoured short, wide inclined planes as a pusher propeller engages to drive it through the air. Even Cayley freely admits that this is more of a conceptual mock-up than a practical flyer and that it would require someone (else) to push the project forward.

> This construction of an experimental machine for mechanical aerial navigation is not offered in the light of a finished model, but more to show, in combination, certain principles which must be attended to in their construction, to give them a fair chance of success.

Who it might be that needed to do the attending, was, according to Cayley's sign-off for his paper, a British aviation society, the absence of which he thought was "a national disgrace."

Even though Cayley rarely edited himself when it came to his publications, we have to ask why he would publish so detailed a model of so untried a flying concept. Suspicion falls on Cayley wishing to push the idea into the public domain in order to prevent a certain American from ever patenting it in Britain: Cayley's moral barometer would never again sink so low.

Though the excitement over the Henson design rose a little higher before it too declined, there was no progress on it because there was no more money to be spent on the project and no enthusiasm in the investment community for that situation to change. So after a suitable period of grace, Henson tried one last time to get the funds he so sorely needed. In September 1846, some three and a half years after Cayley's critique/convertiplane paper, and quite unheralded, Henson wrote to Cayley confirming that he and his partner, John Stringfellow, had not "given it up as a failure." Coming quickly to the point, Henson raises the rather tawdry subject of "that pecuniary assistance necessary to carry on our efforts upon an enlarged scale and with increased energy" while sugar-coating the request for money by referring to Cayley as "the Father of Aerial Navigation." Cayley's reply to Henson's letter is nothing short of brilliant, or as good as a reply can get without actually putting his hand in his pocket.

Cayley expresses his optimism that heavier-than-air flight might be just around the corner, "for the materials are ripe or very nearly so at present." Cayley admits that he thought Henson had abandoned his work but concedes an admiration that was absent in his previous critical paper: "I like your zeal, and as you seem disposed to treat me with your confidence I can only assure you that I shall not abuse it." (Robert

B. Taylor, please note.) Then Cayley condenses the current state of flight science and its near future into the most elegant of nutshells: "As to new principles there are none; of practical expedients there will soon be an endless variety and to select the best is the point at issue." Cayley offers to meet with Henson, but only to discuss what new experiments Henson had conducted, as Cayley explicitly states, "I have not any weight of capital to apply to such matters, [but] I perhaps might be able to aid you in some manner by my experience in connexion with other mechanical persons."

There is a record neither of a response nor of any meeting between Cayley and Henson, but we can assume that nothing came of it. Within two years, Henson had emigrated to the United States with his family to pursue a new career as a civil engineer but not in any sphere known to be connected with flight. Henson's partner, John Stringfellow, took over the designs and went on to build several of the triplane models that Cayley's original critique had suggested. These models, powered by a specially manufactured small-scale steam engine, were sustained in the air from a running wire along their flight path. Though there were suggestions of them having been "launched" after having got up to speed on such wires, there is a suspicion that they "flew" only by virtue of their pre-release momentum being high enough for them to descend at a rate only slightly less than a falling body. They would never maintain level flight so they cannot really be considered successful flyers. Stringfellow's work on aviation soon temporarily ceased, though he briefly revisited it a decade after Cayley's death. Cayley's triplane idea eventually flew (or rather glided) in the hands of Octave Chanute in the late 1890s. Chanute's removal of the lower "deck" to produce a biplane, and his work with Augustus Herring on this very design (rigidly braced with the simple, strong, and effective Pratt truss), provided the strong, light, lift-generating platform for powered flight to be later achieved by the Wrights.

The year of 1846 marked the closure of the least attractive period of Cayley's aviation career, and as if in Divine response, it also marked the beginning of an even darker series of events. With his wife's health continuing to decline, perhaps Cayley hoped that the marriage of his daughter Mary Agnes would give him one less thing to worry about. Instead, his youngest daughter found herself entangled with the despicable Dr. James Alexander and precipitated the "Alexander Affair."

Mary Agnes may have inherited more than just good looks from her mother for she quarrelled fiercely with her eldest sister, Anne – there is even a letter to both of them from Cayley begging them to try to get along. If her temperament was less than appealing, at least Mary Agnes possessed both good looks and a singing voice of pure silver, a combination that attracted a serious amount of attention from the opposite sex. However, she was never in very good health, being afflicted by the untreatable St. Vitus Dance (a movement disorder), and she had had at least one epileptic seizure. She later described herself as being temporarily "an invalid," and from her correspondence there are hints of anxiety and perhaps even paranoia. Mary Agnes's sister Kate referred to her in the family history through the analogy that "the instrument was first rate but never harmoniously strung." At first it might seem that selecting a surgeon and physician for a husband could have been a good idea for Mary Agnes; unfortunately, James Alexander would prove incapable of fulfilling any of these roles.

The early years of their relationship are scantily documented, though there is an undated reference to Dr. James, "fiancé," in a letter from Mary Agnes to Miss Phil. In the letter, Mary Agnes mentions that her father liked James "but he was so frequently against him at first, on account of him being a doctor." The same note also includes plans for a wedding "in mid or late February." The couple were married in the fashionable St. George Church in Hanover Square, London, on March 7, 1846. The exact date takes on some significance – one biographer suggests a shotgun being instrumental in the nuptials: their first child, Mary Isabella, was born barely ten months later on January 15. It could be that the registration of the birth had been delayed to allow a respectable separation between the marriage and christening ceremonies. It wouldn't be the first time that a child "notably larger-than-average" had been registered, and even registration itself was a fairly new administrative procedure at the time. However, there is no documentary evidence to suggest a scandal early in their relationship, and one letter from Cayley to Miss Phil even refers to Alexander as being "amiable." The couple spent their early months not far from the Cayleys' London house by residing with Alexander's father in North Audley Street, Westminster. But soon there were signs of trouble in the marriage and it would all boil down to money.

Mary Agnes's marriage settlement consisted of a hefty down payment and a generous series of instalments, all aimed at establishing house, home, and family. The settlement money was paid out in the handy sums of £500 upfront with a further £4,000 over ten years. It went some way toward eventually purchasing a house in Scarborough, and the couple moved there at some point in 1849. At the same time, Alexander secured a loan from Cayley for the considerable additional sum of £1,880 at five per cent interest per annum – Cayley was a hard-headed businessman in such matters. How it was that Alexander intended to pay back the capital and interest is unclear, for he seemed to have no medical practice, few patients, and little in the way of mar-ketable doctoring skills. What Alexander did have in abundance was an addiction to gambling (at whist and "on the turf") and a violent temper. By the birth of their second child, Walter Cayley in December 1849, there were clear signs of matrimonial distress: Mary Agnes chose to give birth at the High Hall, Brompton, and periodically began taking up residence there.

During this time, the couple were having renovations done on their house in Scarborough, and Mr. Kirby, a local builder and joiner, was a regular visitor to conduct and oversee the work. Alexander accused Mary Agnes of having an affair with Kirby, and news of the accusation reached her father through the convenient action of an anonymous letter writer (almost certainly Alexander himself). Matters came to a head on Christmas Day 1851 when Mary Agnes accused Alexander of having gambled away £150 of railway share certificates that he had intimidated her into giving him. The fact that he had done exactly that did little to calm his temper. Alexander violently brought up the Kirby affair once more, though Mary Agnes "laughed in his face over the absurdity of the thing," which may have not been such a good idea. Finally Alexander exploded at Mary Agnes: "Damn your soul to the bottomless pits of hell. . . . I've a good mind to murder you." His additional threat "to blow Kirby's brains out" was, however, far less sinister than Alexander's reminder of his professional skill "of being able to destroy human life so that no-one could detect the person who was being made away with."

Shortly afterwards Mary Agnes gathered her children and fled to the safety of High Hall, but Alexander was far from finished. He pursued her, raining letters on anyone and everyone he thought might be harbouring her, until Mary Agnes and her children slipped away to Cayley's estate in Scampton, Lincolnshire, where she remained anonymously for several months. Her secret hiding place may not have been that secret. A letter Alexander wrote to Edward Stillingfleet concerning his absent wife, though addressed as having been written in York (Alexander's home city), is postmarked Lincoln, just down the road from Mary Agnes's temporary, hidden residence.

Alexander's threats became ever more persistent and perverse. He insisted that unless Mary Agnes returned to him, he would seek either legal or illegal means of taking the children and then emigrating with them to Australia. The Cayley archives is filled with Alexander's rambling letters, each referred to within the Cayley family as "Alexander manuscripts." These lengthy scrawls slip effortlessly between indignant self-righteousness and unveiled aggression, even though he insists on referring to Cayley as "my father, Sir George." Finally Cayley sought to settle matters in a vocabulary Alexander would truly understand: cash.

The Deed of Separation, dated September 11, 1852, is actually a contract between Alexander and Cayley whereby, for £100 per annum (payable in two six-monthly payments), Alexander agrees to "relinquish ecclesiastical censures and conjugal rights" to Mary Agnes and agrees not to molest or contact her, or live within thirty miles. It adds that "Mary Agnes Alexander may in all things live as if she were sole and unmarried without the restraint or correction of the said James Alexander." By this agreement, Alexander also relinquishes his parental rights and agrees that in the event of Mary Agnes's death, Mary and Walter's sole legal guardians would become the agreement's two trustees: George Allanson Cayley, Sir George's grandson and heir to the Brompton baronetcy, and Sir William Cayley Worsley, another Cayley grandson and the baronet of Hovingham. Alexander signed on the dotted line, pocketed his first instalment, and carried on his reign of intimidation where he had left off.

Most of the internal details of the affair come from a truly epic letter that Mary Agnes wrote in August 1853. This document acted as a record of events and the basis for the second legal attempt to prevent Alexander from carrying out his threats. Through Mary Agnes's statement, which extends over thirty pages, we get some insight into her state of mind, and the view is not a pretty one. Having endured at least two years of threats to both herself and her children, she is quite clearly at the end of a tether that may have been rather short to start with. She forcibly denies the accusation of impropriety with Kirby, then mentions his name more than a dozen times. She talks of her ill health and her invalidity cured through her conversion to the popular quack cure of hydropathy – requiring her to take rigorous early-morning exercise followed by an ice-cold bath. The failings of Alexander's character and behaviour are documented again and again. She admits to having had him followed and even following him herself in order to collect evidence of his infidelity – of which she is convinced, and with some justification, for she claims to have found incriminating letters from at least one female companion. She returns repeatedly to the issue of money and the fact that Alexander "played ducks and drakes upon all occasions with every shilling he could get at." The reports of physical threats are there too, along with his "tyrannical temper and love of command." All this, in a heavily edited form, was the basis for an injunction sought in August 1853. However then, as now, the law had little means of preventing determined and slightly unhinged individuals from pursuing the object of their obsession.

In October 1854, Cayley inserted a codicil into his will making the debt Alexander owed him into a trust for his grandchildren Mary Isabella and Walter Cayley. The harassing, irritating, and sometimes clearly drunken Alexander letters persisted, and fearing things might be even worse otherwise, the half-yearly payments to Alexander continued too. Events progressed unchanged up until Cayley's death in 1857 – but even then there was no end to it. Alexander repeated his threats to exert his (legally strong) rights to not only access but guardianship of his children, who were by now older than infants and less protected from their father's control. The Cayley family rallied round, with the children spending significant time under assumed names with a family friend, Lady Monteagle.

In 1860, at the age of forty-five, Mary Agnes died in Great Malvern, Worcestershire. The only recorded witness to her death was not a relative, but a Mary Anne Towndrow, wife of William

Towndrow, a successful grocer, bonnet maker, and civic improver of some repute. Why and exactly where in Malvern Mary Agnes died is unknown. Her presence there may relate to the local aristocrat, the 3rd Baron of Evesham, who was a member of Parliament at the same time as Cayley, so there may have been some connection through their political association. Why Mary Agnes died is also unclear, because despite there being a death certificate, it specifies the symptoms preceding death rather than any medical diagnosis. Though the certificate quotes the cause as "bleeding from the bowel – certified" this could be as a result of anything from abdominal tumours to poisoning. It can only be hoped that Alexander did not follow through on his insidious threats of a decade earlier.

Even after their mother's death, Mary Isabella and Walter Cayley were not spared from their father's attempts to renege on his sworn intentions. Stalling tactics and semi-legal measures went on for years, until eventually in 1863 Mary Isabella reached the age of sixteen, at which age she could choose whether she would associate with her father – she chose not to. In a typically practical move, Walter Cayley was taken beyond the reach of his father by joining the navy as a teenage midshipman, and he put out to sea that same year. Walter did not make a career as a naval officer, but became a successful brewer in the town of Malton, just a few miles from Brompton. He married the daughter of a local cleric there in 1872 and had four children, three of whom carried "Cayley" as a middle name. Of Mary Isabella and her father James we know little – though Mary was a witness to her brother's marriage. The final document in the "Alexander dossier" is a sterile enquiry from a solicitor dated 1883 concerning the whereabouts of the insurance documents relating to "the late Dr. James Alexander." Sadly the note also refers to "the late Miss Alexander's will," from which it appears that Mary Isabella died some time before her thirty-sixth birthday.

If that had been it, if the trials of the Alexander affair had been the final chapter of Cayley's life, even if the saga spanned beyond his death, it would have been a noteworthy, though intensely gloomy curtain closer. But it wasn't. During and in between the legal wrangling, back-door dealings, threats, and broken promises, somehow Cayley managed to complete his final and triumphant phase of flight experimentation, though even this triumphant phase began with domestic tragedy.

Finding the Pieces VII – Robert B. Taylor, Man of Mystery
Uncloaked by the Internet

Gibbs-Smith, the aviation historian who provides one of the most honest appraisals concerning Cayley's contribution to flight, treats the whole Robert B. Taylor episode with a mixture of fascination and horror. Gibbs-Smith admits to a "sharp pang of regret" on concluding that Cayley has fallen short of what has been hitherto an unblemished moral record, using the minimizing term "purloining" to describe Cayley's intellectual theft. Gibbs-Smith does not seem to have pursued Robert Taylor much beyond determining that Taylor failed to patent anything under his name in New York State and so seems not to have developed his inventions concerning flight or anything else. Without much of a struggle, and perhaps not a little relief, the premier aviation historian of his age leaves further investigation into who Taylor was, where he came from, or where he went well enough alone. Gibbs-Smith concludes his discussion of the whole affair by saying, "It is hoped that some trace of Taylor may turn up in the future. . . ." Fortunately, in my quest to carry the ball forward another yard or two, I had an aid I suspect my predecessor would never have contemplated: the Internet.

The great thing about the Internet is that it is an unconstrained, easily accessible, almost infinitely cross-connected matrix of information about just about everything. The worst thing about the Internet is exactly the same thing. I started with Wikipedia (an excellent first source) where I found nothing about Taylor. I then tried the Google search engine and of course there were 11,500 hits because the Internet is dominated by the English language and American culture, and the name "Robert B Taylor" is common in both. I started adding terms to limit the number of hits, terms derived from what we know about Taylor. I tried his name plus "flight," and then "Cayley," and then "convertiplane," and then "aviation" – then patents and flying and propellers and counter-rotation and New York and Bolton and Mary (his sister's name) and all the other potential proper noun combinations sourced from Taylor's letters that might cut down the hit list to a manageable size. I was still poring through thousands of returns and just about to give up on the shotgun approach and do some proper, subject-specific searching of some real archives when I suddenly found a little local history site in the United Kingdom which said:

> Warrington Academy – Many gentlemen of the medical profession have passed through a complete course of academic learning at Warrington previous to their commencement of the study of physics at university, e.g. Dr. Fair of Bristol, Dr. Parry of Cirencester, Dr. Percival of Manchester, Dr. Taylor of Bolton . . .

And that seems interesting. Robert Taylor had mentioned that his father was a doctor from Bolton and that this father knew of Cayley. So here we had a Dr. Taylor from Bolton who passed through the same kind of institution – the Dissenting Academy of Warrington – that Cayley's tutor (and father-in-law) had attended and even helped run. I pulled this thread with another couple of related searches and up popped another reference:

Taylor, Robert Eveleigh
British physician
An inaugural disputation, concerning the varieties of the
human race, July 1800. 1 vol. (34 pp.). Translated into
English by John Brandreth, 1830.

This is Taylor's dissertation for the degree of Doctor
of Medicine from the University of Edinburgh. It was
published in Latin (Edinburgh, 1800), and Brandreth
made this English translation for a friend later.

Accessioned, 1974
(572.0 T2Li.b)

Now I had Dr. Taylor's full name, including a rather unusual
middle name – and also a connection to Scotland. With the
new terms, I searched some more and within a minute I hit
the jackpot. A certain Jesse Taylor Wallace had posted a
message in 2001 on a genealogical website:

Seek descendants of Robert Eveleigh and Charlotte
(Balshaw) Taylor. Robert (1773–1827) and Charlotte
(1782–1868) arrived from "Bolton-le Moors," Lancashire,
England on 6 Oct 1819 with children: John, Robert,
Franck, Henry, William, Mary and Elizabeth. Last child,
Hudson, born in Poughkeepsie, Dutchess Co., NY. They
were active members of Christ Episcopal Church,
Poughkeepsie. I am a descendant of Franck.

And the facts all matched – the date of emigration (1819),
the father with a son called Robert, and most importantly *also*

a sister Mary, and they *are* in New York State – all mentioned in Robert B. Taylor's letter to Cayley in 1842. There was even a nice little coincidence – Dr. Taylor and Cayley shared the same year of birth so in age at least they were exact contemporaries. More importantly, though four years old, the website message also included a return e-mail address for Jesse Wallace. I sent off a note saying we might be interested in the same guy. In the meantime I had more clues here – the name "Hudson Taylor" (the youngest and American-born son) was a little unusual. The Internet was alive with the name Hudson Taylor! He was an evangelical American of British heritage who went to the Far East to preach the Christian faith. He seemed a fascinating guy – he was one of the first of his profession to assimilate himself into the local culture rather than trying to Westernize it. I soon found out, though, that this is the *wrong* Hudson Taylor, not the American-born son of Dr. Taylor at all but someone else born in England who left to live in America before going to China.

And then I checked my e-mail, and there was a message from Jesse Wallace of Rochester, Minnesota, getting back to me about my earlier message.

Good Morning Richard,

I am indeed interested in Dr. Robert Eveleigh Taylor. He was my G-G-G-Grandfather. I have only recently found some new information on his death, so I am excited that you might have even more information about him.

He did have a son named Robert Burns Taylor, born 8 May 1808, at Bolton-le-Moor, Lancashire, England. I am totally unaware of his designing a flying machine in 1842 and would be very interested in more information on the

subject. I have to admit that I have never heard of Sir
George Cayley. I will check him out after I send this off.
Please let me know what would be of interest to you.
Best wishes,
Jess

So his full name was Robert *Burns* Taylor – the circle was
squared with the Scottish connection – his father's medical
education in Edinburgh was reflected in the choice of the
middle name of his son: we have found our man. Robert B.
Taylor was a lawyer of a well-to-do Poughkeepsie family; he
was married to a Susan Ann Burritt on December 18, 1832, in
Poughkeepsie, and had at least one child, a son, who was bap-
tized in 1839 and named after his father. Robert's own father
probably knew Cayley through his associations with the
Dissenting Academy. Son Robert apparently kept his interest
in flight a secret from everyone except his father, George
Cayley, and those fellow pioneers looking into powered flight
through electro-magnetism. If Taylor's interest ever led to anything material in the way of aviation or other inventions, it's
not readily apparent from what I've found so far.

This sleuthing took just a little under two hours, solving a
160-year-old mystery and I never moved from my seat. All
thanks to Jess Wallace from Rochester.

12

THE BOY CARRIER

The push that Cayley always seemed to need to launch himself into a new project came from a number of different sources over the years. Sometimes it was a local or national need: for increased food production, for calming the rioting worker, for defence or public safety. On other occasions, Cayley's actions were simply in response to someone publishing on topics Cayley felt were his own. Following his less-than-appealing behaviour in the Taylor and Henson episodes, one might think that the repercussions within aviation might have provided Cayley's next external prod. Instead the motivation came about through events much closer to home. The circumstances are recorded through a typical entry dated 1848 from the Cayley family archive as his daughter Emma invites her relations to a quintessentially English event:

> July 21 Wydale
> My dear Father and Mother will you come here on Tuesday next to see a Cricket Match played. It will give us great pleasure if you can come.
> I am your affectionate daughter
>
> Emma Cayley

Our Luncheon is at 2. If you come you should come in and stay in your carriage on the cricket ground. As the only means of preventing your getting cold so should Miss P [Miss Phil] and all elderlies.

On the reverse of this simple and wonderfully culture-stamped letter is a brief entry in Cayley's handwriting: "My Dearest Emma's last note – the poor darling died on 2nd August 1848 only 12 days after."

The early months of 1848 must have seemed one of relative tranquillity for Cayley. Mary Agnes was apparently happily married to the "amiable" Dr. Alexander and had produced a healthy daughter Mary, Cayley's seventeenth grandchild. Though Lady Cayley's mental health was poor, it had been so for such a time as to make its familiarity perhaps bearable. Cayley's widowed daughter Kate had remarried into the local Legard dynasty and had settled in, having produced two more grandsons for Cayley to entertain with his repertoire of conjuring tricks. In fact, all of Cayley's family seemed established in their own pattern of life and seemed, on the surface at least, content enough. Cayley himself was seventy-four but mentally and physically strong. His standing as an aviation authority and as a benefactor for education and learning was at an all-time high. He was also a well-known and well-liked figure in London and Yorkshire society. Cayley had even been recognized by that most enigmatic of organizations when he was elected Master of Scarborough's Old Globe Lodge No. 200 (having been originally elected to the Freemasons back in 1819 just prior to his joining the Whig Party). Cayley could look forward to his autumn years with the satisfaction that his estate and family, their reputation and prospects were in as good a state of health as he was. Though he had a strong and healthy son, Cayley's one regret may have been a lack of an intellectual heir – Digby would not be carrying on his research, and the strictures of contemporary society meant that it would not be appropriate for his daughters to do so. There was, however, another Cayley family member much closer in outlook to the now famous baronet.

The brightest star in the constellation of Cayley's grandchildren was undoubtedly the romantic, multi-talented son of his favourite daughter Emma, the reckless George John Cayley. As early as 1838, at age twelve, he was already writing to his grandfather concerning a familiar Cayley interest: "Papa will not let us shoot bullets except when he is with us but my gun is a cylindrical bore and will shoot shot as well as bullets and I have been out with it today and shot two birds and Ned [his elder brother Edward] shot one. . . ." The letter also discusses another family hobby: "Ned thinks he has invented a new kind of steam engine but I cannot understand it. It is something like this. . . ." The accompanying sketch of Edward's idea for a new source of power is rendered in a fashion that would not look out of place in one of Cayley's early notebooks.

George John's conventional education at England's top-notch Eton College ended rather prematurely at the age of fourteen. He later spoke enthusiastically of his subsequent freedom from the "rustling cloud of dignity and black silk" – the stalking prefects and masters of an institution where corporal punishment was considered more a semi-profession than simply a means of maintaining discipline. Because of concern that such a renegade might fail to find a suitable career, the fifteen-year-old George John was sent to the United States for a three-year visit, staying with the ever-widening international Cayley clan. On his arrival on the new continent, he promptly scaled the Niagara River valley's cliffs just for the thrill of it. The idea behind the visit was for George John to broaden his education but also focus his widely dispersed energies – his grandfather suggested that he use his time there to study the china trade, a booming business at the time. During this period, George John even sent his grandfather an illustration of his own ideas on a flying machine, one that was kept aloft by leg-driven flappers. Cayley must have been ecstatic. More of

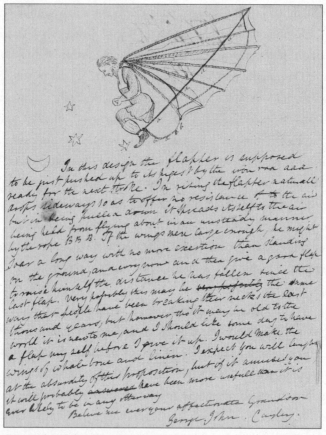

George John Cayley's letter dated 1842 (he was sixteen): proving himself to be a chip off his grandfather's block with his design for leg-powered flappers.

George John's written output, this time a diary detailing his time as an invoice clerk working for John Goodhue of South Street, Manhattan, later found its way into the archives of the New York Historical Society.

On his return to Britain in 1845, the eager young man revisited formal education at Cambridge, where his time centred largely on poetry: he won the chancellor's gold medal for his poem "The Death of Baldur" (the near-indestructible Norse god with a vulnerability to mistletoe). Other of his verses show George John being a little too preoccupied with concerns regarding the reputation of a favoured grandparent and a perhaps less-than-popular recent addition to the Cayley family in the doctor James Alexander:

> Our baronets of late appear to be
>> Unjustly snubbed and talked and written down;
>> Partly from follies of Sir Something Brown,
> Stickling for badges due to their degree,
>> And partly that their honour's late editions
>> Have been much swelled with surgeons and physicians . . .

By the time he was an adult, George John was being described as a striking-looking (but not exactly handsome) daredevil. Though only twenty-two years old by 1848, he had already travelled widely and had shown a clear affinity for informal but voracious self-education. George John was also the keenest of all Cayley's relations when it came to the subject of flight and mechanics. He had inherited his mother's brains and courage and his grandfather's thirst for knowledge and skill with tools. His father, Edward Stillingfleet Cayley, was no slouch either when it came to contributing to his son's education. In addition to the U.S. trip, Edward encouraged his son to take three extended visits with a French colleague during which the Cayley/ Seton/Walker genetic talent for languages had ample time to develop; by his early twenties, George John was fluent in English, French, and Andalusian Spanish.

George John never graduated from Cambridge University, but instead quit his studies there sometime in mid-1848. He entered a new branch of education after being accepted in November 1848 by the Inner Temple law school, where he studied alongside his elder brother Edward, who had started there in May of that year. George John's change in career from poet to lawyer may have been related to the death of his mother in the summer and a need to find a new focus for his energies. Fortunately, the workload to qualify for his new profession would not prevent him from pursuing other interests. Even though George John became a barrister in November 1852, such an impressive-sounding credential does not imply serious study. As long as an accepted student completed nine minor law exercises and, more importantly, had paid for a total of twelve Inn's hall dinners, anyone over the age of twenty-one was entitled to practise at the Bar. However, legal advocacy would not be where George John's future lay.

At the sudden and unexpected loss of his mother in August 1848, George John returned home immediately. Emma was a gentle and empathetic woman who possessed no mean talent as a painter and sculptor. She was also a calming influence on Lady Sarah, despite and perhaps because of her willingness to confront the issue of her mother's temper. Aside from the mournful annotation attached to her final note to her father, the only other surviving description of her death comes in the form of a letter written by Cayley to his long-serving solicitor Arthur Simpson in which Cayley notes the need to amend his will on account of "poor Mrs. Cayley's death." Though reeling from the loss of his favourite daughter, Cayley sought to fill the void left in the highly strung George John. Cayley decided to engage the energies of his grandson (along with his faithful engineer-in-residence Thomas Vick) by embarking on one final series of flying experiments. For the first time, there was a pair of Cayleys set to the task of building an airplane. At last Cayley had what approached an intellectual soulmate in his work.

After his downbeat reaction to Henson's proposals for the Aerial Steam Carriage and the disingenuous communications with Robert Taylor, it would be nice to think that Cayley's burst of energy from 1848 was of a more positive nature. Certainly the newly formed three-man team working at Brompton set about their task with a vigour and singleness of purpose that had been missing from Cayley's solo research for the last thirty years. This turning point was marked by Cayley starting a new notebook, entitled "Egypt." In fact, *Egypt* starts with a brief note on aviation dated June 1848, shortly before Emma's death; the entry was a reference to some independent research Cayley had found concerning resistance of air that matched his own earlier findings. This initial nudge was followed by the trauma of Emma's death, causing Cayley to want to occupy both his own time and that of George John in an aviation endeavour on the grandest scale so far. As we would expect, *Egypt* inevitably diverges into a dozen other subjects, starting with a lengthy evaluation on the effectiveness of transplanted wheat and matters agricultural before it returns to aviation with an entry dated November 29. Here Cayley records the dimensions of a recently shot magpie and "a small yellow brown goose hawk or sparrow hawk (I don't know which)." In between these early summer and late autumn dates there had been a cottage industry in Brompton support-ing Cayley's work. Another Cayley grandson, Henry Frederick Beaumont, spent considerable time in Brompton following his own father's death in 1838. Henry Frederick recalled the summer in which Cayley recruited Henry and as many villagers as he could muster for them to reproduce, feather by feather, a scaled-up, canvas replica of a goose wing – most likely another woeful design on the Degen flap-valve principle. Cayleys were being conscripted en masse for the construction phase of what became his most successful flying experiments.

During the course of 1848 and early 1849, Cayley and his team embarked on an intense period of design and construction. Labour was distributed largely along the lines of seniority: Cayley was the chief designer and works manager, George John the eager apprentice, while Vick carried on with his usual role of doing most of the grunt work of manufacture while applying his long-procured experi-ence as a fabricator of practical, working machines. Perhaps it was the increased nervous energy of both grandfather and grandson that made this a uniquely productive period for the Brompton team, the work being a means of escaping the early traumas of the Alexander affair and residual effects of Emma's death. For whatever reason, the group generated a series of increasingly extraordinary components and eventually completed an aircraft with the singular intention of taking off. During this time Cayley sketched the blueprints for his first full-scale practical flyer since his glider of forty years before.

This new vehicle was a culmination of Cayley's work on the raft of design and technology challenges he'd faced throughout the years: the

The most complete and illuminating sketch of the boy-carrier found in the *Egypt* notebook but which was almost certainly copied from a more detailed schematic now sadly lost. The flapping wings are roughly included along with all the required mechanisms for flight. The upper rudder/elevator could be fixed before flight to "trim" the craft for the required descent, the adjustable rudder/elevator below allowing smaller in-flight corrections.

undercarriage, the dihedral configuration, the multi-plane wing, the streamlined fuselage, and, of course, flappers for propulsion. Cayley roughly sketched these in loose sheets and then took the next necessary step and built the machine that was the sum of his life's work. But he knew that the whole issue of flight rested on the opponent principles of weight and power, so in the absence of a motor to push his craft through the air, he played with the opposite side of the equation by reducing the bulk of the machine and the size of its passenger. So the first man to fly in a specifically designed heavier-than-air machine wasn't a man at all, but a boy.

Exactly when the flight took place is uncertain. What *is* known is that some time in mid-1849 a machine was ready to enter the annals of history as "the boy-carrier." Only a few details of the flight survive, but that some successful flight took place is as verifiable as we could hope for because it is commented on in a dated letter from friend and fellow flying enthusiast Charles Clark writing from Great Footham Hall on June 12, 1849.

> I have never been able to meet with such success as you appear to have met with when experimenting with the boy. Poor fellow. I dare say he feared the fate of some of our earlier aeronauts. I should much like to learn the principles by which this was accomplished, if there is no danger, my dear Sir, of interfering with your patent!

Most importantly, Cayley himself describes the flight and the boy-carrier itself in his correspondence of 1853 with Jules François Dupuis-Delcourt, airship designer and founder of the world's first aeronautical group: Société Aérostatique et Métérologique de France.

In his later cross-channel correspondence Cayley tells Dupuis-Delcourt,

A few years ago, I made the apparatus, the framework of which is represented . . . [in Cayley's accompanying line drawing] . . . but from having my time much occupied with perfecting the air engine as a motive power, combining *lightness* with *energy*, which I consider the point on which efficient aerial navigation now rests, and from the difficulties arising in the way of trying the experiment, I have never had the opportunity of testing the wing waftage. The balance and steerage was ascertained, and a boy about ten years of age was floated off the ground for several yards on descending a hill, and also for about the same space by some persons pulling the apparatus against a slight breeze by rope.

From this account we can deduce that although flappers may have been fitted, the boy in questions either could (or would) not use them as the propulsive mechanism. Quite by accident, then, the boy-carrier's flight transforms from being a rather ill-considered experiment into the application of flappers into a far more useful and, in hindsight, much more relevant exploration of the aerodynamic qualities of history's second successful glider "hop." Since the experiment included another brief flight as a result of being pulled into the air, this also counts as the world's first-ever towed-launch glider flight.

As with so many of the Cayley flying incidents, there is no surviving description of the event (if one *ever* existed), and we have to piece together the facts from the disparate fragments that have been preserved. We can be assured that some flight occurred, but what the reaction to it was, from either Cayley, George John, Vick, or even the hapless young pilot, remains unknown. In a way this is hardly a surprise – though these events are in retrospect historic, they fell far short of Cayley's expectations. These minor successes were simply not enough to be counted by him as major breakthroughs, so they remained largely uncommented on and the machines involved were either cannibalized for reuse or left to rot. (The Wright brothers were similarly unsentimental about their machines. Their first successful glider was abandoned on a Kitty Hawk sand dune, though at least the sateen fabric from the wing was used by the locals as dressmaking material.) Not even Cayley's notebooks provide any description of flights themselves but instead they record the details of calculations and considerations that led up to specific aircraft builds or else the results from previous testing. These were not diaries or daily journals, but acted as a technical *aide-mémoire* for later work or else a record of the almost random series of ideas that occurred to him over time. It seems almost by chance that Cayley saw fit to correspond on the matter with Charles Clark and later Dupuis-Delcourt. There is a similar lack of detail concerning many incidental characters in Cayley's work. The name of the boy who flew is not recorded; he could have been a relative – more likely he was the eager offspring of a High Hall servant or Brompton tenant. Like the bruised child-aviator of Cayley's 1809 flyer, this pioneer joined the nameless ranks of those who flew a little, but neither so well nor so far as to warrant being identified.

As part of Cayley's ethical rehabilitation from the Henson and Taylor incidents, the descriptions of the boy-carrier flight illustrate a welcome return to the understated, honest, and realistic appraisals of his endeavours that had so typified Cayley's earlier written works. Though this undertaking was no doubt a step forward, Cayley makes no great claims for it being anything special and even seems to play down the whole affair as being simply a flight "over several yards." Whatever had encouraged him to act with less than professionalism in his dealings with Taylor seems to have been replaced with an equal and opposite wish to see his work honestly appraised. In any case, this was only the start; this first flying experience drove Cayley and his helpers forward, and in many ways they were just hitting their stride.

In 1849 Cayley extended his long line of flying models with the construction of a new and larger machine. The latest in the series remained,
even if scaled down, of impressive size, being over fourteen feet long.
Cayley also trusted it with a notably wider, though still relatively stubby
wing. This design change is perhaps the result of his exposure to the
dimensions of Henson's Ariel Carriage or of his revisiting his earlier
conclusion that a slender wing was best for "skimming" flight with the
model being a way of testing that supposition. The result was a flying
model with a much improved gliding ratio: the glider would travel much
farther horizontally for any given descent. Cayley later revisited this
model design in 1853, developing another flyer with a wing now over six
and a half feet wide. The later glider has an angled tail plane and a
separate upward-pointing "riding" rudder. This machine, weighing 16
pounds, was nearly 16 feet long and capable of gliding a distance of up
to eight times its vertical fall. It is the most elegant and sophisticated aviation model Cayley ever produced.

John Sproule 1970s replica of the riding rudder glider from the *Egypt* notebook hanging
from the ceiling of the Westminster University – the modern incarnation of the Royal
Polytechnic Institution.

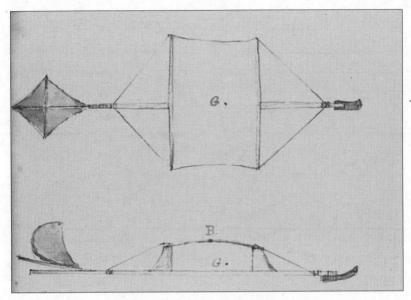

Cayley's 1853 "riding-rudder" glider.

After the success of the boy-carrying craft, but the abject failure of the boy-powered flappers, Cayley briefly returned to an earlier idea concerning how to propel his new machines through the air. Perhaps in desperation over the lack of progress in both lightweight steam and hot-air power plants, Cayley returned to an idea from a half-century before, that of using gunpowder as a fuel, and its explosive action as the means to push a flapper up and down. To test the idea, he drew up plans for a "model apparatus" to see if this quick-and-dirty solution could get a powered machine off the ground. There is no evidence to suggest that the gunpowder-fuelled model was ever built or flown. It may be that the limited number of flapping strokes the engine could produce meant that, even on a small scale, such a machine would be as impractical as it was dangerous. This purely theoretical model also includes his new design for flappers. They now form a concertina-like corrugation through a series of oblique hinges along the flapper's edge

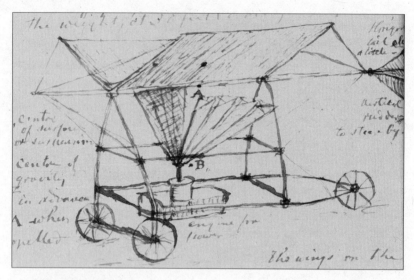

The gunpowder-engined monoplane – the world's first design for a powered flying model.

to increase their pushing surface area in an attempt to generate greater forward thrust for the few downward beats the gunpowder engine might have been able to generate.

Based on his experience with boy-carriers and models, Cayley returned to the laboratory to examine the lifting characteristics of larger wings as well as what has been referred to as "the world's first experiments in streamlining in the service of aeronautics." This involved calculating the drag of differing designs for aircraft components and was conducted on Cayley's new whirling arm of July 1850. This experimental apparatus was his most sophisticated and the one on the largest scale, allowing experimentation on planes and aircraft components of up to ten square feet. Once more, the only details to survive are the volumes of data generated through weeks of research. In all probability this work was conducted by George John and Cayley within the confines of High Hall's stairwell, the site of his first rotational experiments some fifty years before.

During early 1851, George John was preparing for another extended trip abroad, this time to travel the bridle roads of Spain (the title of the book he published on his adventures following his return). Before George John left, he and Cayley spent time together in London visiting the spectacular Great Exhibition housed in the new Crystal Palace. Both men may have been interested in the display of John Stringfellow's wire-supported flying model that was one of the exhibits, though there is no record of them commenting on it. The only mention of the events concerning the exhibition itself refer to the jewel in the crystal crown – the Koh-i-noor ("Mountain of Light") diamond that had been recently acquired (under highly questionable circumstances) from the estate of the Sikh Maharaja of Punjab, Ranjit Singh. The diamond was a "gift" from the recently conquered Punjabi people to the woman who was later crowned (if only in name) Victoria, Empress of India. Koh-i-noor was the major attraction of the exhibition and Cayley sketched it in his *Egypt* notebook, copying the diamond's dimensions from the picture in the *Illustrated Evening News*.

Following George John's departure abroad in the autumn of 1851, Cayley turned from the highly practical experimentation with wing and whirling arm to a mundane, though more important aspect of research: publishing papers. Cayley is momentarily diverted by an article in the *Mechanic's Magazine* concerning John Luntley's suggestion for a rotating balloon. In his brief response to Luntley's idea, Cayley's own *Mechanic's* article of October 1851 includes suggested improvement to the idea, but really this is Cayley keeping his finger on the pulse of publication. He is about to produce his definitive flying design, and this time it would be all his own work.

On Saturday September 25, 1852, the *Mechanic's Magazine, museum, register, journal and gazette* no. 1520 (still only threepence, though a penny more for delivery) placed on its front cover "Sir George Cayley's Governable Parachute." As Cayley was one of its most eminent and regular contributors, we would expect him to receive this kind of prominence from the *Mechanic's* editorial board. It couldn't have hurt that the journal's editor-in-chief was now J.C. Robertson, the man who had so obsequiously written to Cayley during the best-forgotten Robert Taylor incident. In spite of any potential nepotism concerning the publication, Cayley's new machine is nothing short of dazzling. What makes this new flyer so remarkable is the cleanness of the design and the absence of much in the way of distracting flappers. In essence, this is the very first practicable full-scale man-carrying glider, but beyond that, it is the culmination of Cayley's more than forty years of publication and musings captured in a single vehicle.

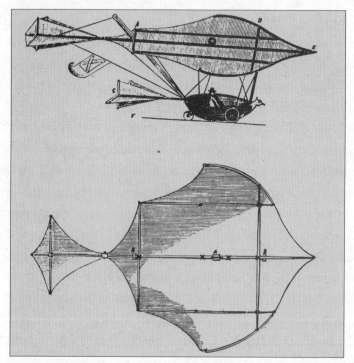

Cayley's governable parachute of 1852. The irritating detail of flag and eagle head may not have been Cayley's idea, but everything else concerned with this extraordinary vehicle certainly was.

As befits his most remarkable publication, this one's external prod, was equally noteworthy. The French aeronautress Madame Poitevin had made a name for herself sitting astride her pony Blanche as they rose several thousand feet suspended from a hot air balloon above Paris. When her attempts to do the same with a bull fell foul of the French authorities, she and her equally adventurous husband had crossed the channel in the hope of English fame and fortune. Her plan to descend by parachute from a balloon raised howls of protest from the London press. Though her announced descent was finally cancelled, by then the news surrounding it had done the job as far as Cayley was concerned, and he put pen to paper.

In the opener to his *Mechanic's* paper Cayley refers obliquely to the whole Poitevin business and then segues effortlessly into his own ideas on the parachuting principle:

> Sir, as the subject of parachutes again attracts the public attention permit me to suggest what would be an interesting addition to the mere hackneyed fact of their descent – their steerage from the moment they are liberated from the balloon to any desired landing-place, within about five to six times the distance horizontally that the balloon is then above the earth.

Cayley then continues to deliver the detailed construction of the vehicle. The all-up weight of the whole machine would be 150 pounds, with the expectation of the same weight again for the pilot, all suspended beneath the 467 square feet of wing area. Such a large supporting sail required each square foot to lift much less than the 1 pound of his earliest machines, giving this new glider a much-improved glide ratio. Cayley states that as well as travelling horizontally, his "parachute" would also be falling vertically through the air, though at a more than survivable "16 1/4 feet per second, which would be equivalent to jumping off an eminence 4 feet high." The vehicle's forward speed would be the Cayley standard 30 feet per second (around 21 miles per hour). He describes how the larger, topmost rudder would be preset before flight to act as a "trimming" surface to "give a straight and steady steerage. . . . It gives the most steady and secure course when slightly elevated, which also tends to secure the parachute from pitching. . . ." The action of the lower pilot-operated rudder/elevator is also described: "The smaller movable rudder . . . is sufficient to effect at will the steerage of the parachute and to elevate or depress its course when occasion requires, or preparatory to alighting to the ground" – another reference to the need to "flare" the glider on landing (first mentioned in the paper of 1810). With an eye to not confusing the reading audience, Cayley explains that his illustration is drawn with the top wing appearing flat though it would actually have the now standard dihedral V-shape: "This form, like the elevation of the rudder, tends powerfully to right the parachute in all cases of accidental disturbance."

Of course it wouldn't be a Cayley paper if it didn't contain a detour, and this one was no exception. The first non sequitur concerns how balloon steerage could be achieved by using a complete governable parachute slung underneath the balloon to act as an inclined plane to control motion vertically, with an additional rudder on the balloon itself for left-right movement. A second false step is a casual description of the wing-folding "umbrella plane," which may or may not have been such a good idea; from the simple illustration and even scantier description, it probably isn't.

Cayley then considers the safety requirement of testing his machines, a matter that preyed heavily on his mind as "no human lives should be put to hazard in these parachutes, until a considerable series of descents have been made with dead weights, exceeding that of the person wishing to try the experiment." He continues with the need to similarly test the trimming mechanisms of the larger rudder, and the controlling sensitivity of the smaller, pilot-operated control surface. He concludes with his statutory lament concerning the lack of an engine for flight, the now customary flip-flopping between flappers and propellers, ending with a typically upbeat (and slightly over-optimistic) message for the future:

> It need scarcely be further remarked that were we in possession of a sufficiently light first mover to propel such a vehicle by waftage, either on the screw principle or otherwise, with such power as to supply that force horizontally, which gravitation here supplies in descent, mechanical aerial navigation would be at our command without further delay.

Readers wishing further information are then referred to his first paper on aerial navigation of 1810, and at this point Cayley's final British publication on the subject of flight abruptly comes to an end. What an exit. As well as being the paper with the lowest gaffe-to-greatness ratio, it is by far Cayley's most elegantly designed machine, and the clarity of his explanation borders on the sublime. It is the crowning glory of his aviation publications, and it was promptly forgotten about by everyone for over a hundred years. There are no references to the governable parachute and no developments on the principles it contains for reasons that will never be adequately explained. Perhaps it was just one of those unhappy situations where nobody who could appreciate or apply its remarkable prescience either read the article or heard about it. Once more it was the archival terrier Gibbs-Smith who uncovered Cayley's work and announced it to the rather limited world of aviation in the 1960s. This final *Mechanic's Magazine* article was not, however, Cayley's final publication altogether.

During the summer of 1853, Cayley produced a series of papers and an eye-catching set of illustrations for publication in the French

Bulletin Trimestriel – Les Annales d'Aérostation et de Météologique.
Unfortunately what is most eye-catching about them is the level of
sophistication and elegance with which Cayley had developed the
flapping ideas of his long-time hero, Jacob Degen. These papers form
another treasure trove of Cayley's thoughts on everything from
balloon flight to weather prediction, but the speculative adventure of
publication in general and aviation publications in particular meant
that the *Bulletin* went out of business before most of Cayley's submis-
sions saw light of day. The much more significant role of these papers
is that through the correspondence between Cayley and the French
editor, we are able to determine when and how Cayley took his
final step on the flying stage. He'd designed and built models and
boy-carriers, done the math, examined the means of constructing
something light and strong, tested it in his circular, whirling wind
tunnel, so all he had to do now was finish it up and make a man fly.

Finding the Pieces VIII – Everyone Did It First

Although the process of invention may be "80 per cent perspiration and 20 per cent inspiration" (Thomas Edison), the math involved in staking a claim to exclusive intellectual ownership of an idea is considerably more involved. When it comes to such a multifaceted machine as the airplane, the devil in the detail makes any one individual's claim to having invented all of it a tough judgement call.

Take, for instance, Emanuel Swedenborg (1688–1772). He was a man who died just a year before Cayley's birth, and as everyone in Scandinavia knows he invented the airplane. His manuscript in *Daedalus Hyperboreus* of 1716 describes sophisticated spring-assisted and cleverly self-folding flappers and a semi-separate wing that has been claimed by some as the first design for a winged aircraft. Swedenborg even suggested having a swinging bob-weight underneath the plane to provide "pendulum stability." Though this idea was a lot less practical than Cayley's alternative suggestion of the V-shaped dihedral wing configuration (a discovery that survives today), Swedenborg had recognized the issue and come up with an alternative answer to it fifty years prior to Cayley. Swedenborg even thought of putting wheels on his vehicle, thus inventing the wheeled undercarriage. To cap it all, Swedenborg suggested testing the whole thing as a ballasted glider rather than heading for nearest cliff and strapping himself in, thus making himself the first person to seriously consider flight testing. The reason this book is about Cayley and not about our newly introduced Swede is that Swedenborg never actually *did* any of the above. Like da Vinci, he just talked a good airplane, but he never built it and he never flew one. Also until recently few people seemed to have heard of Swedenborg or his work, so his impact on the early development of flight was at best slight and in most cases nonexistent. Though potentially a first, Swedenborg is hardly the most influential. The problem with invention is that jingoism, national pride, and the need for iconic individuals who somehow embody those ideals combine with the smokescreen of the fame factory to make finding out who exactly did exactly what unknowable. So who really invented the airplane?

The French have Clément Agnès Ader and the propeller-powered *Avion III*, which to this day hangs proudly from the ceiling in the Musée des Arts et Métiers in Paris as demonstrable evidence of this Gallic wonder being number one on the flight stakes in 1897. Then there's New Zealander Richard William Pearse, the man of near clinical shyness, so backward in coming forward that he dared not tell a living soul of his powered flying experiments during March of 1903 (nine months before the Wrights' first powered flight). Of course if you're Brazilian, then it was Alberto Santos-Dumont who did it first flying his *Bis 14* in 1906 (three years *after* the Wrights). And Germany (Poland really) has the brothers Otto and Gustav Lilienthal. Otto was without doubt the first to demonstrate a practical, robust, and reusable glider, and he conducted thousands of flights before being killed in a gliding accident in 1896.

Everyone in Russia knows that it was Captain Alexander F. Mozhaiski's steam-powered monoplane that was the first to fly in St. Petersburg in 1884 and not the Wright brothers. But then if you read very carefully you'll find that no one said the

Otto Lilienthal on one of his more than two thousand glider flights.

Wright brothers *were* the first to fly or even the first to accomplish powered flight or build an airplane. They were the first to achieve "sustained" and "controlled" flight that was "heavier than air" and "powered." You need all four to qualify, though who it was that decided the criteria I just don't know. The Wrights built the first *practical* powered plane; maybe that's what we mean.

But they all did *something* first – they all contributed a piece or two. Putting all the pieces together is what any invention is all about.

13

LAST FLIGHT

If you search for Sir George Cayley on the Internet, or look inside
any of countless books on early flight or aerodynamics, the story of
the flying coachman will most likely be either the only Cayley incident
related in detail or the one given most prominence. A number of different versions of the incident exist but as with all such tales what we
would really like is a first-hand account. Miraculously one of these
appears to have survived. Mrs. Dora Thompson was the granddaughter
of Cayley through his son, Digby, and she was a resident in High Hall
from her birth in 1844 until shortly before her marriage in 1870. At
some point she decided to record her memories of the coachman flight
in a letter and her eyewitness testimony can be found in the 1926 book
The Legards of Anlaby and Ganton: Their Neighbours and Neighbourhood.
This account of the Legard family, into which Cayley's daughter Kate
had remarried, is written by Kate's son Colonel Sir James Digby Legard.
As both are grandchildren of Cayley, this makes Sir James and Dora
first cousins, though there is no evidence to suggest that they ever dated.
In his chapter dedicated to the Cayley family, Sir James quotes Dora's
account verbatim:

> I have scratched my memory as to the date of his flying machine,
> which I saw fly across the dale. It was 1852 or 1853. Of course,

everyone was out on the high east side and saw the start from close to. The coachman went in the machine and landed on the west side at about the same level. I think it came down rather a shorter distance than expected. The coachman got himself clear, and when the watchers had got across he shouted "Please Sir George, I wish to give notice. I was hired to drive, and not to fly" (of course in broad Yorkshire). That's all I recollect. The machine was put away in the barn, and I used to sit and hide in it (from Governess) when I was so inspired.

This account seems both unambiguous and compelling. Cayley must have built the glider that he had described in his final *Mechanic's* article of 1852, and, just as he had said he would, he sought to test it on a sloping hill before dropping it from a balloon. In part as a result of the comical quality of the story, in part because of the remarkable and counterintuitive nature of the event (manned heavier-than-air flight exactly fifty years before the Wrights), the coachman incident has lodged itself within the aviation psyche and has passed from legend into historical record. Even the aviation historian Gibbs-Smith, our trusty guide for much of the exploration of Cayley's technical work, began not by examining the facts behind the story, but one step beyond, assuming it had happened, and deducing everything else from there. It doesn't appear that anyone has gone back and checked how well the coachman tale holds water. As with so many good stories, while attending to the detail, a faint dripping sound becomes apparent.

We can start by looking at the internal consistency of the Dora account. First there is the date, and in this we seem to be on solid ground, at least as far as the events having transpired in the second of her two alternative years, 1853. Cayley and his team were hard at work during this period, George John had returned from his equestrian adventures in Spain, and Cayley had recently engaged in a detailed correspondence with his aviation counterparts in France. Cayley's correspondence dated June 22, 1853, refers to not only the boy-carrier flight having taken place, but also to his future intentions: "I will again attend to this machine and report any facts of interest which may occur." Early summer 1853 is therefore some years *after* the boy-carrier flight but also clearly *before* his attempt at flight carrying a full-sized man or else Cayley would most certainly have said something about it to his French opposite number. Also there is a detailed entry in Cayley's *Egypt* notebook noting the weights and dimensions of a "new flyer" (assumed to be a development of the boy-carrier), which are dated August 25, 1853. All indications, therefore, point toward this being when it happened; Dora seems to have hit the date on the head.

Then there is Dora's sentence "The coachman went in the machine and landed on the west side at about the same level." This is clearly a mistake, though perhaps a forgivable one. No glider of any kind can take off and hope to fly horizontally. In fact, Cayley's reference to these craft as parachutes rather than gliders is, ironically, more accurate in conveying this fact. The only possibility that Dora's account is accurate would be if Cayley tow-launched his machine head-on into a strong headwind. This seems highly unlikely because of his oft-repeated concerns for safety as well as his habit of testing gliders in either still or very gently moving air. But it is understandable that it might appear, in the excitement of the moment, that level flight had been achieved – especially when one bears in mind that Dora was a nine- or ten-year-old at the time, an issue we will return to later.

The identity of the pilot also seems to make sense. As has been pointed out by Gibbs-Smith, someone familiar with mastering horses would perhaps be the kind of dexterous and physically robust character needed at the helm of the machine's first flight. Wilbur Wright later compared flying to riding a "fractious horse" so the parallel seems an apt one. Dora's quote as to why the frightened first pilot was quitting his job on the spot seems confirmation of his profession – as well as providing the neatest of anecdotal punchlines. The final detail, that of the glider having been put away in a barn where the young Dora would go to escape her teacher, is also partially corroborated from independent sources, as well as having the air of honesty about it. All in all, it seems that Dora's recollections quoted in her cousin's book seem to be standing up well to scrutiny. However, it turns out that this is not Dora's only recording of the facts, and an alternative and, most importantly, original account in her own hand has survived. With its inclusion, things get a little murkier.

The second source of Dora's experiences is contained in her letter dated November 2, 1921, addressed to "Mrs. Hodgson." The recipient is assumed to be the mother of John Hodgson, the first in a short line of Cayley champions and the man who first sought to promote his cause in the early 1920s. The letter is handwritten by Dora who was seventy-six at the time. It's hard to read (in places it's impossible) and made even more difficult by the annotations in the script made later by someone else in pen and pencil. It is only when you see the original, now carefully preserved in the Royal Aeronautical Society archives, that the significance of these later additions becomes apparent. Quoted here, the non-original annotations are in bold and placed within curlicues. Included in square brackets is a best attempt at clarifying some of the meaning of the original, hastily written letter.

2nd Nov {**1921**} {**Coachman Story**}
Southwood, Rhos-on-Sea, Colwyn Bay, N. Wales.
Dear Mrs Hodgson,
. . . I hope I may be useful in sending you a short acct of my grandfather Sir George Cayley's aeroplane efforts of 100 years ago – up to 1856 – when he died – so as to be a help to your son . . . and he will be able to get on [with] the 2nd little pamphlet for aviators early in

258 THE MAN WHO DISCOVERED FLIGHT

May . . . I remember that in later times hearing of a large machine being started on the high side of the valley behind Brompton Hall where he lived & the footman ["footman" crossed out, and in pencil {coachman} inserted above it] being sent out in it & it flew across the little valley about 500 yards at most & came down with a smack what the motive force was I don't know but i think the footman ["footman" crossed out and in pencil {coachman} inserted above it] was the moving element & the result was his capsize & the rush of the watchers across to his rescue – He struggled up – & said – "Please, Sir George, I wish to give notice. I was hired to drive not to fly." This of course in the broadest Yorkshire dialect which I can speak but not write! To carry on the story to present times – one of my nephews who had command [of] a flying line flew down from Scotland & landed on the very spot his great grandfather had for his experiments! I think that's all I can tell you . . .
Dora Thompson
Forgive the mistakes – I was writing in the dark!

This account, in Dora's own handwriting, is singularly less assured than the one reproduced by Sir James, even though his book *Legards of Anlaby and Ganton* was published five years after the date of this surviving letter. This second account doesn't start very well – it gets Cayley's year of death wrong (he died in December 1857) – but then we come to a crunch line. Dora does not claim to be an eyewitness to the flight at all, but says, "I remember that in later times hearing of a large machine being started on the high side of the valley behind Brompton Hall," suggesting that she was told about the incident after the fact. The following detail of the flight being "500 yards at most" is another of those forgivable exaggerations, but this relatively benign error is bracketed by Dora referring to the pilot as a "footman" not once but twice, and on both occasions the word "coachman" has been added by a later hand – we have no idea whose, though John Hodgson could be a candidate. Bearing in mind Dora's seemingly accurate replication of the quote about "driving not flying," it may be that some helpful later reader is merely correcting what they knew to be what Dora *meant* to write; footmen aren't professional drivers, they are general house servants even if the history of the term "footman" refers to servants whose job was to run alongside their masters' carriage. Perhaps this benign interpretation of the reason for the editing is near the truth, though the presence of the word footmen on two occasions raises the concern that Dora wrote exactly what she had meant to write and some later reader found this awkwardly at odds with the flying coachman legend.

Gibbs-Smith, ever the conscientious historian, includes in his discussion of the incident a quote from Mr. K.H. Hardy, a member of the family that owned land close to Brompton. In a letter to John Hodgson dated 1947, which was later passed on to Gibbs-Smith, Hardy recalls what he knew about Cayley and his flight:

> I have never heard any special information about his activities, but can well remember my grandfather pointing out the spot where he launched an experimental glider, carrying his butler. Some mishap occurred and the butler broke his leg.

So now we have a third account. This time a butler was the passenger, but this seems unlikely because Cayley's butler, James Chancellor, was in his mid-forties in 1853 and likely to be in possession of neither the inclination nor the skills required for piloting. However, we are not at the end of Dora's contribution on the subject, and her closing footnote turns out to be yet another water-muddying addition.

Sometime probably in the early 1920s, John Hodgson sent Dora a copy of an illustration for a Cayley flyer, one that had been included in Cayley's French correspondence of the year in question, 1853. In her reply Dora says, "I think I am right in saying that I saw the said flown across the dale in 1852, when I was nine years old. At any rate it was very like it." The illustration Dora says she recognized is a view of the flyer from below, revealing only the pilot's shoes and two pairs of flappers. You can't see the larger supporting wing or the fuselage, and it appears to have one more wheel than is traditionally associated with the tricycle coachman flyer. And yet Dora still says that this is what she saw fly across the dale. Perhaps she was psychic and could have recognized the plane from such an obscure representation; it's far more likely she gave the answer the enthusiastic Hodgson so obviously wanted to hear.

There is one final documentary thread concerning the coachman flight. This was found by the vigilant Gibbs-Smith in the *Encyclopaedia Britannica*, volume IX of the eighth edition from 1855. It is listed not under aeronautics as one might expect, but in an obscure section

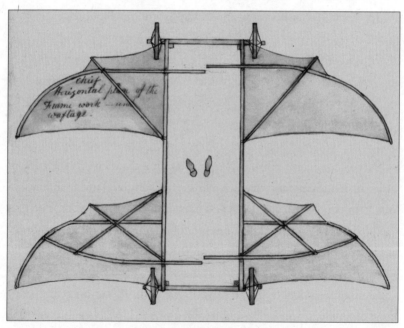

The Cayley flyer that Dora Thompson helpfully identified as flying across Brompton Dale.

labelled "flying," where the article had been languishing, probably unread by anyone, for over a century.

> The flying apparatus constructed by Sir George Cayley can scarcely be considered as a successful experiment, since the wings of that ingenious mechanician acted rather on the principle of the parachute, merely floating the experimenter, who started at a moderate elevation, by very gradual descent towards the earth.

This article is a priceless example of the only near-contemporaneous description of the Brompton Dale flight. It is likely to refer to an actual flight rather than to Cayley's proposals for one (contained within his 1852 paper) because Cayley described the governable parachute as being dropped from a balloon and not "started at a moderate elevation." The *Britannica* article's author appears to have missed the point completely that gliding may have been *exactly* what Cayley had in mind, and so this mighty reference work gains the unique accolade of being the only example of a third party ever criticizing Cayley for *not* attempting to make the wings flap. In its backhanded way the article acts as a much needed independent confirmation that something happened in the early 1850s, but exactly what, and involving whom, we can only speculate. Gibbs-Smith suggests that a Brompton groom who appears in the census return of 1851 could be a contender for pilot because Cayley didn't actually have anyone specifically defined as his coachman. From this supposition, the name John Appleby emerged as a candidate for first adult pilot, and some sources unquestioningly took Gibbs-Smith's guesswork as gospel. Another factoid concerning the coachman flight was born. With the revelation that Dora describes the first airman as a footman, there are even more possible identities for first flyer as at least two footmen were working in High Hall around that time, the forty-seven-year-old John Brown and the twenty-three-year-old Matthew Newby. However there is no evidence, even circumstantial, to suggest that any of these individuals so much as touched the 1853 flyer, never mind piloted it.

If it wasn't the coachman, or the footman, or John Appleby, or even the butler who did it, then who? Suspicion centres on a certain devil-may-care mechanic and horseback adventurer, a flying and Cayley enthusiast – grandson George John.

The idea that George John might have been the man with his hand on the tiller of that first adult flight is not without some support. First, we have an idea of his thirst for adventure, which was evident to the point of foolhardiness – the descriptions of his adventures in the United States, Spain, and the Crimea, and contemporary accounts of his life certainly support it as a dominant characteristic. We also know that George John was not only an active member of the construction team, but positively itching to get the thing in the air. A note from Cayley to Thomas Vick concerning the construction of either the boy-carrier or the "coachman-flyer" was found loose in his correspondence. Which machine it refers to is unknown because the date of the note is infuriatingly illegible and fails to state the year. But whatever it was, it was something big.

> Mr. Vick, If you have not started with the new wheels I think it would be better not to pass the tarred cord through the holes in the wooden rim but to make 8 eyes of iron in the inside and rivet them to a washer on the outside, and then pass the rope through the eyes – thus [Cayley includes a sketch] . . . You must mind, when you couple the flapping wings to the handle that works them, that the connecting rod takes into the butt end of the wing rod at such a distance from the hinge of the wing as to allow the hand of the person working to go through two feet, whilst the tip end of the wing just completes its full range. It is a pity we put the top sail so low, we

should have had 5 or 6 feet of range for the tip of the wing and Mr. George Cayley [George John] says it is only 3 at present. If you want a third wheel look out a young ash tree, the stem of which will give you a straight piece of the length you want; saw it down; shape your piece immediately and bend it round a block and let it dry; don't let me hear of any rash trials with this machine. I will see to it being properly tried when ready. Yours G. Cayley.

Here we have the typical hands-on approach of Cayley seeing to the smallest design detail first-hand, with even a how-to for bent-wood wheel construction – though Vick would most likely have had some ideas of his own on the subject and would have had to dutifully bite his lip. The reference to a "third wheel" is in line with the tricycle undercarriage of both the boy-carrier and the governable parachute, but awkwardly at odds with the four-wheeled design Dora thought she recognized as the coachman-flyer. Also this is obviously a flapping flyer, and it is the flappers that seem to be causing the most problems. It may be that *all* Cayley's attempts at generating thrust with flappers suffered from the same design flaw and this is his latest machine running into similar difficulties. It is clear that the enthusiasm of either Vick or (much more likely) George John needs keeping in check: "Don't let me hear of any rash trials with this machine." A second and once more frustratingly undated note from Cayley directly to George John further emphasizes the same point.

> Dear George I hope I have made my plan intelligible, but it will require your attention with Vick with you, who is quick at receiving from others their plans and executing them. . . . *If I do not get over to see your first trials, I must as grandpapa insist upon the proper precautions* [emphasis added] First it is absolutely necessary that the tail be securely braced up a little, and that the centre of gravity be made to

act steadily on the centre of bulk of the surface so that when weighed up to the weight of the person trying the wings – should it take off, they would skim and not either rise up hill or sink down, but go horizontally. That it will do if it will sail steadily about 1 in 4 down hill. At least that will be so nearly right that a slight turn up of the tail will keep it horizontal and he ought to have some cord at hand to brace the tail. The hill should not be a steep one, but gentle, little more than will make the wheels run. In haste, yours truly G.C.

Here we are teased as to the identity of the potential aviator – the use of the terms "they would skim" and "he ought to have some cord" could be a reference to a third person or simply Cayley's indecision (or foreboding) over who might be the first to try it out. If we take a step back, there is even more support for George John's pivotal role. This is revealed from the sequence of notes in *Egypt* just prior to the second flyer's flight.

The entries in Cayley's *Egypt* notebook during George John's leave of absence in late 1851 quite notably depart from the study of full-scale airplane design for over the next year Cayley turns to the question of a power plant for flight. He touches on the design of furnaces and engines and includes an examination of the qualities of vulcanized Indian rubber and its "remarkable difference in the elasticity . . . with respect to its tension." (In 1852, Cayley was the first to use a rubber band to power a model plane. History usually accords this very minor laurel to Frenchman Alphonse Pénaud in 1871, though it has to be said that Pénaud used the rubber band to power a propeller, whereas Cayley's worked little flappers.) The *Egypt* entries of early 1852 include a discourse concerning wheat production, then return to the subject of furnaces again. The emergence of the potentially aviation-related issue concerning the strength of "hard iron wire N15 gauge .07" is delayed until some time after August 17. We know that George John left Irun in northern Spain en route for Britain on May 21, and it is likely he was back in Yorkshire some time in early August, just in time for Cayley's switch in experimental direction to the use of tension wire – essential for bracing his flying machines. From this point in Cayley's notebook, the entries are largely devoted once more to experimentation in flight: the resistance of spheres to the air, further experiments on the tensioning of wire, the strength and lightness of bird feather quills – though the entries briefly depart on a quick experimental detour concerning the rate of cooling and melting of his recently filled ice house in February 1853. By February 18, Cayley has come back to "the dynamic power of air and steam for Mr Gurney," a theme that continues through March followed by another of his experiments into the strength of wooden timbers. By the end of winter and the beginning of the flying season in May 1853, Cayley is observing crow flight once more "on a perfectly calm day," though his bird-spotting skills are, as ever, a little rusty, for he admits that it could have been a rook. Cayley's notebook then includes his sketches of the boy-flyer copied from an earlier schematic and his comparisons and calculations for his "new flyer."

It may be pure coincidence that during George John's absence abroad, Cayley left aviation construction only to revisit it again on his grandson's return; alternatively it could be further evidence of the young man's role as catalyst for construction and as a test pilot in the making.

Though Gibbs-Smith is taken as the authority on the matter of the 1853 flyer by almost everyone, one of his conclusions concerning the coachman flight seems to have been completely ignored – that Cayley's final flyer was probably not a monoplane, but a multiplane. Cayley's use of the stubby wing meant he had problems getting enough wing area to generate the required lift; his elegant solution to this limitation was the triplane design of the boy-carrier. Though the monoplane governable parachute illustrated in the 1852 *Mechanic's* article is taken as the blueprint for all the replicas of Cayley's 1853 flying machine, it is almost certain that the airplane that flew with an adult pilot did so under a multiplaned, short, fat wing. The second flyer, like the boy-carrier before it, almost certainly also had flappers attached. Dora even refers in her letter to the subject: "What the motive force was I don't know but I think the footman was the moving element. . . ." The presence of flappers for the "new flyer" is also suggested by a tiny sketch in the *Egypt* notebook close to an entry dated May 18, 1853, which compares the flight path of the machine with and without "waftage." Cayley's predictions for potential flight paths are clearly made with the intention of comparing "natural fall" (unpowered, pure glides) with those when flappers are applied. It is also clear from this entry that his calculations predict that "true flight" (i.e., the ability to fly horizontally) is not within his grasp even with hand-powered flapping, despite what Dora Thompson reports.

If we disentangle the evidence we have from the delightful legend of the unnamed flying coachman, a different story emerges. Cayley, George John, and Vick successfully flew a ten-year-old boy in 1849, though this was a pure glider, an unpowered trial that was obviously something of a disappointment for Cayley. Throughout that year and into 1850 and early 1851, the Brompton team continued its refinement and enlargement of the boy-carrier, which had originally weighed a carefully calculated "132 1/2" pounds. During George John's absence overseas, Cayley turned to his publications, including his timely *Mechanic's* discourse on parachutes and their governability. Cayley did not return to the construction of the enlarged second flyer until after George John's return in mid-1852. By August 25, 1853, the second prototype, which by then weighed in at "164 1/2 lbs," was nearing test-readiness. That it had not flown before that date is evidenced by Cayley's correspondence with Dupuis-Delcourt in June 1853, at which time Cayley is still looking forward to the first flight. This machine was

It must ever be dependent on engine power
& with waste weight of engine &c probably
it will take a 5 horse power to effect it.!!
a man can exert a two horse power for
a minute & as a preliminary experiment
it would be expedient to find how much he
could make the downward path, the
machine takes, with his weight alone, divert
towards the horizontal by waftage. This
would furnish practical in lieu of theoretical
data
Horizontal path, —
or true flight —
waftage fall
natural fall

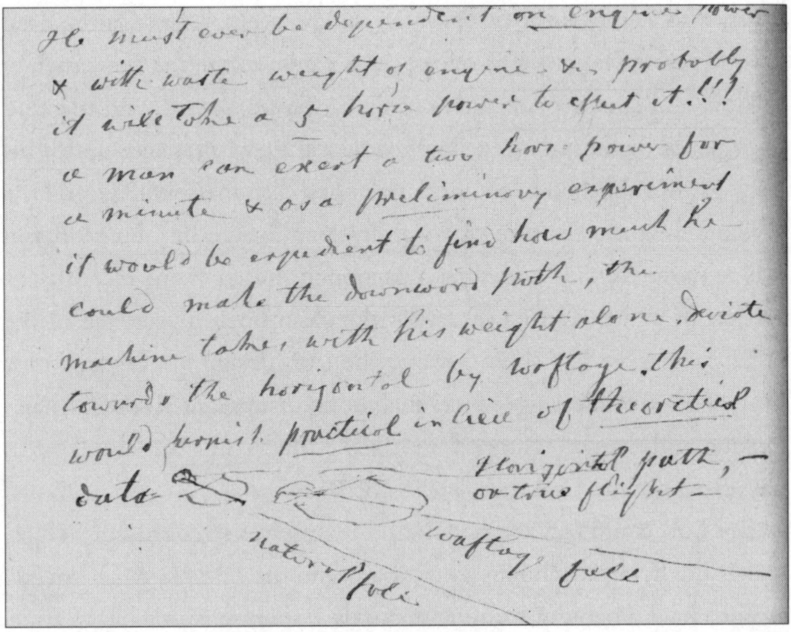

The *Egypt* notebook entry of 1853. The text reads "... a man can exert two horse power for a minute & as a preliminary experiment it would be expedient to find how much he could make the downward path the machine takes with his weight alone divert towards the horizontal by waftage. This would furnish practical in lieu of theoretical data."

The sketch below shows the steep "natural fall" of the machine, the shallower "waftage fall," and "horizontal path – or true flight."

not a construction of the 1852 monoplane design from the *Mechanic's* paper, but a multiplane, probably a triplane, fitted with flappers and designed to fly higher than the glide path expected from an unpowered vehicle, but below that of "true flight." This was because despite the fitness and enthusiasm of the pilot, George John Cayley was unable to generate more than two horsepower for the duration of even this short flight. The *Encyclopaedia Britannica* account is the most authoritative one we have – the flight was a glide or at best flapper-assisted, and so fell short of some people's expectations, or at least those of the editor at *Britannica*. However, the event did cause a significant stir among those who witnessed it or heard about the event. Dora Cayley, aged around ten at the time, was one of those caught up in the generation of folklore and later provided her cousin Sir James Legard with the kind of evidence he most desired: an unequivocal eyewitness account for his soon-to-be published book. Dora was not a dishonest woman, and the account she provided directly to professional historian John Hodgson was a more candid, and thus a seemingly much more inconsistent version of events. On its discovery, the clean-lined illustration of the 1852 governable parachute became the icon design for Cayley's final flyer. This eye-pleasing conceptual design supplanted the archaic-looking and flapper-equipped multiplane that is much more likely to have been the machine that flew in 1853.

But how could fact and fiction find themselves so confused? Why is it that the flying coachman account arose in the first place? Of course, legends have a habit of forming themselves spontaneously all the time, but this one may have had some additional help. For instance, George John knew the qualities of a good tale. By his own admission in the preface to *Bridle Paths*, he left it up to the reader to sift fantasy from truth, and even his friends and admirers labelled him capricious. Whatever the source, like the explanation for the tongueless lion of the Cayley coat of arms, a good punchline helped the coachman story along in spite, rather than because, of the facts. As the tale grew in the telling, no one wanted to admit that it could, perhaps, be an embellishment of the real events, especially when it put Brompton and Britain on the aviation map. There was a flight and it was a world's first, but almost certainly not the one of folklore. And the reason the identity of the pilot has remained a mystery for so long is that researchers have been looking for a coachman who didn't exist.

Finding the Pieces IX – The Bridle Roads of Spain
by George Cayley

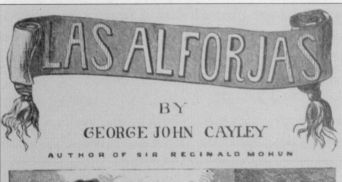

George John and companion with their Spanish saddlebags. The text loosely
translates as "After some consideration Don Juan announced finally that there is
no book so bad that it doesn't contain some good."

Research is sometimes a case of "how come I didn't see this before" and sometimes just dumb luck in stumbling over hidden treasures. The discovery of George (John) Cayley's long-lost classic *The Bridle Roads of Spain* is a little of both. Though the Cayley family pedigree describes George John as the "author of several works," I initially took these to be his output of poetry. Then I discovered that The Long Riders' Guild Press had chosen the year 2004 to republish George John's travelogue of 1852, and I found myself in the researcher's motherlode: an honest autobiographical account of a key character. The contribution *Bridle Roads* can make is that we get an idea of what kind of man George John was. We discover he lies somewhere between the classic English eccentric and an out-and-out fruit loop.

Bridle Roads takes us on a journey across Europe and into the depths of nineteenth-century rural Spain in the company of a young man comfortable, confident, and mature enough to consider such an adventure second nature. There is little evidence of naiveté about him for he is a twenty-six-year-old multilingual with a decade's worth of foreign travel behind him and a man born to a world where some money and the right credentials could get a body a long way. For those occasions when these are not enough, he also carried a brace of multi-barrelled pistols, powder, and a more than sufficient supply of balls. He and his travelling companion, the Right Honourable Henry Coke, disguise themselves as caballeros, mount a couple of stubborn ponies, and trek the length of the Pyrenees on the equivalent of five dollars a day. Throughout their travels, they sketch scenery and portraits, disturb the peace, and generally act in the way one would expect of two impetuous representatives from the era's proudest and most belligerent nation. Though the detail of the journey is fascinating, the same cannot be said about the general quality of the prose. Even George John's own aunt, Mary Agnes, has little positive to say about the work:

> It is an idle book, some parts of it are interminably dull, that is it is evident the author who writes is brighter than what he puts on paper and therefore he insults the public by giving them his worst.

Contemporary critics also took unkindly to George John's habit of casually setting fact and fiction on an equal footing and leaving the reader the task of separating one from the other. George John's intention of following in the footsteps of his hero Don Quixote appears both literal and figurative. The book isn't a straightforward travelogue, though there are times when its rough self-deprecating charm gives rise to laughs-out-loud:

> . . . poets and novelists – an officious set of fellows, who never can inform their readers that something does something without gratuitously adding that it does it in the same manner as some other thing does something else.

All in all, the book is a faulted seam of semi-precious jewels and a unique insight into the writer's roguish character and risk-taker's bent. George John's mantra is that you make life as exciting as you want, for "how very flat the world would be if one only did what one has any business to do." He is a seeker after truth and adventure, though not necessarily in that order. *Bridle Roads* contains few references to his life in England, and no discussion of his grandfather or their work together; the account of his Spanish travels is mainly just another contribution to filling in the blanks concerning a young man running riot through his life.

Immediately on returning from Spain in 1852, George John published his diaries in the magazine *Bentley's Miscellany* (of which Charles Dickens had been an editor and in which the first serialization of *Oliver Twist* appeared). These articles were then republished as a book in two volumes, *Las Alforjas* (The Saddlebags) in 1853. By 1854 George John was heading off to the Crimean war as a reporter for the *Daily News* and this pattern of casual employment and foreign travel was one he followed from then on.

As additional fodder for those interested in George John himself, later editions of the *Bridle Roads* include not only a preface by the author (roundly berating critics of the first edition and their complaints concerning his deliberate inclusion of fantasy) but also two letters as footnotes to George John's later life. The first is from Lady Anne Thackeray Ritchie, a writer and eldest daughter of author William Makepeace Thackeray. The second letter is from Ellen Cobden Sickert, another author and friend of George John in his final years. These two biographical essays paint a portrait of a wild-eyed linguist and handyman with

> nervous, gentleman's hands, the fingers scarred and
> stained with many experiments, with work on anvil, with
> acids and varnishes. . . . To seek his society was to court

surprise, for he was eccentric and unconventional, steadfast and capricious, made up of contradictions. He was a wayward philosopher.

Returning to Naples direct from the Crimean war, George John stumbles upon a grand ball (and the young Lady Anne), where he mingles effortlessly with the polished nobility in spite of his roughened appearance: "He wore a loose black necktie which I dare say had been in battle with him." There is an intriguing reference to a mysterious falling out with the Cayleys in general but he had apparently "made it all right with his family," suggesting that his untamed ways and radical views might have become eventually accepted. In other ways George John was the victim of the family's reputation; even though he married a non-relative, Lady Anne assumes his wife, Mary Ann Wilmot, was his cousin. George and Mary's married life was as unconventional as it was tragic and short. In her description, Lady Anne poignantly recalls her winter visit to see the young Cayley family. Four-year-old son Artie is seriously unwell, and Lady Anne is greeted despondently at the door by George John saying,

"... Come in and share our dismal jollity. Artie is very ill, there is hardly any hope for him, but he wanted to see the Christmas-tree lighted up, and so we are having it tonight instead of waiting for Christmas." We followed him upstairs to the drawing room, where the tree was beginning to shine with its candles, the two other children were excitedly running to and fro, little Artie was lying back on his pillows between his mother and his nurse; then George

Cayley, with tears running down his cheeks, went steadily lighting the candles and looking to it all.

Artie died, aged six, on Boxing Day 1868. This year also marked George John's fifth and final attempt to become the Conservative M.P. for Scarborough. Following the death of his son and the end of his political aspirations he, his wife Mary, and their two remaining children, Hugh and Violet, indulged their wanderlust by summering on the Mediterranean island of Majorca, followed by wintering in north African Algiers. This is where Ellen Cobden first met them. The encounter made a considerable impression.

Mr Cayley took the common things of every day and made of them adventure and romance. . . . They listened while Mr Cayley, in Arabic, exchanged greetings with the coffee-makers. . . . He often wore some modification of Arab dress, which became him very well. So clothed he could be seen hammering metal, gold, silver or brass – into strange and beautiful shapes.

Like his grandfather, George John's publishing output was varied and sporadic. In addition to verses (including an anonymous work *Indignant Rhymes by An Illused Candidate* recounting one of his many political defeats), he published on political and financial reform as well as the iniquities of promotion in the Royal Navy. He was also a regular contributor to *Fraser's Magazine for Town and Country* on the subject of travel and craftsmanship. His final publication, on lawn tennis, was published by the *Edinburgh Review* in 1875. Despite his avid thirst for adventure, George John's physical condition had never been particularly good. After a long period of declining health, he died on October 11, 1878, at Munton Rectory in Kent while en route to his family and their beloved Moorish house above Fontaine Bleue in Algiers. He was fifty-two.

As far as his grandfather was concerned, George John could do no wrong. In 1840 Cayley wrote with immense pride of his two grandsons, George John and Henry Frederick Beaumont, having "killed 30 brace of partridge on Friday

George John Cayley.

which at this season of the year is considered a sort of feast." In his will, Cayley bequeathed George John the considerable legacy of £500, five times the amount left to even his own daughters though the unmarried Anne and troubled Mary Agnes also received annuities for their upkeep. It was as if George John became everything Cayley wished to be had he not been weighed down by aristocratic title and tied to the responsibilities of tenants and estate.

During the brief period between Emma's death and George John's pony trek along the Pyrenees, grandfather, grandson, and Thomas Vick formed the team that laid the groundwork for a unique contribution to flight. On his return, George John had played his part in the first flight and perhaps made his own quixotic contribution to the story of it. George John was every inch the warrior-poet of Miguel de Cervantes Saavedra's fictions, though the quality of the Englishman's verse and the ferocity of his battles were moderated through the charismatic sentimentality that was a Cayley family trademark.

14

THE END

In a draft letter to an unknown recipient we get a brief glimpse of Cayley's life on Christmas Eve 1853. Even after this most extraordinary of years, we see Cayley in an insular mood. We also see that like many Yorkshiremen of legend, he would never shrink from calling a spade a bloody shovel.

> Brompton Nr Pickering,
>
> Dec the 24th: 53
>
> Dear Sir, I have little to say that will be of interest to you – I stay tolerably well in health and spirits and shall soon reach my 80th birthday two days hence (the 27th). My wife, I am sorry to say 'tho in tolerable bodily health has sunk into total mental imbecility.

As his domestic world continued to fray, with concerns for Mary Agnes and her children compounding Sarah's illness, Cayley still found time to engage in litigation with the Church over tithes for his estate in Scampton, Lincolnshire, and retain control over the daily range of estate-related business. Even in his ninth decade Cayley was toying with his ideas on flight in the form of complex, multi-winged aircraft with alternating flappers, though these remained confined to paper and did not approach construction. Over the next few years, even his *Egypt* entries became sparser and ever more varied.

> A ready method for making volute of any given proportions and dimensions . . . Furnace lining . . . Torsion in small iron rods . . . Shaving straps . . . Agricultural statistics . . .

As ever, there is the fascination with birds: "young Digby Cayley [he was forty-seven at the time] shot a heron – weight 3 1/4 pounds each wing 2 feet 7 inches long." Even as his own health waxed and waned, Cayley never stopped recording for posterity what he experienced: "March 29th: 54 I have lately observed a sort of speck in the retina of my left eye which being exactly in the axis of its direct vision is not a pleasant omen – It is of but small dimension extending over an angle of about one in 43.6." If it slowed him down at all, he didn't admit to it.

By October 1854, as Cayley was inserting the codicil into his will to ensure that Dr. Alexander's debts to him would both accrue interest and require repayment to Mary Agnes's children, Cayley also found the time to include in his notebook an opportunity to berate a group of contemporary scientists and their inability to consistently calculate absolute zero: "It is obvious that no confidence can be placed in any of the procedures used. . . ." Two months later, on December 8, Lady Sarah finally gave up her enduring struggle and died, aged eighty-one. She and Cayley had been married fifty-nine years, Sarah had borne him ten children, and of those who survived to adulthood, most seemed to have been completely alienated from their mother, or at best left exasperated with her decades of erratic behaviour. There is so little documentary evidence from or concerning Sarah that it is difficult to get anything beyond a caricature of this wild-tempered, intelligent, mentally fragile woman. Though Cayley's own erratic output of charming and dreadful poetry includes odes to his wife up to her eightieth birthday, it is hard to say what kind of relationship they had or really could have had during Sarah's final years. Even in death, the family would, publicly at least, gloss over the details of her life. Sarah's official newspaper obituary seems a poignant illustration of her family's discomfort with her.

> The Late Lady Cayley (From a Correspondent). This lady, who died on the 8th inst. at the residence of her husband, Sir George Cayley, Bart, Brompton Hall, Yorkshire, was the only daughter of the Late Rev. George Walker, for many years the minister at High Chapel in Nottingham whose memory she tenderly revered, and some portion of whose abilities, and whose noble and generous spirit she inherited. To most of the present generation this excellent man was personally unknown but to the few still surviving who enjoyed the privilege of his acquaintance and to perhaps some others who have only heard of him from their parents or older friends, it may not prove uninteresting to read a portion of the tribute paid to him by an intimate friend, the late Rev. and learned Gilbert Wakefield who in his volume of Autobiography speaks in the following terms of Mr Walker who was then living . . .

Sarah's own obituary goes on to laud the intellectual prowess of her late father, but fails to so much as mention her name a second time. As there are no surviving letters mourning Sarah's death, mirroring the level of documentation of her life in the family archive, it is unclear exactly how Cayley felt about his loss, though there may have been some considerable relief mixed with his grief. With the Alexander saga dragging on, and with Cayley now in his early eighties, he may have had little to spare of the energy that so characterized his earlier life.

Occasionally, however, his health allowed him to engage in further experiments. In October 1855, with the Crimean war continuing and George John reporting on its disastrous progress, Cayley can once more be found responding to the situation. Cayley writes to Mary Agnes on his latest "breech loading gun, on the most simple plan possible." In the same letter, he bemoans the loss of his illustrations through the collapse of the Dupuis-Delcourt French *Bulletin* of two years previously, as well as making reference to a series of early photographs: "I agree with you about those daguerreotypes. Can you tell me where the whole cargo of these articles are deposited? You had them to look at and I cannot find them anywhere."

The prospect of there being perhaps a photographic record of a Cayley flyer is another alluring mystery, though its existence is remote, bearing in mind their controversial nature. Digby, by now the de facto lord of the Brompton manor, was embarrassed beyond words on the subject. One stern and ancient photographic image of Cayley does survive from around this time, though it fails to capture him as well as the Henry Briggs portrait painted a dozen years before.

This year, 1855, also saw Cayley's final contribution to aviation, and it was a singularly fitting one. Sixty years after first building his Chinese flying top and forty-five years after first describing it in his seminal flying publication, Cayley patented his "*improved* Chinese flying top" and provided a watercoloured illustration of his device to support the claim. This toy with which he had amused himself and countless friends and relations forms the bookends to his life in print on the subject of flight. Though this patent was his final publication, even as his health failed his experiments and notes in *Egypt* continued.

> Dr Leigh in his dictionary of arts manufacturing and mines (article cable) gives the following table of the strength of chain and rope cables for reliable uses....Rough estimate on the height of the atmosphere...Weight of dry soot....On the strength of iron bars....On *The living triangle* a work on human longevity and the amount of life on the globe....

Cayley captured (badly) in one
of the earliest forms of portrait
photography from the early 1850s.

A much more compelling, and
certainly more complimentary
representation of Cayley: the
copy of the Henry Perronet
Briggs R.A. portrait from 1841,
which hangs today in Cayley's
great-great-great-granddaughter's
house in Brompton.

Even when he was confined to bed, *Egypt* faithfully records Cayley's critical discussion of his reading materials, even when the book in question was "the good one" and his views, as usual, far from orthodox: "Mathew Chapter 1 – the laborious list of the progenitors of Joseph the Husband of Mary here given seems idle [irrelevant] if Jesus is the offspring of Mary alone. . . ."

A letter from this period sent by Cayley to Mary Agnes stands as testament to his enduring concern for the welfare of his family. Neither

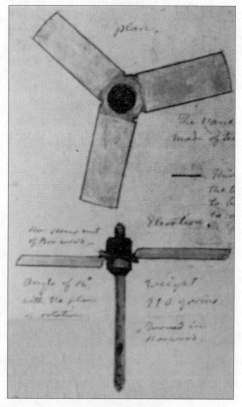

Cayley's final contribution to aviation science – his improved Chinese flying top. Cayley gave this model, which he built himself from these plans, to his granddaughter Dora Thompson of Ripon.

of them were in good health at the time but Cayley, as always, took on the role of supporter and adviser to his distressed daughter: "Let us, then, hold ourselves in peace and smile at the terrific masks that would scare us from our equipoise – for love will banish the frowns of the fancied demon."

In a letter to his cousin Edward Stillingfleet Cayley dated early December 1857, Digby writes, "My father is much the same this morning, he is no better. . . . I see no prospect of him rallying. . . . There is no pain, no seeming struggle. . . ."

Cayley's final notebook entries, barely legible pencil marks pressed faintly against the paper, reflect his continued critical studies of the Scriptures. On the last page of all, his bed-bound commentary on the New Testament collides with his previous notes made from the back page of *Egypt* working forward. As his reflections on Christ's approach to Jewish law meet up with Cayley's earlier musings on the erosion of marble through the action of rainwater, the record of his thoughts on anything at all comes to an end. He would probably have continued had there been more space, but there wasn't, so the written witness to almost seventy years of extraordinary mental activity ended there.

Cayley died on December 15, 1857, twelve days before his eighty-fourth birthday; he was buried in the family vault of All Saints Church close beside High Hall. As we might expect, Cayley's affairs had been set in order long before his death. His legacies were thoughtful, if prudent, making his gift of £500 to George John all the more note-worthy. Cayley's other brother-engineer, Thomas Vick, received Cayley's iron lathe and £25. More practically, Cayley had arranged for his lifelong friend Sir Goldsworthy Gurney to take Vick on as an engi-neer at the Palace of Westminster's heating and ventilation plant. Cayley's last will and testament left no loose ends and generated few surprises. Within ten months of Cayley's death, the ever present Miss Phil had also passed away, and so their generation ended.

Once the public eulogizing had died down, the new Brompton Baronet, Sir Digby, took over the few strands of estate management that had remained in his father's control in his final months. One of Digby's early acts was to remove from sight the relics of the flying machines that had so diverted his father's attention. A Brompton man named Richard Tyson recalled Sir Digby "using the darkest terms and ordering the remains of one of Sir George's flying machines from the Low Garden." Tyson, then only a child of eight, helped lead the horse that dragged these remnants into a series of disused barns where they acted as chicken coops and hideaways for truant Cayley children. Sir Digby went on to become an effective, if unimaginative head of household, and through good luck and some application, the Cayley finances reached something of a peak during his tenure.

If Cayley's flying endeavours were considered best forgotten in Brompton, this was not the case elsewhere. As the world's second aviation organization, the Aeronautical Society of Great Britain, was established, there were occasional references to Cayley's earlier publications. In 1876 an abridged (some say butchered) version of his triple papers of 1809–10 was reprinted in the society's annual report; a French translation of the same appeared in L'Aéronaut the following year. The triple paper was again reprinted in 1895 through The Aeronautical Annual of Boston, Massachusetts, and this publication was where Americans Octave Chanute and the Wright brothers first encountered Cayley's work. However, even as Cayley's scientific reputation continued to grow, his domestic legacy began to show signs of distress.

In Britain, the fortunes of the agricultural community were being hard pressed by the onset of recession. Now receiving no subsidies through legislation like the Corn Laws, and with the innovations in transport of the last fifty years helping to dramatically lower the price of imported grain, the British rural economy entered a tailspin. Though the Brompton finances were healthy enough when Sir Digby died in late 1883, by the time the 8th Baronet, Sir George Allanson Cayley, died in 1895, the family coffers were draining fast. Unfortunately the 9th Baronet, George Everard Arthur Cayley (Sir Everard) was blind to the haemorrhaging effect of his extravagances. He once engaged the services of an entire train and crew to ferry friends and relations from Sawdon Station to Doncaster by rail for the famous St. Leger race meeting. In order to finance his losses, Sir Everard eventually mortgaged the contents of High Hall for £5,000 to banker and family acquaintance John Coulthurst. This loan was finally defaulted, passing the furniture, paintings, statues, carvings, coaches, glassware and flatware, tools, and miscellanea of more than three centuries of life at Brompton to the Coulthurst estate at Gargrave House in nearby Skipton. Though the Cayley family retained many personal items, what had once been the single legacy of a tight-knit household was now dispersed among a dozen residences.

By the year 1907, as the Wright brothers were amazing French crowds with their flying displays (and rebutting the accusation "The Wright Brothers: flyers or liars?" in the most satisfying and spectacular way), Sir Everard Cayley had moved out of High Hall with the Brompton estate in receivership. He was also publicly defending his spending habits in the British press as his bankruptcy hearings continued. By the time of Sir Everard's death in November 1917, High Hall was acting as a temporary Red Cross station for recuperating British soldiers from World War I; Sir Everard's elder son, Francis, had died in action barely six weeks before; his only surviving son, Kenelm, was already wounded and a POW. After over two years as a military prisoner, and some months spent interned in neutral Holland, Sir Kenelm, 10th Baronet, returned to Britain in 1918. Within six years, High Hall had been cleared completely prior to its sale to a hotel chain. There are rumours of fourteen trunks of Cayley family papers that younger rel-atives rummaged through to cut out the precious penny-black stamps of the previous century; a fraction of the remainder found its way to the family archive preserved by the local government in Northallerton. Not only the attics were cleared, but the contents of the barns were dragged into a local field and what was left of Cayley's flying machines were unceremoniously cremated. It was during this period that the mysterious bearer of Cayley's silver disc appeared at the Scarborough Silversmiths to add another piece to the documentary puzzle of Cayley's lifework.

During Sir Kenelm's twentieth-century stewardship of the baronetcy, Cayley's name finally emerged from the shadows. Credit goes to a series of enthusiastic aviation advocates who used their mild indignation at Cayley's obscurity as motivation to the cause of restoring his reputation. In the best British tradition, John Hodgson, honorary librarian of the now *Royal* Aeronautical Society, started the ball rolling with a letter to *The Times* in March 1927. This letter outlined Cayley's aviation accomplishments and was followed up through the *Newcomen Society's* 1933 publication of Cayley's earliest notebooks. In 1955, the Royal Aeronautical Society published the now restored version of Cayley's triple papers of 1809–10. This was the year after the inaugural "Cayley Memorial Lecture" was delivered at the Royal Aeronautical Society by the next Cayley torchbearer, the impressively qualified Captain J. Laurence Pritchard (Commander of the British Empire, Honorary Fellow of the Royal Aeronautical Society, Honorary Member of the Flight Information Advisory Service, Meteorological Research Institute). This event came some three years after Sir Kenelm was forced to sell the remaining estates around and within Brompton itself; in Elizabeth II's coronation year – 1952 – the last landed interests of the Cayleys in Brompton finally ended. Hodgson also died that year. Though he had started work on a Cayley biography, he failed to begin the project proper. Fortunately, his voluminous notes were made available to Pritchard, as was the willing cooperation of Sir Kenelm and his wife, Lady Elizabeth. Pritchard produced a series of short publications on Cayley before his most complete work, a full biography in 1961. The following year, Pritchard's friend and colleague Charles Gibbs-Smith produced his own detailed description of Cayley's work on aviation. As a result of one of those rare "finding the pieces" moments, during his preparation for his book Gibbs-Smith was informed by Lady Elizabeth that she had recently rediscovered a further two Cayley notebooks, including the priceless *Egypt*. Gibbs-Smith could now follow Cayley's notes from his late teens to early eighties, finding the boy-flyer in the lost notebook, though Gibbs-Smith independently uncovered the 1852 governable parachute publication and much more besides. Lady Elizabeth, with journalist Gerard Fairlie, produced the third book dedicated to Cayley's life in 1965, just two years before Sir Kenelm's death. Though Sir Kenelm and Lady Elizabeth had seven healthy offspring, all were daughters, so the succession of the Brompton baronetcy had to be traced back through the male line in order to determine who would be 11th Bart. This turned out to be Sir Kenelm's second cousin (once removed) and a man with a familiar name. Sir Digby William David Cayley, the current baronet, inherited the title on December 27, 1967, the 194th anniversary of Cayley's birth.

As the Royal Aeronautical Society continued its annual lectures, the name and work of Cayley maintained a steady profile, though it was largely confined to Britain and some aviation circles abroad. Academic institutions honoured Cayley occasionally; my own sister was a resident of Cayley Hall at the largely engineering university of Loughborough. During the 1970s an ex-Royal Navy pilot, John Sproule, took on the task of spreading the word, producing the model of the 1853 riding rudder glider and helping oversee the construction of the governable parachute, which actually flew for a British TV documentary on Cayley in 1975. Another replica of the same machine flew across Brompton Dale in 2003 in part to commemorate the 150th anniversary of the flying coachman, as well as to counterpunch the celebration of the much better documented achievements of the Wrights a mere one hundred years before. One of the pilots that day was Sir Richard Branson, millionaire entrepreneur, transatlantic balloon pilot, and the money behind *Spaceshipone*, the first planned commercial service for suborbital space tourists. Closer to home, the Cayley anniversary marked the first time that Sir Digby, 11th Baronet, had ever stepped inside High Hall, renamed Brompton Hall and by then a residential school under local government control.

The Internet is the most prolific source of articles on Cayley these days, though they largely parrot the legends and poorly reproduce Cayley's illustrations of his hoppers and flyers. Several instances of serious literature on Cayley's contributions to aerodynamics and flight can be found, but rarely do they stray into the myriad of subjects that filled his life.

Summarizing a man like Cayley and his work is not an easy task, though one place to start might be that he proved Sir Isaac Newton wrong. Although he wasn't the first, last, or only one to do so, pulling a rug from under Mr. Gravity still counts for something special. Newton had said that when an inclined plane passed through the air, the upward force it generated would decrease exponentially as the angle of the plane's incidence increased. This conclusion, expressed as Newton's "sine-squared *law*," stopped any serious work on wings in its tracks because the law predicted that an inclined plane could never generate the required lift for flight. By doing his whirling arm experiments, Cayley showed that the law wasn't a law at all and that a moderately inclined plane could support considerable weight in the air. Fixed-winged flight was a practical proposition, bird flight could now be explained, and Newton's preoccupation with squaring everything to find his answers was shown to be just that. Of all his discoveries, it is this one that sets Cayley apart from his peers; those simple schoolboy doodles irrevocably changed the world. The other characteristic that puts Cayley up there with the best scientists is that he never assumed experimentation in the lab equated to experience in the field. In fact, quite the opposite. He always tested his lab findings for real; he got his hands dirty building models and airplanes to prove his theories, and his 1804 glider is the best example of that: it was simple, it was robust, and it flew.

In the years following his first glider trials, Cayley positively tripped over aerodynamic discoveries, so many in fact that he failed to follow up on many of his own ideas. Cayley's moments of insight are so numerous as to make their retelling border on the tedious, but here goes anyway: the dihedral structure of the wing; the cambered wing cross-section; the benefits of a high-aspect ratio wing; the fact that the centre of lift is at a position well forward of the wing's physical centre; tubular construction for lightness and strength; streamlining through the solid of least resistance; trimming of the elevator and rudder for stable flight; the biplane and triplane; wheeled undercarriage; the fundamental need for a light engine . . . the list goes on. If his thoughts on airships were included as well, never mind his work in related mechanics, and in the dissemination of his own and everyone else's knowledge through the Royal Polytechnic, mechanics institutes, philosophical societies, and British Association, then the series becomes a litany, and of that Cayley would have disapproved. More importantly, just detailing all he did means we begin to lose sight of the man, and it is not through Cayley's successes that we get the keenest insight into him, but from his failures.

More than anything else it is in Cayley's stubborn refusal to apply propellers to his machines that we see his most obvious blind spot. It is easy to see his lapses as profoundly flawed, in hindsight almost comical. An alternative is to see them as symptomatic of Cayley's lack of an intellectual partner, someone who shared his passion and his talent but who could also challenge him enough to at least consider other means of propulsion. The Montgolfier *brothers*, the Lilienthal *brothers*, the Wright *brothers* – these are instances where the idea of peer collaboration worked so well in early aviation. But we can turn this around. We can get something from the flappers preoccupation if we see it as providing a unique view into Cayley's mind or, better still, a window into his soul.

Cayley believed in nature, *truly* believed in it. His was not some superficial acceptance of nature as a law-giver. He did not see nature as an arbitrary source for setting the boundaries within which the world worked. Cayley thought there had to be some *sense* to it and that sense centred on his belief in the Divine. Cayley saw God as a benign and intelligent provider whose creations obeyed rules and whose gift of human curiosity meant those rules were there to be discovered. Cayley's firm and forceful religious beliefs coloured much of his adult life but these same beliefs set in place a fundamental conflict between his intellect and his spiritual intuition. Cayley *knew* that propeller-driven ships worked, he *knew* his model helicopter flew, he saw the future of the airscrew but whenever he considered his own personal conquest of the air he looked to the hundred flying creatures for which nature had decided that flapping was the solution. Cayley would, again and again, return to this same theme: "The one way that presents itself is to copy nature. . . ."

Although Cayley and his contemporaries were gripped by the idea of "invention," Cayley was not an inventor, he was an explorer. Flight was not there to be invented, it was all around him: herons skimmed, crows flapped, and sycamore chats spiralled down while floating for a dozen yards. It was just a case of finding out *how* flight was achieved, so

Cayley stripped the wing down to its most elementary working component, a task that had defied the attempts of everyone for the previous three thousand years. When it came to deciding on propulsion, Cayley found himself confronted by one of those "dark" problems that had him returning instinctively to Mother Nature. Cayley's uncharacteristically sour dealings with Robert B. Taylor are perhaps the paradigm example of what could happen: a new breed of scientist, clearly realizing that propellers were the future, meets head-on with the established authority figure whose gut feeling was that flappers were the way. Taylor's forthright and intellectually unassailable argument in favour of the airscrew sent Cayley into a huff and then on to his least constructive correspondence and publication. But what turned Cayley around was the other central theme in his life: his love of family. Their needs, particularly those of soulmate George John, provided the impetus that combined with Cayley's own all-consuming curiosity, so his swan song became a fable that survives to this day. Beyond the folklore, the facts are *still* the stuff of legend, even when distilled into the amiable flying coachman myth.

Like the romantic view of nature contained in the verses of Wordsworth, the man whose brief association with Brompton included getting married there but little more, Cayley would always see natural design as the blueprint for success. With one foot in the age of enlightenment and his other planted firmly in the cold objectivity of the new industrial sciences, Cayley sought somehow to bridge the gap. But really his heart remained tied to his love of the land, its sustaining qualities, and the creatures who inhabited it.

As to whether Cayley was a genius . . . the term is bandied around so often these days as to render it largely meaningless. Perhaps he was the opposite – *ingenious* to a fault. What he certainly possessed was an infectious eagerness and an uncanny ability to peel away the incidental from the fundamental, then to explain the remaining kernel with a child-like simplicity. The essence of his intelligence lay in these plain homilies; he was an unedited spokesman of his outlandish ideas and damn the torpedoes. It's why his publications contain as many errors as they do insights, for he wrote to inform rather than to impress and chose those journals by and for amateur enthusiasts like himself.

He discovered the secret of flight, but that discovery came too soon. Had he been around forty years later things might have been different, for by then Cayley's "prime mover" was a reality. If he'd had the power of the internal combustion engine to drive his flyers, who knew what he could have achieved. Instead his legacy became the groundwork that secured for others the eventual conquest of the air.

The Last Piece – The Common Cold and Cayley's Ornithopter

Colds are bad at the best of times, but a really bad cold on Christmas Eve has got to be the worst. My wife struggled on for a couple of days, but finally succumbed and wrapped up on the couch with lemon tea. She was idly flicking through the few channels we get while I was in the basement trying to explain why Cayley, inventor of the airplane, could never really get over the need for it to flap to fly. Upstairs, my sofa-bound spouse came across a Discovery Channel special on the use of thin-film solar arrays and ionic polymer-metal composites. Realizing its significance, she called me up from the den to watch it too.

Thin-film solar arrays are light, flexible mosaics of solar panels that can generate electric power but require uninterrupted sunlight to do so. Ionic polymer-metal composites are a new material that can be made to bend, warp, and flex in whatever complicated manner you wish. It is a material that can be made to flap like a bird, just so long as there is an appropriate electrical power source handy to induce the required distortions. By combining these two technologies, you get the efficient, lightweight power source and the light, strong, flexible structure to mimic the lift and thrust-generating motion of a bird's wing. This engineless flying machine with an unlimited fuel source sounds like science fiction, but its potential is enough to attract a sizable research contract from NASA. Such vehicles would be ideal for upper atmosphere exploration of not only Earth but Mars and even Jupiter. These environments have little or no oxygen, so a conventional aircraft motor wouldn't work, but a solar-powered ornithopter would work pretty well. Perhaps Cayley's flapping obsession was actually on the right track after all, just on the wrong planet.

EPILOGUE

GEORGE CAYLEY: A VERY BRITISH DA VINCI?

His family deposited most of the Cayley papers into a public records office in a small town in northern England in the 1960s. The archive consists of boxes of letters, along with legal papers, receipts, bills, and the miscellanea that such collections always seem to contain, but this is only part of the written record. All those papers relating to his flying machines and other inventions were extracted and placed on permanent loan with Britain's Royal Aeronautical Society (RAeS) in London. This is where you can find the jewel in the Cayleyana crown, the personal notebooks that came to light in the mid-twentieth century and in which he jotted down what was interesting him on any given nineteenth-century day: the best recipe for ginger beer, how to estimate the yield of corn in the lower dale field, how the wheels of his manned glider were coming along. These notebooks have been examined by researchers, and I've read accounts of their contents, but to get their real sense you have to read them first-hand. The notebooks are held securely in the safe of the Royal Aeronautical Society at their headquarters near Piccadilly, just down from the Green Park tube station – turn right at the Hard Rock Café and there you are. That is the only place where you can see the original notebooks, and so there I went.

The home of the RAeS is a striking multistorey Georgian townhouse with a grand and exhausting central staircase. It spirals up through an arresting selection of portraits of famous aviators and prints showing a hundred years of flight. Near the top is the neat library crammed with journals and jumbo volumes on everything from stress-induced fractures in carbon-fibre structures to menus from the first flying boats to cross the Atlantic. I had decided to save the famous Cayley notebooks until last of all so I went through the catalogue of other, non-notebook Cayley items and ended up requesting nearly all of them. Among the catalogued articles, letters, and etceteras was an unassuming reference to a school exercise book of Cayley's. When it arrived, I opened it up to see what he, like every other schoolboy in history, had thought to doodle on the inside cover.

I stared at it for a while. I've had some iconic moments in my life, and this was one of them.

"He's bloody da Vinci," I said.

I actually said it out loud, and a fellow researcher shuffled in his chair and gave me something approaching a look. Admonishment indeed in such surroundings.

I'm not saying that Cayley was a brilliant artist – far from it. That he could exhibit an artistic bent of sorts, occasionally, when he took his time, is probably the case, but that isn't what I saw in these sketches. What I saw was an unquenchable inquisitiveness at work, a teenage mind firing off in half a dozen directions. I saw an intellectual energy that seemed to echo the same sense of what I get from those famous da Vinci cartoons. I tore myself away from the exercise book and buckled down to get on with the mundane work of combing through the other papers to get as many first-hand facts as I could, but at the back of my mind was an idea.

When I stepped away from it for a while and calmed down a little, I realized that Cayley isn't da Vinci, or even close. But there could be an equivalence in their lives. There are coincidences between the two in abundance: no one knows of either's exact place of birth; neither had a relationship of any kind with their father; both were sent away from their rural homes to be schooled in the major cities; both were intrigued by nature, the countryside, and in particular birds from an early age; both were Freemasons . . . the list goes on. But there are just as many differences: da Vinci was homosexual, or maybe bisexual, well definitely very *demonstrably* sexual, whereas Cayley was by all accounts the quintessential English gentleman – a discreet, devoted, and faithful partner to a woman whose volcanic temper and later mental illness would have tested the patience of Job. Da Vinci avoided obligation. His list of unfinished works and half-promised commissions is a rich seam for art historians, whereas Cayley was simply Mr. Commitment. Cayley started as a radical liberal, ended up as a bit of a soft-touch capitalist with his heart in the right place. Da Vinci remained on the seething edge of Borgian back-stabbing until his dying day. Everyone thought da Vinci was a genius (da Vinci included). Most contemporaries thought Cayley was something akin to an eccentric old fool and Cayley himself seemed to care not a jot what anyone thought about him. So if there are as many divergences as parallels in their lives, where am I going with this?

I went back to psychology 101 and a truism: our environment influences who we are. What happens if two people with similar innate talents, similar kinds of intellects grow up in radically different environments? Could there be a point in considering da Vinci and Cayley something like, for want of a better term, "twinned-souls, raised apart"?

The problem with starting with such an idea is that it is possible to find parallels of almost anything in almost anything else. This is readily achieved by starting with a premise and then carefully separating what is "relevant" (i.e., supportive) from what is "irrelevant" (i.e., awkwardly unsupportive) and your self-fulfilling prophecy duly meets its destiny. In general, the occurrence of startling analogies increases in direct proportion to the eagerness of the seeker to find them, and writers tend to be a pretty eager breed. So why would I go down this route? My only defence was that it wasn't my fault; Cayley made me do it.

The conclusion I came to was that although they shared much in the way of capacity for scientific investigation and talents in pursuing them, each was nevertheless an undeniable product of his place and time.

Da Vinci was a Renaissance Man, *the* Renaissance Man if you like to think that way, and many do. However, his start in life was tough. He was the illegitimate son of a well-to-do Florentine banker-cum-lawyer, though Leonardo spent much of his early life living with his thuggish stepfather on the wrong side of the Vinci village tracks. The redeeming factor was that da Vinci's one way out from this domestic strife happened to be one of the best ways possible. He was brought up in an era where art in all its forms was big business, and a career within it offered high prestige. Italy was crammed with art and artists and everyone wanted in: it was a boom that had no bust. Patrons just couldn't get enough of good quality art, and they had more money than could be (easily) spent in a lifetime. If you were talented, you could be schooled in the production-line techniques of the art business. If you had real skill, you could go on to be an independent artist running a workshop and become an art-school master yourself. If you were exceptional (and/or had a reputation as such), there was literally more work than you could possibly cope with. This was why half a dozen artists would often be required to finish a single painting and wealthy patrons would specify in the commissioning contract exactly how much of a given work a given artist would contribute.

Da Vinci certainly knew how to trade on his marketable talent. He was an extraordinary artist, though I wouldn't be the first to suggest that his skills as a draughtsman exceeded those as painter. He was also a notable poet and a professional musician who was highly praised in his early days. Da Vinci even claimed the title of civil engineer when the likelihood of employment could thus be improved. He was a libertine and extravagant socialite with a talent for drama and melodrama, a man fascinated by beauty, including a somewhat morbid obsession with his own attractiveness and that of his young male friends. As a sideline, he was a dab hand at the near-profession of riddle and pun production. Later, when his manuscript notes came to light, he became known above all else as the inventor of almost everything: armoured cars, snorkels, siege engines, parachutes, flying machines, the aerodynamics of birds, the fluid dynamics of water . . . he didn't seem to have missed much.

The problem is that he didn't actually build much of anything, and the things he did design were notoriously disastrous. His plans in 1504 for diverting the river Arno to cut off supplies for the rebellious city of Pisa cost 80 lives and 7,000 ducats. It might have looked good on paper but it didn't work out in practice.

Leonardo had a thousand ideas, and his heady mix of skills as an enigmatic writer and graphic artist allowed these imaginings to take life. The problem was that it stopped there. He didn't construct an armoured car, and if he had it wouldn't have worked. It couldn't move. It would have suffocated and/or crushed anyone inside it who fired its cannons, which were in any case rather oddly arranged in a complete circle (so at least half of them were facing away from the enemy and toward the friendly troops behind). Another thing da Vinci didn't build was a flying machine, and even if he had built what he'd drawn it wouldn't have got off the ground. There is one enigmatic reference in one of his notebooks to having tried and failed to fly, but we have no idea how the attempt was made. His ornithopters suffered from the same flaw as all his contemporaries in that none of them provided an upward-lifting force and means of control.

Da Vinci's other celebrated invention was his helicopter. This was derived almost directly from an Archimedes fluid screw and had the singular disadvantage of also not generating anywhere near enough lift. This was probably a good thing because da Vinci also didn't know about counter-rotation (even though other engineers of the day certainly did). If the helicopter had ever got off the ground, the fuselage would have counter-spun at an equal rate and opposite direction to the rotors with fairly uncomfortable consequences for the pilot. His helicopter also had neither intrinsic stability nor stabilizing controls so that if it did ever take off, the delirious spinning crew could not have stopped it from crashing instantly.

Even da Vinci's design for a parachute remained unconstructed in his lifetime. When it was built in the year 2000 by English skydiver Adrian Nicholas, he discovered that the construction weighed nearly two hundred pounds – so if you were hanging underneath it when you reached the ground, the thing would likely kill you. Nicholas tested it by strapping himself in to the da Vinci parachute, which was then dropped from under a balloon. After he had descended a few thousand feet, Nicholas quickly unstrapped himself, fell free, and deployed a *real* parachute in order to reach the ground unscathed.

Da Vinci's most focused work on flight is *Sul volo degli Uccelli*. Again we see the hand of the elegant artist plus the mind of almost terminal curiosity at work. What we fail to see are any substantial conclusions as to how bird flight was achieved or calculations as to how it might be emulated. Da Vinci was a great observer, perhaps one of the finest, and an extraordinary illustrator of what he saw. But did he understand the science of the flight he recorded so elegantly? Unfortunately not.

One thing that we do know is that da Vinci's designs and writing on flight (or anything else) had little impact on science. This was due to a combination of factors. The first was the snobbish assumption by his contemporaries that da Vinci's lack of formal education meant he would have little to contribute. The second was the fact that hardly any of his 13,000 pages of notes were ever made publicly available before the end of nineteenth century. By then, even his most original ideas had been overtaken by the natural progression of science and invention in the preceding three centuries.

And yet da Vinci remains a subject of constant fascination and the man to whom the term genius seems most commonly applied. Could it be that the accessibility of his mind is what is so attractive, with that avenue into his keen intellect being through his visually stunning cartoons? When we look at the da Vinci drawings, we judge not their practicality, but their innovative and visual qualities. And originality and aesthetics were definitely Leonardo's strong suit, though it has to be said that he borrowed a number of these ideas from other sources. We must remember, though, that he never said they *were* his idea in the first place. That claim came from the da Vinci reputation factory following his death. Though Renaissance man, he wasn't industrial man, or a fabricator of his musings. He was a collector of concepts, a thinker, and an ideas man with a gift for illustration – and there's nothing wrong in that, especially as he had an exceptional talent for it. The problem is that it's hard to argue with the contention that he never actually invented *anything* associated with flight that worked. It's equally hard to argue that Cayley's influence on early flight science was anything less than pivotal.

Cayley was born into wealth and privilege. If he'd wanted to, he could have sat back and lived off the rents his tenants paid to scratch a living from agriculture. Many of his contemporaries did exactly that, but something lit a fire under Cayley. Without doubt there was an internal source of combustion – his fascination with the natural world was evident from an early age. He started to indulge his interests in his teens and his early passion was flight. He actually built a model helicopter that flew rather than just drawing one. It was small scale, a toy rather than a machine of war or a vehicle for self-aggrandizement, so all it did in a practical sense was amuse the observer. But it flew, and later versions acted as an inspiration for the Wright brothers, so that seems achievement enough.

The Muston Drainage scheme is a lot less exciting than da Vinci's siege works and river diversions around Pisa, but it does have the advantage of having worked (it still works today). There's nothing glamorous about moving a thousand cubic yards or two of mud and sand to build a flood wall – it's just one of those dirty, thankless jobs that needed doing. The annals of history aren't going to ring with Cayley's praises over Muston, because the rural Yorkshire tenants who got their own acre of tillage land out of the scheme aren't the ones whose voices determine who makes it into the halls of the great and the good.

When Cayley moved on to his experiments on bird flight, he started to think about how to build a machine to measure the lift generated by a wing, and then he went on and did just that. He constructed the world's first glider, and flew it, and tested it, and redesigned it until it flew the way he wanted it to. There was no new technology here, just fabric and wood. It was the *idea* that was new. And then he did the best thing of all – he published his results for the world to see. No hidden, semi-cryptic musings here, no reliance on the processes of a few centuries of posterity to uncover, translate, and perhaps edit and reshape, re-interpret, and amplify his inner thoughts. Cayley just put them out there, warts and all. Some people thought he was nuts – most people thought he was nuts – but a few said they thought he might be on to something.

Cayley published works on air engines, steam engines, optics, gliders, parachutes, bird flight, balloon flight, caterpillar tracks, airships, railways, prosthetics, politics, economics, religion, ballistics, helicopters, and ornithopters. He founded local political parties, philosophical societies, scientific institutions, and educational establishments. He fought inside Parliament for the rights of inventors and out of Parliament for

the need to fund invention and innovation. He was a friend and colleague of those who invented everything from steel processes to the
computer, from a thesaurus to the conoidal propeller. Over the course
of his life he had financial, legal, and moral responsibility for one
headstrong mother, one mentally unstable wife, ten children, eighteen
grandchildren, twenty-five farms, a couple of hundred tenants, and more
than a few thousand acres. His life spanned the period from before the
American Revolution to the middle of the industrial revolution. As far
as we know, he lied about his inventions exactly once, but pointed out
his own failings and acknowledged the contributions of others on countless occasions. His jokes were corny, his verses trite, his illustrations
functional, his politics liberal, his religion conservative, and his economic
philosophy was low tax, hard work, and thrift. He made people laugh
and encouraged almost everyone he met to do and to be the best they
could. Perhaps the best way of summing him up was that he was thoroughly nice – not an adjective that captures headlines.

When Cayley died in 1857, most people, his son and heir included,
tried to forget about Sir George's rather embarrassing "aerial crotchets."
It took the best part of three-quarters of a century before an aviation
historian found one of his notebooks, and Cayley became briefly
famous in the 1920s, and again in the 1970s, before descending into
near-obscurity once more. And then one day in 2005 a would-be biographer saw a doodle in a schoolbook in a library and said something
out loud he shouldn't. So here I am, more than two years later, trying
to say something I should, and that thing is this.

As much as the stunning natural splendour of Tuscany and
Lombardy, the aesthetics and frenetics of the Renaissance, and the
internecine politics of the Medici and Borgias helped produce da Vinci,
Britain's dark, satanic mills and an acre or two of green and pleasant
land helped sculpt the man who built the first plane and made it fly.
Cayley was an eccentric enthusiast who was just too busy building

things, forming societies, managing his estates, and performing conjuring tricks for his grandchildren to spend all day writing about it. When he did have the time to record events, he was just as likely to jot down his thoughts on recipes for boot polish and home-made beverages, and that's just not the way to get posterity to label you a genius. But it *is* rather British.

USING *all the* BUFFALO

Brad Bird, animator, film director, and a man described as "very strong coffee" by his colleagues (a compliment by the way), said that you should follow the example of the Native Americans and always use all the buffalo. With this in mind, I have created a bibliography that not only documents my sources but also includes what I thought about them. Their order here is determined by the sequence in which I wrote up their descriptions, on the basis that an alphabetical list would be helpful to only me, who knows what is in the list, and useless for the first-time reader.

Fermat's Enigma by Simon Singh. Penguin Books, 1997. A lovely little tome that makes super-complicated math cool and interesting. It's an informative and exciting peek into how the science of mathematics progressed from the ancient Greeks to the modern day. Just skip the really involved bits and take in the appendices as and when you can. Well-written and pacey, it has the benefit of being a short book with a happy ending: a quick, easy, enjoyable read.

Whiggery and Reform, 1830–1841 by Ian Newbould. Stanford University Press, 1990. This is a clear, crisply written description of the most influential period of Whig politics. It has a tendency to assume a considerable amount of prior knowledge concerning the individuals and incidents involved, but it is a rich seam of hard facts concerning early nineteenth-century British politics. Essentially a textbook on the subject, perhaps even *the*. Oh, it's fantastically dull.

Whig Renaissance: Lord Althorp and the Whig Party 1782–1845 by Ellis Archer Wasson. Garland Publishing, Inc., 1987. If you want a detailed blow-by-blow account of the Great British Reform Act printed from the camera-ready copy that came straight off a frontstroke typebar Underwood upright typewriter, this is your book. Essentially it's a political biography of Althorp (later Lord Spencer of the Lady Diana Spencer family fame) and there doesn't seem much missing in the way of political detail. It continually mentions in passing some fascinating historical asides and then fails to tell you about them, a tendency that suggests it was written by either a serious tease or by an even more serious academic (I suspect the latter). A book for non-partying undergrads or perhaps biographers needing a crash course in early nineteenth-century politics.

Benjamin Franklin, a Biography by Ronald W. Clark. Castle Books, 2004. It felt like at least one-third of this book was extended verbatim quotes from Franklin and his contemporaries, which is great if you like that kind of thing, but I don't. Not so much a "warts and all" bio as one that includes the occasional zit here and there. It's never a good sign when I'm eagerly counting down the years to the subject's death. The book has the disadvantage of being very long with the redeeming feature of having plenty of bits you can scan through without losing the thread of the story.

The Map That Changed the World: William Smith and the Birth of Modern Geology by Simon Winchester. Harper Collins, 2002. An

306 THE MAN WHO DISCOVERED FLIGHT

inspirationally good book about a fascinating subject, the truly roller-coaster life and times of the man who invented geology. This is a biography written like a solid novel by an informed and enthusiastic author. A must-read for anyone interested in the social impacts of pre-reformed Britain on an individual and his work or for lovers of a good tale well told.

Charles Babbage: Pioneer of the Computer by Anthony Hyman. Princeton University Press, 1982. This book includes, by way of rec-ommendation, a quote from a reviewer that describes the work as "intellectually subtle but enormously entertaining history." I think this is a pretty poorly disguised insult, but then perhaps my thinking so shows a little intellectual subtlety all of my own. As a record of Babbage's life, it's fairly pedestrian and not really a critical evaluation of the man, his work, or his times. The author wrote it while being salaried through the kind of sinecure fellowship at Cambridge University of which Babbage would have passionately disapproved, which is rather fun. Its most notable feature is perhaps the most garish dust jacket of any book I ever saw – a lime-green line drawing of Babbage on an ebony background.

Wellington: The Years of the Sword by Elizabeth Longford. Harper and Row, 1969. A biography in the old school – incredibly detailed and referenced, voluminously written, and without a scrap of criticism or honest evaluation for its subject (hagiography is, I believe, the accepted term). Wellington was a hero, he beat Napoleon and saved Europe from a despotic leader, but to suggest that the Iron Duke was a sensi-tive intellectual closely wreathed in a tough leathery exterior is simply too hard to believe; such conjecture is certainly unsupported on the evidence presented here. Wellington *did* say that British soldiers were the scum of the earth, which, even if they were is hardly the most kind or diplomatic comment – the poor wretches died in their thousands for the man. A great historical record, but you don't feel any closer to knowing who he was. A first-rate source for a second-rate essay.

The Miracle of Flight by Stephen Dalton. Firefly Books, 1999. This is a visual gem of a book, a sumptuously illustrated celebration of all things flying that leans toward the insect world. The photos are stunning, and the unusual combination of coffee-table-book looks and detailed examination of the biology and aerodynamics of natural flight make this a must-read for anyone even vaguely interested in the subject and an even better starting point for those who aren't. It's a low-priced, high-value bargain.

Leonardo da Vinci: Flights of the Mind by Charles Nicoll. Viking Penguin, 2004. Virtually all you need to know about this book can be judged by its cover. Under the dust jacket, the volume is bound in a highly impractical pale cream, which stains on contact with anything, it weighs the best part of two pounds, and the initials of the author (*not* the subject) are inlaid with half-inch-high gold letters on the front cover. The constant amateur psychologisms suggest Nicoll was clawing for something new to say about a man who has been better captured elsewhere. By the end of it, I felt sorry that da Vinci, a man of innumerable talents, should be described by an author whose many talents don't seem to include writing an insightful book about da Vinci. Good for detail, pretty good for illustrations, useful for some of the demystifying of the post-mortem fame factory that has grown in the last hundred years, but I still yearned for it to be over.

The Life of a Genius: Sir George Cayley, Pioneer of Modern Aviation by Gerard Fairlie and Elizabeth Cayley. Hodder and Stoughton, 1965. This biography takes a quite unusual approach to the whole subject of describing someone's life. Unconfined by the shackles of documented fact or any sense of chronological or thematic structure, the unholy alliance of a British tabloid journalist and the wife of George Cayley's great-great-grandson produced what amounts to a fantasized description of a series of conversations between Cayley and his cousin "Miss Phil," loosely reconstructed from their "old, platitudinous letters written in fading ink" (to quote the authors in their introduction). Having explained that there was no need to go into detail concerning Cayley's inventions, the work continues to go into detail concerning very little at all save for how mad, bad, and beautiful Cayley's wife, Sarah, was and how it is a crying shame that no one currently cares about George Cayley: genius, theologian, and all-around good guy.

Sir George Cayley: Inventor of the Airplane by J. Laurence Pritchard. Horizon Press, 1962. This is the most detailed and comprehensive Cayley biography bar none. It covers all the main points with an archivist's eye for detail and with considerable background concerning the events and individuals involved in Cayley's life. The notable exception to this is the coverage of Cayley's family life, which is nonexistent. This omission is explained perhaps by the very cozy relationship between the author and Cayley's then living descendants and the deferential approach of British biographers to aristocracy in the 1960s. Though sympathizing with the problem, it's difficult to follow a clear chronology of events as the bio progresses; the information is there, it just needs a little digging. It is largely uncritical of Cayley, which is a pity, and it occasionally shows a shocking lack of sensitivity – for instance, choosing as the front-cover illustration the one and only invention Cayley wantonly plagiarized seems a little off. Suggesting that Pritchard's treatment of the story "tends towards the dry" is akin to suggesting that the Dead Sea "tends towards the salty" – though many will find it typical of mainstream biographies of the time. Good, solid work, though now appearing dated in style and tone. I was lucky to have such a thorough source to cross-check my own research against.

Sir George Cayley's Aeronautics 1796–1855 by Charles H. Gibbs-Smith. HMSO, 1962. Not a biography, though it can act as a partial one, this is a specialist examination of the aviation-related inventions, notes, and publications for Cayley. Gibbs-Smith, though obviously a devotee, gives an honest, critical, and perceptive account of Cayley's contributions to flight as well as his shortcomings. Aimed at the airplane enthusiast, it nevertheless deals in a down-to-earth manner with Cayley's work in lay terms. It benefits from (though makes no self-aggrandizing claims for) the fact the Gibbs-Smith suddenly gained access to the two "other" Cayley notebooks discovered during the writing process, sources not available for Pritchard's earlier bio. Solid, reliable, and charmingly nostalgic in its own way – I'm sure it reflects the author, who I understand was a thoroughly nice man.

For God and Glory: Lord Nelson and His Way of War by Joel Haywood. Naval Institute Press (Annapolis, Mass.), 2003. A collection of essays concerning Nelson's approach to a series of subjects from the admiral's own perspective, which assumes you know the chronology of the man's life, so the author deals purely thematically with the subject matter. It is tightly written by a professional military historian who earnestly believes there are modern military lessons to be learned from two-hundred-year-old battles and even older warriors. Though critical of Nelson by way of its inclusion of fact, it still leans toward the hero-worship precipice a little too often in tone. The importance attributed to religion in Nelson's life is heavily emphasized, though in order to maintain the appearance of objectivity the author should perhaps have thought twice about putting "God" as the first entry in his acknowledgements section.

Aviation: An Historical Survey from Its Origins to the End of the Second World War, Second Edition, by Charles H. Gibbs-Smith. Science Museum (London), 1985. This is a meticulous documentation of aviation history written in a way that appears simultaneously disinterested and interested. Well put together and typically well illustrated (as aviation literature tends to be), this is another of those books aimed at the enthusiast with a penchant for the historical record.

Taking Flight: Inventing the Aerial Age from Antiquity Through the First World War by Richard P. Hallion. Oxford University Press, 2003. So far the definitive record of the early history of aviation – essentially taking up from the work of Gibbs-Smith, Hallion constructs a well-written, objective, and once more meticulous account of the progression of flying from its earliest days. Balanced and sympathetic to even those less-than-likeable characters of the past, it is rich in detail of individuals and events in a way that will satisfy even the most critical reader. The book has that rare quality of being both a good read *and* a great reference work.

Early Developments of Modern Aerodynamics by J.A.D. Ackroyd, B.P. Axcell, and A.I. Ruban. American Institute of Aeronautics and Astronautics Inc. (Virginia) and Butterworth-Heinemann (Oxford), 2001. This is a book for the mathematically talented (a group to which I was refused membership some years ago), though the brief snatches of history along the way are interesting in filling in the personal details and chronology of aerodynamics. This critical and academic treatment of the subject forms an excellent introduction to its complexities. Note that from Chapter 10 onwards the ratio of formulae to prose exceeds 2:1. Not a book to be read aloud at bedtime – on the other hand, some insomniacs out there may disagree.

Sir George Cayley, the Father of Aeronautics Part I: The Invention of the Aeroplane by J.A.D. Ackroyd (2002). Notes Received by the Royal Society of London, volume 56, part 2, pages 167–181. This academic paper includes a potted biography of Cayley and goes on to examine the aerodynamic science of Cayley's earliest work. Though written for a scientific audience, the general reader should find it accessible enough. It is good to see a serious and critical examination of Cayley's contribution by an author qualified and knowledgeable enough to do the subject justice. It even corrects some of Gibbs-Smith's more complimentary claims for Cayley's work. A short and effective introduction to Cayley and his work, with some heavyweight aerodynamics, but not impenetrable to anyone interested enough in the subject to pursue it beyond the superficial level. A handy addendum to Ackroyd et al.'s *Early Developments of Aeronautics and Astronautics* (above).

Gentlemen of Science: Early Years of the British Association for the Advancement of Science by Jack Morell and Arnold Thackray. Clarendon Press (Oxford), 1981. This is it: the definitive history of the early days of the British Association. Though the world may not have found its breath necessarily baited while awaiting this publication, those with an interest in how, when, why, and who formed the British Association will find this a treat. Those interested in a well-expressed narrative concerning the early days of British science may be slightly less than satisfied – this is an academic book written with the aim of not making any mistakes rather than drumming out a rattling yarn. I have to admit to not having read all of it, but the first half a dozen chapters certainly seemed to be delivering a detailed (and well tabulated) list of facts.

Delta Papa: A Life of Flying by Derek Piggot. Pelham Books (London), 1977. Though essentially a book by and about plane spotters (flying enthusiasts), it comes in the form of an autobiography of the man who probably flew more types of vintage aircraft than any other pilot. Among those types flown by "Delta Papa" was the replica of the Cayley governable parachute, which was filmed for the Anglia Television documentary in 1975. Being a book from which anything even remotely controversial or unsavoury is wholly absent, it doesn't so much keep you on the edge of your seat as plump up the cushion behind you before warming up your slippers and going off to make a nice hot cup of cocoa. Not many non-plane-spotting readers will find it that interesting but I was charmed.

Bridle Roads of Spain: A Journey from Gibraltar to the Pyrenees in 1852, Second Edition, by George Cayley; The Long Riders' Guild Press, 2004. This is the republished memoir of John George Cayley, grandson of Sir George Cayley (6th Bt) produced as a celebration of the long-lost art of cross-country horse travel. As an unvarnished auto-biographical sketch of George John, it is unparalleled; as a travelogue it is picturesque and frank; as an advertisement for the qualities of the Briton abroad, it is pretty embarrassing and perhaps all too accurate. The heavily armed and relentlessly pompous Cayley spends six months setting back British diplomacy a decade or two as he sketches portraits while leaving the landscapes to his travelling companion and fellow artist, The Right Honourable Henry Coke. Even reviewers of the day took issue with the seamless interleaving of fact and fiction, a point that Cayley, in his preface to the second edition, saw as the baseless whining of the intellectually subtle. Though the casual xeno-phobia that pops up regularly throughout the book is probably another honest reflection of its times, a modern reader may find the author losing some of his appeal as a result. An ideal gift for the forgiving equestrian with a yearning for a view of rural nineteenth-century Spain seen through the eyes of a genuine British eccentric.

The Measure of All Things: The Seven-Year Odyssey and Hidden Error That Transformed the World by Ken Alder. The Free Press, 2002. A description of the internecine scientific politics of revolutionary and Napoleonic France as two men (one a self-deprecating detail fanatic, the other a worldly-wise, egotistic detail fanatic) triangulate France in order to determine an earth-derived basis for the calculation of the metric metre. I should have loved this book, for it has everything I'm interested in: history, politics, revolution, science, personalities, and a great story. It's difficult to put my finger on why the book doesn't fly but it doesn't. It could be the rather long-winded style Adler adopts (though this may sound like pots and kettles comparing each other's relative hue) or it could be that it is a little too earnest about itself to carry the narrative. Bits of it are good (and the actual story is fascinating) but the good bits are just too sparse to keep up the momentum of my enthusiasm for the whole thing.

Yeager: An Autobiography by General Chuck Yeager and Leo Janos. Bantam Books, 1986. An entertaining and impressive autobiography written from the hip. Yeager was the man who bridged the gap between basic, simple-wing, low-speed flight and the supersonic. It is written in an easy, self-deprecating style; how much of it was Yeager and how much the ghost-writer I don't know and I don't care. The book is a great story that is both informative and fun. The man's life reads like a novel. A must-have for anyone interested in modern aviation or in good old-fashioned heroes.

Wind, Sand and Stars by Antoine de Saint-Exupéry (translation by Lewis Galantiere). Time Life Books, 1965. Along with having perhaps the most exotically romantic name of any writer who ever lived, Saint-Exupéry was one of those classic warrior/poets in the great Gallic tradition, with his particular form of warfare being in the air. Many hail the author as the possessor of the only true voice of the aviator, and this powerful documentary of his flying experiences will no doubt inspire some and be appreciated by many more. I assume that the wholly unmoved state I found myself in having read it is evidence of my lack of anything even vaguely approaching a soul.

History in Hansard: 1803–1900 by Stephen King-Hall and Ann Dewar. Constable and Company Ltd. (London), 1952. I thought I was buying the History *of* Hansard 1803–1900 – one of those online ordering mistakes. The short introduction describes a little of the history of the publication, then continues to quote a series of the dullest, least relevant, and at times pointless speeches in parliamentary history. Some are clever, most are not, and almost all of them are too long to be an efficient source of quotes. I hope this is reflective of a failure of selection rather than a shortcoming in the source. The length of its original print run was almost certainly determined by the number of M.P.s and their descendants willing to pay for their honeyed words to be so preserved.

Wish You Were Here: Biography of Douglas Adams by Nick Webb. Headline Books (London), 2003. The rags-to-riches story of the author of the *Hitchhiker's Guides*; the man hailed as the P.G. Wodehouse of his generation. The reason I include a summary of this book here is that I learned a compelling lesson from reading it. Though well and wittily written, sympathetic and knowledgeable of its subject, the author is just too emotionally close to Adams to be able to step back far enough to describe him. A biographer should sift the wheat from the chaff but make sure that they talk a little about *both* because that's what makes people people. The book resembles its subject: clever, energized, and funny, but I found the result strangely unsatisfying.

Life in Georgian England by E. Neville Williams. English Life Series (Ed. Peter Quennell), London, 1962. This is a potted summary of the social, economic, and political turmoil that was England for most of the eighteenth century and the beginning of the nineteenth century. At first Williams comes across as either being a superficialist, or else someone forced into that role by editorial strictures that required over one hundred years to be compressed within fifty thousand words. However every now and then he surprises you with some compelling observations that make you realize what a pivotal period this was in British social history. In the end I realized how much I'd enjoyed the book: sometimes lightweight just works.

The World on Fire by Joe Jackson. Penguin, 2005. The search for oxygen was a cat fight between a Yorkshire dissenting minister in the form of Joseph Priestley and the aristocratic Lavoisier, tax collector, liar, and cheat. Another book containing all I could wish for: science, personality clashes, story line, and the French revolutionary wars. It comes in at around a B- on the basis that Jackson seems to make up just a little too much of the back story and commits his own kind of heresy by getting some basic facts wrong. Jackson gives it a good go, and there is much to commend the book as a thorough documentation of events.

Longitude: The True Story of a Lone Genius Who Solved the Greatest Scientific Problem of His Time by Dava Sobel. Walker (New York), 1995. The story of a talented, tenacious, and bad-tempered Yorkshire clockmaker fighting the system and everybody in it in order to get the reward and reputation he deserved. Another shockingly well-written book with just the right mix of history and histrionics. It is the ideal house guest for your head: it doesn't dawdle at the door but gets in, entertains you, then exits smartly, leaving you wanting just a little bit more. Near enough faultless as far as I can tell.

INDEX

320 THE MAN WHO DISCOVERED FLIGHT